The Chassidic Dimension

Interpretations of the Weekly Torah Readings
and the Festivals

Based on the Talks of
**The Lubavitcher Rebbe
Rabbi Menachem M. Schneerson**

Vol. II

Published and Copyrighted by
"KEHOT" Publication Society
770 Eastern Parkway, Brooklyn, N.Y. 11213
5755 • 1995
הי׳ תהא שנת נפלאות הגאולה

The Chassidic Dimension

Interpretations of the Weekly Torah Readings
and the Festivals

Based on the Talks of
The Lubavitcher Rebbe
Rabbi Menachem M. Schneerson

Vol. II

Compiled by Rabbi Sholom B. Wineberg
Edited by Sichos In English

THE CHASSIDIC DIMENSION
VOL. II

Published and Copyrighted by
"KEHOT" PUBLICATION SOCIETY
770 Eastern Parkway, Brooklyn, N.Y. 11213
Tel. (718) 493-9250, 778-0226

5755 • 1995

Printed in the U.S.A.

Library of Congress Cataloging-in-Publication Data
Schneersohn, Menahem Mendel, 1902
  [Likute Sihot, English Selections]
  The Chassidic dimension vol. 2:
  interpretations of the weekly Torah readings based on the talks of the
  Lubavitcher Rebbe, Rabbi Menachem Mendel Schneerson/compiled by
  Sholom B. Wineberg: edited by Sichos In English.
    p. 304   15 X 22 1/2 cm.
    Translation of: Likute sihot.
    Includes bibliographical references.
    ISBN 0-8266-0684-9
    1. Bible. O.T. Pentateuch—Commentaries. 2. Hasidim. 3. Habad. I. Wineberg,
Sholom B. (Sholom Ber) II. Gale, Gershon. III. Title.
BS1225.3.S362513   1995
222'.107—dc20   90-4076
                                                                      CIP

Table of Contents

Table of Contents
Sefer Shmos

Table of Contents
Sefer Vayikra

Table of Contents
Sefer Bamidbar

Table of Contents
Sefer Devarim

Publisher's Foreword

The Rebbe has stressed on numerous occasions that one of the best ways to be *Mekushar*, bound up and connected, with him is by studying his Torah. If this was vital at all times, how much more so after *Gimmel Tammuz*.

Surely, the Rebbe's *magnum opus* is *Likkutei Sichos*, from which the essays in The Chassidic Dimension are culled. They transmit, albeit with much brevity, kernels and gems of thought on the Torah portions and the Festivals that are found at greater length and with much more profundity in *Likkutei Sichos* proper.

It is our fervent hope that the study of the Rebbe's Torah as compiled in The Chassidic Dimension will serve as a step in hastening our generation — "the final generation of exile and the first generation of redemption" — to once again merit very speedily the Rebbe offering us wonders from his Torah, "a 'new' Torah shall come forth from Me."

Vaad L'Hafotzas Sichos

Chai Elul, 5755

ספר בראשית

Bereishis

Bereishis

בראשית

"Who Knows Ten?"

The Torah portion of *Bereishis* speaks about the creation of the world. All of creation came about, as the *Mishnah* states in *Avos*,[1] as the result of ten Divine utterances. Indeed, continues the *Mishnah*, creation could have resulted from a single utterance, were it not for G-d's desire to offer mankind more opportunities for reward and punishment.

So significant is the number ten — "the complete number"[2] — that the *Mishnah* enumerates other times the number occurs, such as the ten tests of Avraham and the ten miracles performed for our forefathers in Egypt.

But why does the *Mishnah* fail to mention that the Torah itself was given in *Ten* Commandments? Our Sages note,[3] after all, that the ten Divine utterances of creation correspond to these Commandments!

The significance of the number ten lies in the fact that G-d, having brought about Creation through ten utterances, thereby imbued the world with a nature such that ten units signify a complete state, corresponding to the ten supernal *Sefiros* from whence the material universe emanates. The number ten is thus considered a "complete number" because it signifies a complete state.

However, this in no way implies that G-d found the number ten to be an indispensable characteristic of completion; it is merely that G-d chose the number ten to indicate completion. G-d could have employed a different number of supernal *Sefiros*, and thus a different figure — corresponding to that number of *Sefiros* — would signify completion.

---

1. *Avos* 5:1.
2. See *Pardes, Sha'ar* 2, chapters 1-2; *Iben Ezra, Shmos* 3:15.
3. *Zohar I*, p. 11b; see also *Zohar II*, p. 43a, 93b.

The relevance of the number ten to the Torah's Ten Commandments can be understood accordingly:

The *Midrash* states[4] that the Torah served as G-d's blueprint for creation. Understandably, this blueprint contained all of creation's parameters, including the fact that its state of completion finds expression in the number ten.

Thus, the fact that the Torah was given in *Ten* Commandments is not a function of this number per se. Rather, the opposite is the case: ten is "the complete number" only because the Torah was given in the form of Ten Commandments. This in turn led to a universe that finds fulfillment through the number ten.

Hence, the *Mishnah* could not possibly list the Ten Commandments as one of the things reflecting the consummate state of ten, for the fact that the Torah was given through Ten Commandments does not serve to indicate the complete state of Torah. Rather, because the Torah contains the aspect of ten — the Ten Commandments — the importance of the other things enumerated in the *Mishnah* is established.

But even though G-d decided that the number ten would constitute a completed state within creation, He is in no way limited by this. For inasmuch as G-d defies any and all limitations, He is not limited even by His own actions, and can create things whose states of completion do not find expression in the aspect of ten at all.

This is similar to those miracles that change the ordered nature of existence; although the world obeys the "laws of nature," it does so only because, and only for as long as, G-d desires it to do so. He can just as easily suspend these laws in order to perform miracles. Thereby G-d amply demonstrates that even after He has established the rules by which nature operates, He is by no means limited by them.

This concept is indicated in the *Mishnah* when it states that the world need not have been created with ten Divine

---

4. Beginning of *Bereishis Rabbah.*

utterances; it could have been created with only one. The Mishna speaks not only of G-d's ability to create the universe with one utterance, but informs us that even after He created the world using ten utterances, He is still entirely capable of changing the rules.

Based on *Likkutei Sichos, Bereishis* 5747

Creation — A Lesson in Time Management

In telling the story of Creation, the Torah relates that "G-d finished on the seventh day His work which He had done, and He rested on the seventh day from all His work which He had done."[1]

In commenting on the words "G-d finished on the seventh day," *Rashi* notes: "Rabbi Shimon says, 'A human being can never be sure of the exact time, thus he must supplement the holy [day of Shabbos] by adding to it from the mundane [weekday]. G-d, however, who knows His exact moments and seconds, can enter into it [Shabbos] by a hairbreadth.' It thus *seemed* as if the work was concluded on that day."

Rashi goes on to give another explanation: "What was the world lacking? Tranquillity. When Shabbos arrived, tranquillity came as well. The work was then concluded and complete."

To indicate a tiny amount of space, the term "hairbreadth" is appropriate. However, a phrase like "the blink of an eye" seems more applicable when one is speaking about a minuscule unit of time. Why does *Rashi* use the former expression rather than the latter in explaining that G-d labored on the seventh day for only "a hairbreadth"?

"A hairbreadth" describes something so inconsequential that it is not perceived in and of itself. A single strand of hair

---

1. *Bereishis* 2:2.

is so fine that it is almost invisible; it is only when many hairs are close together that they can readily be seen.

Rashi therefore uses the expression "a hairbreadth" to explain that G-d's "labor" on the seventh day cannot be construed as prohibited work. For when *"everything* was [already] done on the sixth day,"[2] the labor done on the seventh was but "a hairbreadth," i.e., were it not for the absolute completeness of the work done on the sixth day, the seventh day's "labor" would not have been discerned at all. This is indeed "labor" that is permitted on Shabbos.

The following question, however, begs to be asked: Granted that labor of a mere "hairbreadth" is permitted on Shabbos, why was it necessary for G-d to labor so long and hard that He entered even "a hairbreadth" into Shabbos; why not complete it *all* on the sixth day?

This was done in order to teach man a priceless lesson concerning the value of time: As long as an individual has the opportunity to fulfill the purpose for which he finds himself in this world, he is to do so to the best of his ability and until the last possible moment.

For "G-d created nothing without a purpose."[3] Each and every thing which G-d created — including every iota of time and space — has a purpose. If G-d grants an individual a measure of time for the fulfillment of Torah study and the performance of *mitzvos*, and the person does not make full use of it, this unused time — be it only a twinkling — is considered wasted.

The preciousness of every moment is emphasized to an even greater degree by *Rashi's* additional question: "What was the world *lacking*? Tranquillity. When Shabbos arrived, tranquillity came as well. The work was then concluded and *complete.*" Until the actual arrival of Shabbos and the concurrent "hairbreadth" of labor, all that had been achieved was considered "incomplete" and "lacking."

---

2. As indicated ibid. verse 1:31.
3. *Shabbos* 77b.

This teaches us that using every moment wisely and well is so crucial that if an individual has occasion to do but another "hairbreadth" and wastes the opportunity, he is lacking completion in all those aspects of the work and service which he has fulfilled until then.

When all our moments, like G-d's, are so precious that none of them are wasted, when all are filled with positive accomplishments, then, like Him, we are able to enjoy the tranquillity that comes from knowing we did our best.

Based on *Likkutei Sichos*, Vol. V, pp. 24-34.

Noach   נח

Blessed Waters

The *Midrash* states:[1] "At the very beginning of the
world's creation, G-d's praise came solely from the waters....
When the generation of the Flood arose and rebelled against
Him... G-d said: 'Let these [rebels] be removed and the former [i.e., the waters] arise and come [in their stead].' Hence
it is written: 'And the rain was upon the earth 40 days and
40 nights.' "

Accordingly, it is to be understood that the world's
status at the time of the Flood was similar to the exalted
state it enjoyed at the very beginning of creation, when it
was "one mass of water,"[2] entirely involved in praising G-d.

How can this *Midrash* be reconciled with the fact that the
waters of the Flood were clearly meant to "destroy all flesh[3]"
— just the opposite of praising G-d?

It has been noted by our Sages[4] that "Torah preceded the
world," i.e., although Torah as studied in this physical
world is to be understood in its plain context,[5] it preceded
the world. For every letter of Torah also possesses inner and
esoteric meaning. Such meaning emanates from the study of
Torah in the higher spiritual realms — worlds that transcend
physicality.

Understandably, this applies not only to the Torah's
commandments, but to its stories; although all the stories
recounted actually transpired in all their detail, still, since
Torah *preceded* the world, we must perforce say that these

---

1. *Bereishis Rabbah* 5:1; see also *Eichah Rabbah* 1:52.
2. Ibid. 5:2.
3. *Bereishis* 6:17.
4. *Shabbos* 88b; *Pesachim* 54a; *Bereishis Rabbah* 1:4, *et al.*
5. *Shabbos* 63a.

tales also contain meanings found in the higher, spiritual worlds.[6]

This gives rise to the following inescapable conclusion: Since "No evil sojourns with You,"[7] we must say that even though the Torah contains things that in their simple context seem undesirable — such as misdeeds, punishments, and the like — in the world above, where it is impossible for evil to reside, these selfsame events are understood as being entirely desirable, holy and good.[8]

This principle will help us understand a seemingly inexplicable phenomenon associated with the reading of the Passage of Admonition (in the portion of *Savo*) by the *Alter Rebbe*, Rabbi Shneur Zalman of Liadi:

The *Alter Rebbe* used to serve as a Torah reader. It once happened that he was not in town during the Shabbos of *Savo*, so his son, the *Mitteler Rebbe*, heard the Torah read by another. His anguish upon hearing the maledictions in the Passage of Admonition was so great that it profoundly affected his health.

When the *Mitteler Rebbe* was asked: "But don't you hear this reading every year?" he responded: "When father reads, one does not hear any maledictions."

Surely, when the *Alter Rebbe* read the Torah the plain *text* was heard. What, then, did the *Mitteler Rebbe* mean when he said "one does not hear any maledictions"? How could he have failed to discern the simple meaning of the verses?

In light of the above, the matter is readily understandable: Maledictions exist in the Torah only as it is studied in this corporeal world. In a completely holy world, utterly divorced from evil (and thus also from the punishment that stems from evil behavior), even such things as maledictions are entirely holy and represent blessings.

---

6. See *Likkutei Torah, Tazria* 23b and onward.

7. *Tehillim* 5:5. See also *Likkutei Torah, Bamidbar* 3c.

8. See *Sefer HaMa'amarim 5679* (p. 515ff), where this concept is discussed at length.

Thus, when the *Alter Rebbe* would read the Torah, his level of inflection was such that his son could perceive even the Section of Admonition as it existed Above — in complete goodness and blessing.

The same is true with regard to the comment of the *Midrash* concerning the Flood: That the floodwaters came in order to punish the people of that generation was only so in this world. Since the incident of the Flood is related in the *Torah*, it follows that the event also transpired "above," in the spiritual world that is wholly good and utterly removed from any vestige of evil, sin, and punishment.

The *Midrash* thus informs us that the Flood was (also) entirely good and holy, similar to the "very beginning of the world's creation," when the entire world was but "one mass of water" and "G-d's praise came solely from the waters."

Based on *Likkutei Sichos, Noach* 5747.

In Praise of Noach

The Torah portion *Noach* begins with the words: "These are the children of Noach. Noach was a righteous individual...."[1] But only in the second verse does the Torah mention his three children, Shem, Cham and Yafes.

Rashi[2] explains this seeming incongruity by noting that the phrase "Noach was a righteous individual...." is a parenthetical statement inserted in the first verse — "Since he [Noach] is mentioned, his praises are extolled, for it is written,[3] 'the mention of a righteous individual should be accompanied by his praise.'"

This, however, gives rise to the following question: Noach's name was already mentioned in *Bereishis*;[4] seem-

---

1. *Bereishis* 6:9.
2. Ibid.
3. *Mishlei* 10:7.
4. 5:29-30; 5:32; 6:8.

ingly, it is there that his name should have been accompanied by praise. Why does the Torah refrain from praising him until the portion *Noach*?

Additionally, what is the reason for and the benefit of lauding the virtues of a righteous individual?

The *Gemara*[5] informs us that *Lashon Hara*, slander, harms not only the teller and the listener, but the person being talked about as well.

Now it is quite understandable that spiritual harm befalls both the speaker and the hearer of slander, for both are engaged in an act which our Sages liken to the combined sins of idolatry, incestuous relationships and murder.[6] But why is the object of the slander spiritually affected? Why should he suffer when he had no part in this sin?

Consider. Speech reveals that which was previously concealed as thought. Speaking of another's evil may thus have a detrimental effect on the slandered person; if the person's evil had not been spoken about, it might have remained "concealed" and not come to realization.

The reason this is so is that man's every action — especially speech, whose purpose is to reveal the concealed — has an effect. This may be felt either in a physical sense or on a spiritual plane, where the damage is perceived with higher and more refined senses.[7]

Thus it is related[8] that a person was once quarreling with another in the Baal Shem Tov's *shul*. In the heat of the moment, one of the disputants shouted that he would tear the other to pieces. The Baal Shem Tov revealed to his disciples how this act of dismemberment actually took place on a spiritual plane.

Yet "a good attribute is far more efficacious than a harmful one."[9] If speaking of another's evil has a detrimental ef-

---

5. *Erchin* 15b.
6. Ibid.
7. *HaYom Yom* p. 100.
8. Ibid.
9. *Sotah* 11a.

fect, then surely speaking of another's good qualities has a salutary effect on the person being spoken of; he is more likely to realize his goodly potential and qualities.

If this is so with regard to praise by human beings, how much more so with regard to G-d's praise of an individual, especially when this praise is included in the Torah itself!

This is why "the mention of a righteous individual should be accompanied by his praise"; by praising a person, one is actually assisting him in his righteous behavior.

The reason why Noach is first praised in the portion *Noach* rather than in *Bereishis* will be understood accordingly:

While it is true that Noach's name is mentioned earlier, it is specifically in the portion *Noach* that the Torah speaks of Noach with regard to the good deeds and spiritual service he attained on his own, as opposed to that with which he was favored from Above.

Since the reason for praising a righteous individual is to assist him in his divine service, and since Noach's service begins in the Torah portion *Noach*, it follows that it is here that his name be "accompanied by his praise."

The lesson to be derived in terms of our own service is obvious: A Jew should do his utmost to perceive the goodness of his fellow, and speak of his good traits and qualities. By doing so, he assists in revealing the goodness of the other, and at the same time helps the other in his spiritual passage through life.

Based on *Likkutei Sichos*, Vol. V, pp. 36-46.

Lech Lecha   לך לך

Three Altars

The Torah portion of *Lech Lecha* relates that Avraham built three altars to G-d.[1] *Rashi*, basing his commentary on the *Midrash*[2], explains that Avraham built the first altar "upon hearing G-d's promise that he would have children, and that they would inherit the land of Israel."[3]

Rashi goes on to state that he erected the second altar — in the vicinity of *Ai* — because "he saw in his prophecy that his progeny would stumble there through the sin of Achan. He therefore prayed for them there."[4]

However, no explanation is given by *Rashi* as to the reason for Avraham's third altar, since Avraham built it out of his simple love of G-d upon his arrival in the city of Chevron.

Our Sages inform us[5] that "G-d gave Avraham a sign that all that transpired with him will transpire with his children as well." This is so because the actions of the Patriarchs serve as an antecedent and a *catalyst* for the subsequent actions of their descendants.

Thus, the altars built by Avraham empowered his progeny to successfully bring offerings upon the altars in the *Mishkan* and the first and second *Beis HaMikdash*.

How did Avraham accomplish the building of these three altars?

The *Gemara* relates[6] that the altars performed three primary functions: they provided sustenance to the entire

---

1. *Bereishis* 12:7, 12:8, 13:18.
2. *Bereishis Rabbah*, conclusion of ch. 39.
3. *Rashi, Bereishis* 12:7.
4. Ibid. 12:8.
5. *Tanchuma, Lech Lecha* 9; similarly in *Bereishis Rabbah* 40:6.
6. *Kesuvos* 10b.

world; they negated any harsh decrees against the Jewish people by bringing about atonement for their sins; and they caused the Jewish people to be loved by G-d.

These three functions correspond to the three general categories of offerings: *Olah* — which were wholly consumed upon the altar; *Chatos* — atonement offerings; and *Shelamim* — peace offerings:

The *Shelamim* — parts of which were eaten by those who brought them — symbolize the altar's function of providing the world with sustenance; just as the owners were able to physically sustain themselves by eating parts of the offerings, so too is the "entire world sustained in the merit of the offerings."

Chatos — offerings that brought atonement — served to negate any and all harsh decrees, and caused the Jewish people to be forgiven for their sins.

The wholly consumed *Olah*, offered "entirely for G-d's glory,"[7] without any ulterior motive, served to make the Jews even more loved by G-d.

The bringing of offerings was deemed to be so important that the generic term "service" (*Avodah*) is applied to it.[8] It thus follows that in our day-to-day service to G-d, which mirrors the "service of offerings," we will also find the three above-mentioned categories:

First and foremost is the ongoing service of Torah and *mitzvos* — similar to the *Shelamim* offering — which continually provides a Jew with his physical and spiritual sustenance.

The second general aspect of Divine service — similar to the *Chatos* offering — is that of repentance and atonement; even when one — G-d forbid — transgresses, one is able to gain forgiveness through repentance and atonement.

However, a Jew achieves total unification with and attachment to G-d only through the service of *mesirus nefesh* —

---

7. *Midrash Tadsheh; Sefer Raziel HaMalach.*
8. See commentaries on *Avos* 1:2.

complete, absolute and selfless dedication, similar to the wholly consumed *Olah* offering.

In this state, a person dedicates himself to G-d not for the sake of physical or even spiritual reward, but solely for the sake of G-d's glory, with no thought of self. By acting in such a manner a Jew becomes "ever the more loved by G-d."

Avraham's building of three altars and their effect on his progeny can be understood accordingly: he thereby laid the foundations for the three general aspects of Divine service practiced by the Jewish people throughout history.

The first altar — built upon hearing G-d's promise about children and the land — relates to the physical and spiritual sustenance achieved through the ongoing service of Torah and *mitzvos*.

The second altar — wherein he prayed that the sin of Achan be forgiven — involves repentance, atonement and forgiveness.

The third altar — for which *Rashi* provides no reason at all — symbolizes that aspect of service which transcends reason: the service of *mesirus nefesh*.

Based on *Likkutei Sichos, Lech Lecha* 5747

"Down Is Up"

The name of a Torah portion is, of course, indicative of its general content, inasmuch as the title applies equally to all its verses. This is also true regarding *Lech Lecha*, "Go for your own sake" — a title that implies a continual moving forward.

The general meaning of forward movement in the life of a Jew, prefigured by the journey of Avraham — the first Jew — is a constant spiritual elevation through divine service, the reason for which man was created.[1]

---

1. Conclusion of tractate *Kiddushin*.

The beginning of *Lech Lecha* describes how Avraham fulfilled G-d's command to "move forth from your land, birthplace and father's home,"[2] by completing his father's journey to Eretz Yisrael. It then goes on to chronicle how Avraham continued to journey in the direction of Jerusalem and the *Beis HaMikdash*.[3]

The above facts thus detail Avraham's constant spiritual climb, forever attaining more sublime spiritual levels.

However, soon afterwards the Torah relates how a famine in Eretz Yisrael forced Avraham to *descend* to Egypt, a land whose spiritual degradation was such that is was called the "abomination of the earth."[4]

How does this descent conform with a title that refers to continual spiritual ascent?

Our Sages inform us[5] that "All the events that transpired with the Patriarchs serve as a sign to their progeny." This means that not only were these events the forerunners of similar ones involving the Jewish nation, but also that the trailblazing of the Patriarchs *brought about* those ensuing events.

Thus the *Zohar* says[6] that Avraham's descent to Egypt led to the subsequent exile of the Jewish people there, and understandably, Avraham's ensuing ascent from Egypt made possible the Jewish people's subsequent exodus and elevation. Similarly, since Avraham left Egypt "heavily laden with livestock, silver and gold,"[7] the Jewish people would leave Egypt with great wealth.

Accordingly, it is to be understood that the *ultimate* meaning of Avraham's descent into Egypt is indeed alluded to in the title *Lech Lecha*; his descent into Egypt was a necessary prerequisite to his subsequent ascent, "heavily laden

2. *Bereishis* 12:1.
3. *Bereishis Rabbah* 39:24.
4. *Bereishis* 42:9.
5. See *Tanchumah, Lech Lecha* 9; *Bereishis Rabbah* 40:6.
6. *Zohar, Lech Lecha*.
7. *Bereishis* 13:2.

with livestock, silver and gold." Therefore, this descent was part and parcel of his later *ascent*.

The same holds true with regard to our own spiritual debasement in the present Exile — an exile rooted in the Egyptian exile, the source of all later exiles.[8]

The ultimate intent of this exile is the enabling the Jewish people — through their spiritual service under the most trying circumstances — to reach an even loftier level than that attained during the time of the *Beis HaMikdash*.[9] Thus, the present descent is in itself truly part of the coming ascent.

The above helps immeasurably in terms of our own spiritual service. When one ponders the current state of the world, one may well despair of ever vanquishing the spiritual darkness and illuminating the world with the light of Torah and *mitzvos*.

In truth, however, all these descents and concealments are merely external. On a more sublime level, since G-d conducts the world according to His will and since He desires that all creation attain spiritual perfection, even those things that *seem* to indicate darkness and a headlong fall are but a prerequisite for refinement, illumination and soaring ascent.

Thus, since the present state of affairs is truly part and parcel of the coming ascent. The world overall is indeed becoming holier day by day, and ultimately will attain completion as a wholly fit dwelling place for G-d.

Based on *Likkutei Sichos*, Vol. V, pp. 57-63.

---

8. See *Likkutei Sichos IX*, p. 178, fn. 28.
9. See *Pesachim* 87b; *Torah Or*, 6a; *Or HaTorah, Lech* 86a.

Vayeira   וירא

Two Forms of Kindness

The Torah portion of *Vayeira* begins by relating that G-d appeared to Avraham at the entrance of his tent. But when Avraham observed three strangers standing nearby, he got up, asked G-d to wait, and ran to greet the strangers and offer them hospitality.[1]

Thus, for the sake of hospitality to strangers, Avraham left G-d waiting. Indeed, our Sages glean from Avraham's conduct that "Hospitality to wayfarers is even greater than receiving the Divine Presence."[2]

Such hospitable behavior has become an integral part of Jewish conduct — another example of the abovementioned pattern described by our Rabbis.

Yet Avraham himself had no such commandment. What led him to feel that it was proper to forsake G-d for the sake of strangers?

Kindness toward others can be motivated by either magnanimity or humility:[3]

An example of the former would be the favor shown by a great king or wealthy individual. Their feelings of self-worth and importance lead them to act in a generous and benevolent manner, "showering beneficence on all."

An example of kindness that results from humility is the charity exhibited by Avraham, who said of himself: "I am mere earth and ashes."[4] Because he felt himself to be less

---

1. *Bereishis* 18:1-5 and commentary of *Rashi*.
2. *Shavuos* 35b.
3. See *Likkutei Torah, Eikev* 17c and onward; *Toras Chayim, Toldos* 4a and onward; *Or HaTorah, Vayeira* 90a and onward; *Ma'amar Kotonti 5679*.
4. *Bereishis* 18:27.

significant than all others, he felt it natural to extend kindness and honor to all.[5]

Kindness that results from such self-effacement is superior to that which emanates from magnanimity in two important ways:

Kindness that comes from the feeling that everyone else is more worthy will cause an individual to give everything away to others, sustaining himself on their leavings. But kindness that stems from magnanimity will see the giver keeping the lion's share for himself, giving only the leavings to others.

Moreover, magnanimous kindness is only extended when the benefactor will not suffer from his own generosity. Self-effacing kindness, on the other hand, will inspire a person to give even when doing so causes him suffering and deprivation.

Because Avraham's kindness and hospitality stemmed from humility and self-effacement, he not only placed his physical life in jeopardy by battling mighty kings to save the lives of others,[6] but was even prepared to put his *spiritual* life in jeopardy — something much more important to him than his physical life.

This superior brand of kindness is what motivated Avraham to leave G-d waiting while he went to greet passing strangers.

The above sheds light on a saying of our Sages, who note[7] that: "In the merit of our father Avraham saying 'I am mere earth and ashes,' his children merited the commandments of the ashes of the Red Heifer and the earth of *Sotah* [used in the ritual of examining a suspected adulteress]."

It is axiomatic that "G-d rewards measure for measure."[8] Aside from the innocuous connection of the words "earth" and "ashes," what inner relationship exists between Avra-

---

5. See places cited in fn. 3.
6. *Bereishis* 14:14-17.
7. *Sotah* 17a; *Chulin* 88b.
8. See *Sotah* 8b and onward.

ham's statement and the two abovementioned commandments?

The connection is as follows: the performance of both these commandments is bound up with the humility and spiritual self-sacrifice that come from the awareness that one is "mere earth and ashes."

The ashes of the Red Heifer, used to purify individuals defiled by contact with the dead, caused some of those involved in its preparation to themselves become mildly defiled.[9] Thus, purifying an individual with the ashes of a Red Heifer necessitated a spiritual self-sacrifice upon the part of those who did the purifying.

The ashes of *Sotah* were also used in a ceremony that necessitated spiritual self-sacrifice, for the ritual required the erasing of the Divine Name. For the sake of bringing peace between husband and wife, the Torah indicates that G-d's name may be erased[10] — an act of self-sacrifice that echoes the kindness of Avraham.

Based on *Likkutei Sichos* Vol. XXV, pp. 79-83.

---

9. Mishnayos *Parah* conclusion of ch. 4; *Bamidbar Rabbah* beginning of ch. 19; *Rambam, Hilchos Parah Adumah* beginning of ch. 5.
10. *Shabbos* 116a.

Vayeira   וירא
Chof Cheshvan   כ' חשון

The Crucial Decision

When Rabbi Sholom Ber of Lubavitch was four or five years old, his mother escorted him to see his grandfather, the *Tzemach Tzedek*, on the Shabbos of the Torah portion *Vayeira*, in order for him to receive his grandfather's birthday blessing.

Upon entering his grandfather's room the child began to cry. When his grandfather asked him why he was crying, he answered that he had learned in *Cheder* that G-d appeared to Avraham. He was crying because he could not understand why G-d appeared to Avraham but does not appear to us.

The *Tzemach Tzedek* responded: "When a Jew at the age of 99 decides that he should circumcise himself, he is deserving that G-d should appear to him."

The lesson of the *Tzemach Tzedek*'s statement is that even a person who has engaged unremittingly in divine service for 99 years — as did Avraham — must also circumcise himself, i.e., he must take precautionary measures to guard against the coverings and concealments of the corporeal world and seek to remove them.

There is an additional factor involved: Adam was given six *mitzvos*, Noach received a seventh, and Avraham was given the *mitzvah* of circumcision. Since this *mitzvah* began with Avraham, it can be understood that it applied to him in particular.

Thus, Avraham's decision at the age of 99 to circumcise himself not only involved a refinement in his manner of service, but made him realize that even after all those years he was still lacking something vital. Moreover, from this time on all his deeds would be accomplished in a higher manner.

This is in line with the comment of our Sages on the verse, "and be unblemished,"[1] that G-d told Avraham that as long as he was uncircumcised he was considered blemished.[2] It is obvious that the difference between being blemished and unblemished applied to all aspects of Avraham, and not only to his "blemished" organ.

One of the meanings of "All the events that transpired with the Patriarchs serve as a sign to their progeny" is that the conduct of the Patriarchs in their performance of *mitzvos* paved the way and provided the fortitude for the Jewish people to perform the *mitzvos* after the Torah was given.

In order that the *mitzvos* performed by the Patriarchs be connected with those performed by the Jewish people after the Torah was given, there had to be at least one *mitzvah* that was similar to those performed by their children. This was the *mitzvah* of circumcision.

As opposed to Avraham's performance of other *mitzvos*, this *mitzvah* was commanded by G-d. Therefore the sanctity of the *mitzvah* remained in the physical object with which it was performed, similar to the sanctity remaining in objects with which *mitzvos* are performed subsequent to the giving of the Torah.

The commandment of circumcision was thus the one *mitzvah* that connected *all* the *mitzvos* performed by the Patriarchs with the *mitzvos* performed by their progeny after the Torah was given. It was specifically this *mitzvah* that made it possible for the *mitzvos* performed by the Patriarchs to provide fortitude to their children.

Accordingly, it is to be understood that Avraham's decision to circumcise himself after 99 years of spiritual service involved much more than the realization that he was missing something vital, and that from now on all his actions would be whole and unblemished.

---

1. *Bereishis* 17:1.
2. *Rashi* ibid. See also *Nedarim* 32a.

For it also involved the realization that all his *previous* actions were lacking; it was necessary that he circumcise himself so as to transform all his previous *mitzvos* as well, making them complete and unblemished.

There is a lesson here: A person must know that no matter how great he may be, he has yet to perform that degree of service which will render all his previous labors whole and complete.

Based on *Likkutei Sichos*, Vol. V, pp. 86-90.

Chayei Sarah   חיי שרה

Immediately Answered Prayers

In the Torah portion of *Chayei Sarah* we read[1] how Avraham sent his servant, Eliezer, to find a wife for Yitzchak. Arriving in Aram Naharayim, Eliezer prayed that his mission be crowned with success. The Torah goes on to say:[2] "He had not yet finished speaking when Rivkah appeared...."

Regarding the alacrity with which Eliezer's prayer was answered, the *Midrash* states:[3] "There were three individuals whose prayers were answered immediately: Eliezer the servant of Avraham, Moshe, and Shlomoh.

"Eliezer — [as written:] 'He had not yet finished speaking when Rivkah appeared'; Moshe — [as written]:[4] 'No sooner had he finished speaking these words [that the earth would split and swallow up Korach's rebels if he, Moshe, was indeed G-d's messenger], than the earth split; Shlomoh — [as written]:[5] 'And as Shlomoh concluded praying [that the Divine Presence grace the *Beis HaMikdash*], a fire descended from Heaven....' "

In light of the fact that Eliezer's prayer was likened to the prayers of such giants as Moshe and Shlomoh, and that other individuals of great stature did not have their prayers answered with such dispatch, we must perforce say that the immediate response was not so much dependent on the person doing the praying as on the uniqueness of the prayers.

---

1. *Bereishis* 24:1-14.
2. Ibid. verse 15.
3. *Bereishis Rabbah* 9:4; *Yalkut Shimoni, Remez* 108.
4. *Bamidbar* 16:31.
5. *II Divrei HaYomim,* 7:1.

In what way were these prayers so exceptional that they, and they alone, were answered with such speed?

The amount of time it takes for something to be transferred from one person to another depends entirely on the distance between the giver and the recipient; when they are utterly united, the transfer takes no time at all. It thus follows that the petition of one entirely united with G-d will result in an immediate response.

Just as the degree of closeness to G-d will affect the swiftness of response to one's prayer, so too will the content of the prayer have a direct effect on the speed of the answer — the more the prayer emphasizes the concept of unity and closeness to G-d, the more immediate the response.

In light of the above we can understand the uniqueness of the three abovementioned prayers: they encompass the three general manners whereby G-dliness is united with creation — within the *world*, within *man*, and within *Torah*.

The proof that G-dliness abides within the world was the manifestation of the Divine Presence in the *Beis HaMikdash*.[6] There it was possible for the naked eye to perceive that the material world was nullified before G-dliness, so much so that physical space transcended finite boundaries, as our Sages state:[7] "The space of the Ark was not [capable of being] measured."

It was for this measure of unification and revelation of G-dliness within the world that Shlomoh prayed at completion of the *Beis HaMikdash*, and that is why his prayer was answered immediately.

The revelation of G-dliness through unification with *man* finds expression in prophecy. This state is achieved when a prophet cleaves to G-d,[8] meriting to have G-d's words re-

---

6. See *Or HaTorah, Vayeitzei* 178a and onward; *Ma'amar Reb Brachya 5643*, chs. 2-3, 14 and onward; *Ma'amar Padah B'Shalom 5680* and *5687*.

7. *Yoma* 21a.

8. See *Rambam, Hilchos Yesodai HaTorah* 7:1.

vealed to him clothed in his own intellect, in his thought and speech.[9]

Moshe's prayer in response to the rebels' clamor:[10] "Why are you setting yourselves above G-d's congregation?" addressed itself to this issue, as the verse states:[11] "This shall demonstrate to you that *G-d sent me* to do all these deeds, and I did not make up anything myself."

Because Moshe's prayer dealt with the critical issue of uniting with G-d through prophecy, G-d's response was instantaneous.

The third manner of revelation of G-dliness — in a manner of complete unification — is the Divine revelation within *Torah*, for Torah and G-d are entirely one.[12]

When G-d gave the Torah to the Jewish people, He brought about the unification of the highest with the lowest — transcendent G-dliness uniting with the physical world — thereby making it possible for parchment, for example, to become a sacred object.

The incident that paved the way for the unification of the most lofty with the most base was the marriage of Yitzchak to Rivkah, for the actions of the Patriarchs serve as an antecedent to the actions of their progeny.[13] Yitzchak's marriage to Rivkah mirrored the joining of the most high with the most low.

Marriage is the highest form of union. In order for Rivkah (a child of the nefarious idolater Besu'el and sister of the infamous swindler Lavan) to marry Yitzchak (a living "sacred offering,"[14] the ultimate in holiness), a true union of the loftiest and lowliest had to be achieved. This marriage served as the forerunner of the union represented by the Torah.

---

9. *Shaar HaYichud VeHaEmunah* conclusion of ch. 2, quoting the *Ari Z"l.*
10. *Bamidbar* ibid. verse 4.
11. Ibid. verse 28.
12. *Tanya* chs. 4 and 23 quoting the *Zohar.*
13. See source cited in *Likkutei Sichos V*, p. 79, fn. 20.
14. *Bereishis Rabbah* 64:3.

It was for this union that Eliezer prayed. Little wonder, then, that "He had not yet finished speaking when Rivkah appeared."

Based on *Likkutei Sichos* Vol. XX, pp. 91-96.

Aging Gracefully

In chronicling the life of Avraham, we are told in the portion *Chayei Sarah* that[1] "Avraham was old, well advanced in days, and G-d blessed Avraham in all things."

Seemingly, "old" and "well advanced in days" are synonymous. Why does the verse repeat itself?

Our Sages interpret the qualities of "old" — *zakein* — and "well advanced in days" — *ba bayamim* — in the following manner: "Old" alludes to the acquisition of knowledge,[2] while "well advanced in days" refers to the filling of each and every day with the performance of *mitzvos*.[3]

"Old" and "well advanced in days" thus allude to two distinct things: "Old" relates to the superior quality of Avraham's *soul*, for he acquired much wisdom and insight; "well advanced in days" relates to Avraham's accomplishments with regard to the world as a whole, since the world is a composite of time and space.

This is in keeping with the general difference between Torah and *mitzvos*.[4] Torah, G-d's wisdom, is both intellectual and spiritual. By acquiring this wisdom, one enhances the quality of one's soul. *Mitzvos*, on the other hand, are clothed in physical things, and their main purpose is not so much to enhance a person's spiritual standing as to illuminate the physical world and transform it into a dwelling fit for G-d.

---

1. *Bereishis* 24:1.
2. *Kiddushin* 32a.
3. See *Zohar I* 224a; *Torah Or* 16a, 79b.
4. See *Tanya* chapters 23, 37. *Iggeres HaKodesh* conclusion of section 20.

Thus, with regard to gaining wisdom the term "acquisition" is used, for a person acquires wisdom. With regard to performing *mitzvos*, however, the term "days" is used, as it indicates the effect that *mitzvos* have on the world at large.

Herein lies the special quality of Avraham. He was able to harmoniously combine the ability to perfect himself and the ability to perfect and elevate the world. Moreover, Avraham accomplished both in a flawless manner — he was "blessed in *all* things," "old" and "well advanced in days."

An additional matter now becomes clear. The *Gemara* relates[5] that the 2,000-year period of Torah began with Avraham, for Avraham's manner of service was such that it served as a preparation for the giving of the Torah. What aspect of Avraham's service served as a forerunner to *Mattan Torah*?

The *Midrash*[6] informs us that prior to *Mattan Torah*, physicality and spirituality were separate entities. The novel quality of *Mattan Torah* was that from then on it became possible to fuse the physical with the spiritual through the performance of Torah and *mitzvos*.

The process of blending the sacred and the mundane began with Avraham's perfecting of his own spirituality while perfecting the spirituality of the world as a whole, to the degree that the world could attain such perfection prior to *Mattan Torah*.

As with all accounts in the Torah, there is a lesson[7] here for our own spiritual service:

There are individuals who constantly busy themselves with rectifying and improving the world, yet forget about their own self-improvement. Then there are others who are entirely immersed in perfecting themselves and do nothing to illuminate the world around them. Avraham's manner of service teaches that we must combine the two.

---

5. *Avodah Zarah* 9a.
6. *Shmos Rabbah* 12:3.
7. See *Zohar III* 53b.

Although both these aspects of service are necessary, greater emphasis is placed on illuminating and improving the world. Why?

Creator and created are separated by an infinite gulf. Perfecting oneself enhances the quality and increases the joy of created beings; perfecting the world at large and fulfilling G-d's desire of transforming it into a dwelling place for Him through the performance of *mitzvos* causes G-d pleasure and delight.

It is thus understandable that no matter how great the pleasure an accomplishment brings to created beings, it can in no way compare to the delight and gladness of the Creator Himself.[8]

Based on *Likkutei Sichos*, Vol. III, pp. 773-778.

---

8. See *Hemshech V'Kachah 5637* ch. 12.

Toldos   תולדות

To Give and Give Again

In the Torah portion of *Toldos* we read of the blessings
that Yitzchak bestowed upon his son Yaakov, beginning
with the words:[1] "And may G-d give you...." Comments the
Midrash:[2] "May He give you, and May He give you again."

Man is inherently limited, so his gifts are inherently limited. Even if a person were to give as much as he can, his gift
would be limited, and thus he may add to his gift by giving
once again.

G-d, however, is truly limitless. Surely, His original gift,
emanating as it does from his infinite kindness, is also without limit. What possible need could there be for G-d to give
and then give again?

The transmission of knowledge from teacher to student
can be achieved in one of two ways: a) the student may understand his master's teachings, but not thoroughly enough
to arrive at novel concepts; b) the disciple may completely
master his teacher's discourse, so that he is able to amplify
on these teachings and come up with novel thoughts of his
own.

Examples of the above are found in the *Mishnah*,[3] where
R. Yochanan ben Zakkai speaks of the qualities of his disciples, comparing R. Eliezer ben Horkenus to "a cemented cistern which does not lose a drop" and R. Elazar ben Arach to
a "fountain which flows with ever-increasing strength."

It is readily apparent that the latter student is superior to
the former. Thus Abba Shaul goes on to say in the name of
R. Yochanan ben Zakkai: "If all the Sages of Israel, including

---

1. *Bereishis* 27:28.
2. *Bereishis Rabbah* 66:3.
3. *Avos* 2:9 (according to the Alter Rebbe's version in his Siddur).

even Eliezer ben Hurknus, were on one side of a scale, and Elazar ben Arach were on the other, he would outweigh them all."

The reason for this superiority lies in the fact that even if "not a drop" of knowledge is lost, such a disciple will never have more than he received from his master.

However, a student who "flows with ever-increasing strength" will be able to use his master's teachings as a springboard to gain ever-increasing amounts of knowledge.

Nevertheless, it goes without saying that even the student who "flows with ever-increasing strength" owes his gains to the teachings of his master. After all, it is upon those teachings that his subsequent knowledge is based. In fact, this ability in his student represents a teacher's crowning achievement, for the ultimate objective of a teacher is to get his students to think for themselves.

Herein lies the meaning of "May He give you, and May He give you again": G-d's blessings are so splendid that not only is the person blessed with unlimited bounty from Above, but he is inspired to make use of these blessings on his own, thereby gaining yet again.

In terms of man's spiritual service, these two types of students correspond to the righteous individual and the penitent:

The righteous individual follows the path of Torah and *mitzvos* as they were transmitted from Above, while the penitent, having deviated from the path, transforms iniquity into merit.[4] His method of service uses his power of repentance — the arousal of which is also granted to him by G-d[5] — to perform an additional measure of service, a service not readily available to the righteous.

Furthermore, just as the student who is likened to "a fountain that flows with ever-increasing strength" is superior to a student who is similar to "a cemented cistern which does not lose a drop," so too is the service of the penitent

---

4. *Yoma* 86b; see also *Tanya* ch. 7.
5. See *Chagigah* 15a; *Berachos* 3a; *Likkutei Torah, Bamidbar* 6c.

superior to the service of the righteous. Our Sages express it thus:[6] "On the level that penitents stand, the completely righteous are unable to stand."

Their superiority is similar to that of the preeminent student: just as he is capable of endlessly increasing his knowledge, so too is the penitent's manner of service on an infinite level, while the service of the righteous, however excellent, is merely finite. The penitent thus serves in a manner of "May He give you, and May He give you again."

Based on *Likkutei Sichos* Vol. X, pp. 80-83.

---

6. See *Berachos* 34b.

Sowing the Physical and Reaping the Spiritual

In the Torah portion *Toldos* we read[1] that "Yitzchak sowed that land, and reaped that year a hundredfold." The *Midrash* notes[2] that Yitzchak measured the yield in order to tithe his crops.

In *Pirkei d'Rebbe Eliezer,*[3] however, we find the following comment: "Can it be that Yitzchak planted grain, Heaven forfend?! Rather, he took a tenth of all his wealth and implanted *tzedakah* — he distributed it to the poor."

Why does *Pirkei d'Rebbe Eliezer* find it so difficult to imagine Yitzchak planting crops? Commentaries explain[4] that since the Patriarchs were shepherds and wandered from place to place, it would have been impractical for any of them to sow seeds, as that requires remaining in one area for a considerable time.

---

1. *Bereishis* 26:12.
2. *Bereishis Rabbah* 64:6.
3. Beginning of ch. 33.
4. *Biur HaRadal* ibid.

But even if this were so, what is so devastating about the idea of Yitzchak's planting crops that the expression "Heaven forfend!" is used?

Moreover, we see that according to the *Midrash*, Yitzchak did indeed plant crops. Even if we were to say that these are two different opinions, they cannot be diametrically opposed.[5] How is it possible that according to the *Midrash* Yitzchak did plant crops, while according to *Pirkei d'Rebbe Eliezer*, "Can it be that Yitzchak planted grain, *Heaven forfend?!*"

We must perforce say that according to *Pirkei d'Rebbe Eliezer* as well, the simple meaning of the verse is that Yitzchak planted crops, for a verse can always be understood in its simple context.[6]

When *Pirkei d'Rebbe Eliezer* states "Can it be that Yitzchak planted grain, Heaven forfend?! Rather, he... implanted *tzedakah*" it intends to reveal the inner content and purpose of Yitzchak's planting:

With regard to the Patriarchs it is stated:[7] "The Patriarchs are truly the [Divine] Chariot,[8] for all their organs were completely *holy* and *detached* from mundane matters. Throughout their lives they served as vehicles for the Divine Will."

Thus, with regard to our Patriarch Yitzchak, *Heaven forfend* that the ultimate purpose of his planting was merely to raise crops. *Pirkei d'Rebbe Eliezer* therefore states that although Yitzchak's physical actions were surely those of planting crops, his inner purpose was to tithe the harvest and distribute *tzedakah*.

Pirkei d'Rebbe Eliezer, however, does not pose its question concerning the Patriarchs' chief physical occupation; it never asks "Were the Patriarchs shepherds, Heaven forfend?!" They chose to become shepherds for the very fact that shep-

---

5. *Tosfos, Beitza* 13a. See also *Darkei Shalom, Klalei HaShas, Klal 415*.
6. *Shabbos* 63a.
7. *Tanya* ch. 23.
8. *Bereishis Rabbah* 47:6; 82:6.

herding is not taxing, and they were thus able to concentrate on their service to G-d.[9]

Farming, however, is both physically and mentally taxing, something that in itself inhibits divine service. It is thus necessary to inform us that Yitzchak's labor was not, Heaven forfend, one of simple farming, but a preparation for the *mitzvah* of tithing, since tithes must be given from one's own crops.[10] Yitzchak's planting was thus not one of "planting grain" but truly that of "implanting *tzedakah.*"

Yitzchak's physical planting of crops may indeed be linked to the statement in the *Mishnah*[11] that if one carries out food on Shabbos in a vessel holding less than the amount necessary to incur guilt for carrying from a private domain to a public domain, he is then not only guiltless of carrying the food, but is also guiltless of carrying the vessel; since the vessel is wholly subordinate to the food it holds, it is considered as if he did not carry it at all.

Yitzchak's physical planting, too, was so subordinated to the spiritual goal of *tzedakah* that he did not "plant grain," rather he "implanted *tzedakah*" — throughout their lives, the Patriarchs served as "vehicles for the Divine Will."

Based on *Likkutei Sichos*, Vol. V, pp. 68-74.

---

9. See *Toras Chayim, Vayechi* 102b.
10. *Rambam, Hilchos Ma'asar* 2:2.
11. *Shabbos* 93b.

Vayeitzei   ויצא

The Jewish People — Sons and Sheep

The portion of *Vayeitzei* relates at length how Yaakov, while sojourning with Lavan, was involved with sheep. He was both shepherd and sheep owner, for he received sheep as payment for some of his years of service.

Every detail in Torah serves as an eternal lesson for all Jews at all times and in all places. This is especially so with regard to the actions of the Patriarchs, since these serve as an antecedent to the spiritual service of their offspring.[1]

Surely this is so regarding the lengthy story of Yaakov's involvement with sheep. What spiritual lesson is to be gleaned from sheep?

The *Midrash*[2] speaks of the relationship between G-d and the Jewish people in the following manner: "He is unto me a father, and I am unto Him as a son; He is unto me a shepherd and I am unto Him as sheep."

Obviously, the relationship between father and son goes far beyond the relationship between a shepherd and his flock. Once the *Midrash* states that Jews are like G-d's children, what additional bond is the *Midrash* hinting at when it states that G-d loves the Jewish people as a shepherd loves his sheep?

Describing Jews as G-d's children implies that they are looked upon as a distinct entity.[3] Although every Jewish soul is inseparably bound to G-d[4] — unlike a physical father-and-son relationship, which can be broken — the very

---

1. See *Likkutei Sichos V* p. 69ff.
2. *Shir HaShirim Rabbah* 2:16 (1).
3. See *Or HaTorah, Re'eh* pp. 784-785, p. 795ff.
4. *Likkutei Torah, Rosh HaShanah* 62d.

fact that a Jew is called "son" implies that he is another entity — he is not the Father.

Therefore, while as "children" of God our existence and our love for our Heavenly Father is important to Him, we remain created beings; entirely different from the ineffable Presence that is G-d. With regard to this essential state the verse states:[5] "He has no son...."

This unbridgeable gulf is better described by likening the Jewish people's relationship with G-d to that between a shepherd and his sheep; there is no comparison at all.

Nevertheless, this latter relationship also serves as an illustration; there is a fondness between the Shepherd and His flock. But in this context, our belovedness stems from the intensity of our *self-nullification* rather than from our state of *being*.

This self-effacement is alluded to in the metaphor of sheep, for we observe that sheep possess a greater degree of self-effacement than do other animals.

The two descriptions of the Jewish people — sons and sheep — allude to two forms of spiritual service:

The level of "son" results from the service of Torah study, which involves an individual's comprehension. Though increased Torah learning brings increased closeness to G-d, it also brings increased awareness of the fundamental and unbridgeable distance between created and Creator.

The level of "sheep" is attained by purifying, refining and elevating the physical world. For the Hebrew word for sheep, *tzon*, is related to the word *yetziah*, or departure,[6] referring to the "departure" from one's intellectual self and the occupation of one's body with worldly matters in order to transform the world into a dwelling fit for G-d.

It is specifically this manner of service that evokes true self-nullification to G-d, for in this form of service, the Jew serves not for his own benefit and spiritual elevation, but

---

5. *Koheles* 4:8.
6. *Torah Or, Vayeitzei* 23c; *Toras Chayim, Vayeitzei* 38b.

strictly for the sake of realizing the Divine goal of transforming this world into a dwelling place for G-d.

Based on Likkutei Sichos Vol. XV, pp. 252-254.

Shabbos — An Unlimited Heritage

In the Torah portion *Vayeitzei*, G-d blesses Yaakov, declaring to him:[1] "You shall spread out to the west, to the east, to the north and to the south." The *Gemara* comments:[2] "Whoever delights in the Shabbos receives an unlimited heritage, as is written:[3] 'Then you shall delight in G-d... and I will nourish you with the heritage of Yaakov,' of whom it is written: 'You shall spread out to the west, to the east....' "

The reward for the performance of a *mitzvah* is, of course, measure for measure.[4] What aspect of the *mitzvah* of Shabbos causes its reward to be "an unlimited heritage"?

Shabbos differs from all other *mitzvos* in that the performance of other *mitzvos* is achieved through labor and action. There are thus differences between the manner in which a very righteous individual will perform a *mitzvah* and the manner in which it will be performed by a simple person.

For example, *tefillin* are to be placed opposite the heart and upon the head so as to "bind" the head and heart to G-d. Understandably, there is a vast difference between the spiritual head and heart of a truly righteous individual and that of a less righteous one. The same is true with regard to other *mitzvos*.

Observing Shabbos, however, consists of a *cessation* from labor. With regard to "not doing," all Jews can be equal.

---

1. *Bereishis* 28:14.
2. *Shabbos* 118a.
3. *Yeshayahu* 58:14.
4. See *Sotah* 8b, 9b. See also *Tanya* ch. 39: "From its reward one knows its essence...."

Although the cessation of labor of simple folk involves refraining from menial tasks while the cessation of labor of the lofty involves a pause in the spiritual refinement of the physical world, these people only differ with regard to the manner of labor they are resting from; with regard to the resultant *cessation* of labor, all Shabbos-observant Jews are equal.[5]

Superficially, it would seem that the same would be true regarding *all* prohibitive commandments; like Shabbos, they involve *not* doing something. But upon closer reflection, the difference between the cessation of labor on Shabbos and the keeping of negative commandments is obvious:

Prohibitory commands are a direct outgrowth of positive ones. For example, the prohibition against idolatry stems from the positive command that a Jew is to have faith and knowledge only of G-d; the prohibition of eating non-kosher animals is a direct result of the *mitzvah* of *kashrus*, etc.

The cessation demanded by Shabbos, on the other hand, is the actual and entire commandment, as the verse states:[6] "You shall not do any work... For [in] six days G-d made the heavens and earth... and rested on the seventh day."

The reason why all Jews are entirely equal with regard to the *mitzvah* of cessation of labor on Shabbos stems from the fact that the *mitzvah* of Shabbos touches the essence of the Jewish soul. Differences between one Jew and another exist only on an external level; with regard to their essence, they are all equal.

This, too, is the meaning of the statement in the *Minchah* prayer of Shabbos: "May Your children recognize and know that from You is their rest, and by their rest they sanctify Your Name." Shabbos rest derives from G-d's very Essence — "from *You*." This causes each Jew's rest to be bound up with the essence of his soul.

---

5. See *Ma'amar Atah Echad* of the *Mitteler Rebbe*.
6. *Shmos* 20:10,11.

It is also from this level of essential soul that a Jew finds the strength to offer his life for the sanctification of G-d's Name — a power found in all Jews equally.

Thus, both Shabbos rest and ultimate self-sacrifice arise from the same source. It thus follows that "by their rest" i.e., by the very power that enables all Jews to rest equally on Shabbos, comes the ability to "sanctify Your Name."

The connection between the blessing "And you shall spread out..." and Shabbos will be understood accordingly. "And you shall spread out..." is an *unlimited* heritage that derives from G-d's limitless Essence. This is achieved through observing Shabbos, for Shabbos too stems from G-d's Essence.

Based on *Likkutei Sichos*, Vol. XV, pp. 226-229.

Vayishlach　　　　　　　　　　　　ויַשׁלח

"Today I Become a Man"

In the Torah portion of *Vayishlach* we read about Dinah's brothers, Shimon and Levi: "each *man* took his sword,"[1] in order to avenge their sister's violation by Shechem. Shimon and Levi were at that time 13 years old.[2]

According to some opinions,[3] since at the age of 13 Shimon and Levi were deemed "men" — a term that denotes maturity, as the verse states:[4] "Strengthen yourself and become a man" — we derive the law that "at the age of 13 one becomes obligated to perform the *mitzvos*."[5]

In other words, by the age of 13 one has acquired the intellectual characteristics and attitudes of an adult — maturity of intellect and *discernment*. It is for this reason that a person is then obligated to perform all the commandments.

Although it is possible to be intellectually acute even before the age of 13, maturity is still lacking, both with regard to the dearness and merit of performing *mitzvos*, as well as with regard to the severity of the sin in their non-performance.[6] Accordingly, a pre-teen is not held responsible for his conduct and actions, and the obligation of *mitzvos* cannot be placed upon him.

According to another opinion, however, the source for the obligation to perform *mitzvos* at age 13 is a dictate

---

1. *Bereishis* 34:25.
2. *Bereishis Rabbah* 80:10; *Midrash Lekech Tov* and *Sechel Tov* on this verse.
3. *Rashi, Nazir* 29b; *Bartenura, Avos* 5:21; *Machzor Vitri* ibid.
4. *Melochim I*, 2:2. See also *Sefer HaShorashim* of the *Radak* under the heading *Ish*.
5. *Avos* ibid.; *Rambam, Hilchos Shevisas Asor* 2:10.
6. See *Kuntres HaTefillah* ch. 5, p. 15ff.; *Sefer HaMa'amarim 5670*, p. 115; *Hemshech 5672 III*, p. 1227.

handed down by G-d to Moshe at Sinai.[7] As such, it follows along the lines of other supra-rational edicts regarding measurements and amounts. According to this opinion, the obligation to perform *mitzvos* at 13 has nothing to do with maturity or discernment; it is a supra-rational law.

One of the Halachic differences between these two opinions is the age at which a non-Jew becomes obligated to observe the Seven Noahide Laws.

If the obligation of *mitzvos* at the age of 13 is dependent on the age at which (most) people reach maturity, then it should apply to Jew and non-Jew equally. If, however, it is one of the supra-rational Laws of Measures — which do not apply to non-Jews[8] — then the age at which non-Jews' are obligated to perform their seven commandments depends entirely on individual maturity.[9]

In terms of spiritual service, the difference between these two opinions relates to the manner in which a Jew is to approach the performance of Torah and *mitzvos*:

According to the first opinion, the approach is one of serving G-d logically; if the age at which one becomes obligated to perform *mitzvos* depends on one' intellectual maturity, it is understandable that the service commences with logic and comprehension.

According to the second opinion, however, the obligation to begin performing *mitzvos* at 13 is supra-rational — because G-d has so commanded. It therefore follows that the approach to the performance of *mitzvos* involves the supra-rational acceptance of the Divine Yoke.

Nevertheless, even those who hold the first opinion — that the age for beginning one's service is gleaned from the verse "each *man* took his sword" — also agree that the performance of *mitzvos* is bound up with *mesirus nefesh*, i.e.,

---

7. *Responsa* of the *Rosh*, beginning of general principle 16; *Responsa* of the *Ma-Haril*, sect. 51; second comment of *Rashi* in *Avos* ibid.
8. *Rambam, Hilchos Melochim* 9:10.
9. *Responsa* of the *Chasam Sofer, Yoreh Deah*, sect. 317.

serving G-d in a self-sacrificial manner that transcends the bounds of intellect.

That this is indeed so is amply demonstrated[10] by the fact that those who hold this opinion derive it from the verse "each man took his *sword*" — an action that demands self-sacrifice.

This in no way contradicts the earlier statement that this manner of service demands comprehension and intellect, for though they maintain that the action should be performed with understanding and discernment, they agree that the *foundation* of Divine service lies in acceptance of the Divine Yoke. Then, and only then, can a person be assured that he will not be *blinded* by his own logic, and that his performance of *mitzvos* will be done in an entirely proper manner.

Based on Likkutei Sichos Vol. XV, pp. 289-292.

10. See *Likkutei Sichos V*, p. 162 fn. 74; ibid. p. 421.

"An Abode for G-d in the Nethermost Levels"

The Torah portion *Vayishlach* begins by relating how Yaakov sent messengers to his brother Esav.[1] His underlying purpose in doing so was to rectify and elevate Esav by revealing the good concealed within him.[2]

This is similar to the mission entrusted to every Jew, for all Jews are G-d's messengers,[3] charged with the mission of "making an abode for G-d in the nethermost levels"[4] — this physical world.

In order for a Jew to be able to transform the physical universe into an abode for the Creator, G-d caused Torah

1. *Bereishis* 30:4.
2. See *Torah Or* and *Toras Chayim* portion *Vayishlach*.
3. See *Likkutei Torah, Vayikra* 1c.
4. See *Tanchuma, Naso* 15; *Tanya,* beginning of ch. 36.

and *mitzvos* to descend to this world.[5] By studying Torah, performing mitzvos and spreading their light, a Jew is able to perform his mission.

To make an abode for G-d "in the nethermost levels," however, two seemingly opposite things are necessary:

First and foremost, an individual must be completely self-effacing, aware that he is merely G-d's emissary, and as such may not, Heaven forbid, act in a manner contrary to G-d's desire as expressed in the Torah, even when he thinks that by doing so he can have a greater effect on his environment. If an emissary acts contrary to the dictates of the one that appointed him, he ceases to be an emissary.[6]

On the other hand, in order for an individual to succeed in disseminating the light of Judaism and influencing others, he must use his *own* intellect — the opposite of self-efface-ment. This ability to use one's own faculties is also a precondition to becoming an emissary, as it is clearly stated[7] that an emissary must be mentally competent.

These two attributes, so essential to the mission of "making an abode for G-d in the nethermost levels," reflect the two components of that mission: "an abode" and "in the nethermost levels."

The concept of "an abode" stresses that the revelation of G-dliness in this world must have the same qualities as a person in his own home. When a person is among others he is constrained and cannot be truly himself; when he is at home the restraints are lifted and he reveals himself fully.

The concept of "in the nethermost levels" emphasizes that this revelation is so intense that it permeates the very essence of the nethermost levels.[8]

This also explains why there are two aspects to the mission of "making an abode for G-d in the nethermost levels":

5. See *Tanchuma, Vayigash* 6; *Tanya* ch. 5.
6. *Rambam, Hilchos Shluchin v'Shutfin* 1:2 and onward; *Shulchan Aruch, Choshen Mishpat* 182:2 and onward.
7. *Gitin* 23a.
8. See *Maamar Tik'u 5667; Likkutei Sichos XII*, p. 73, *XV*, p. 88ff and fn.

On the one hand, all Jews are entrusted equally with this mission; on the other, each has his specific tasks to fulfill.

With regard to the preparation of an "abode," all Jews are entirely equal, in that they each possess a soul that is "truly a part of G-d above,"[9] and are thus G-d's emissaries. Therefore every good deed performed by a Jew serves to reveal G-d's essence, helping make an "abode" for Him.

However, in order to permeate the many entities that constitute the "nethermost levels" with this intense degree of holiness, it is necessary that actions be undertaken appropriate to each entity and level. Here, each Jew has his own mission through which he purifies and elevates his portion in the world.

In light of the above, we can readily understand why it is necessary to display both complete self-effacement and independent thought in order to "make an abode for G-d in the nethermost levels."

In order to be a proper emissary, a person must be wholly dedicated and nullified before G-d, for G-d resides only among the humble.[10] At the same time, in order to better influence the "nethermost levels" a person must be able to reach out to them — something that requires applied intelligence.

Based on *Sefer HaSichos 5748*, pp. 138-143, *Likkutei Sichos*, Vol. XXV, p. 364.

---

9. *Tanya* ch. 2.
10. *Yeshayahu* 57:17. See also *Sotah* 5a: "G-d says of the arrogant individual, 'He and I cannot reside in the same world.' "

Vayeishev   וישב

A Jewish treasure hunt

The Torah portion of *Vayishlach* concludes by briefly listing the kings of Edom — the descendants of Esav — and their settlements. This is followed by the portion of *Vayeishev*, in which we are told how Yaakov settled in Canaan, and where the story of his progeny is related at great length.

The connection between *Vayeishev* and the conclusion of *Vayishlach* is explained by our Sages with the following parable:[1]

"It is analogous to a king who had a pearl that was cast in earth and thorns. The king had to probe the earth and thorns in order to recover the pearl. As soon as the king recovered the pearl he discarded the earth and thorns and occupied himself with his treasure."

Here, too, it was impossible to describe Yaakov's settling in Canaan and tell the story of his children without first summarizing the section about Edom, the descendants of Esav.

Why, indeed, was such a preface necessary? Also, the parable seems to imply that Jacob was "hidden" among Esav's descendants, yet almost all the Edomites come on the scene after Yaakov's passing. Additionally, why was the "pearl" found in the midst of both "earth" and "thorns"?

The purpose of Yaakov's settling in Canaan was not only so that he and his children might inhabit Eretz Yisrael, but also, as Yaakov told Esav, so that he might remain within reach of his brother "until I come to [you], my lord, in Seir,"[2] which refers — as *Rashi* explains[3] — to the fulfillment of the

1. *Tanchuma, Vayeishev* 1.
2. *Bereishis* 33:14.
3. Ibid.

promise "at the time of Mashiach's coming... that 'deliverers[4] will go up to Mount Tzion to judge the mount of Esav.' "

It is this that our Sages imply with the parable of the pearl: The allusion is not merely to Yaakov's settling in Eretz Yisrael, but to Yaakov's ultimate goal — "coming to *Seir*." Since this can be attained only by working within "the settlements of Esav and his progeny," i.e., purifying and elevating the sparks of holiness concealed within physicality, Yaakov's pearl is described as being concealed within the "earth and thorns" of Esav.

Herein lies a vital lesson for Jews during times of exile: The purpose of all exiles, and particularly of this final Exile, the exile of Edom, is to purify and elevate the sparks of holiness (the pearls) found in physical things[5] — the earth and thorns.

Within physicality itself there are two distinct categories, alluded to by our Sages as "earth" and "thorns:"

"Earth" denotes permissible things that merely conceal sparks of holiness found within them. A Jew is able, through his spiritual service, to purify these sparks and elevate them.

"Thorns," however, refer to material things that are prohibited, and that so profoundly conceal the holiness within them that in the normal course of events they must be cast aside.

Moreover, even after a person "recovers the pearl," he must "discard the earth." I.e., it is necessary for the person to indicate that the physical things in and of themselves are of no importance. He occupies himself with them *only* so that he may gain access to the sparks of holiness concealed within.

This is why "discarding the earth" is necessary in order to obtain the pearl: As long as physicality itself is important to the seeker, not only will he be unable to properly extricate

---

4. Conclusion of *Ovadiah*.
5. *Torah Or*, beginning of *Lech*; ibid. 117b. See also *Likkutei Sichos III*, p.826.

the pearl, but it is quite possible that his occupation with physical matters will lead to his spiritual downfall.[6]

Only when a person's every physical act is performed in a manner such that he that he disregards their corporeality will he be able to elevate the sparks of holiness concealed within matter. By doing so a person's own spiritual stature is immeasurably enhanced as well.

Based on *Likkutei Sichos* Vol. XV, pp. 302-307.

---

6. See *Likkutei Torah*, Naso 26c, Balak 72a, *Pinchas* 79d, et al.

How To Increase Your Luck

The Torah portion *Vayeishev* relates at length[1] about Yosef's trials and tribulations in Egypt, first being forced into slavery and then incarcerated in an Egyptian prison. In both instances G-d was with Yosef, blessing him with good fortune.

The Torah, however, clearly distinguishes between his good fortune as a slave and his good fortune as a prisoner: With regard to the former, the verse states:[2] "and G-d made it so that all he did was favored with good fortune — *matzliach* — in his hand." With regard to Yosef's fortunes as a prisoner, the verse merely states:[3] "and that which he did, G-d favored with good fortune," deleting the term "in his hand."

Why do the verses differ?

The *Tzemach Tzedek* explains[4] that the word *matzliach* means good fortune — something granted as a gift from above, independent of a person's own labor.[5]

---

1. *Bereishis* 39:1 and onward.
2. Ibid., verse 3.
3. Ibid., verse 23.
4. *Or HaTorah, Vayeishev* 278a-b.
5. See *Moed Katan* 28a; *Zohar, Vayeishev* 181a.

There are, however, two kinds of "luck": One is realized *within* and *through* a man's actions. For example, a person who succeeds at *whatever* he does owes his continued success to G-d's ongoing gift.

There is, however, an even greater kind of luck, wherein the reward for a person's labor is so out of proportion to the effort expended that one can immediately perceive G-d's hand at work.

Herein lies the difference between Yosef's two kinds of luck: During the time that he was a slave, the verse states:[6] "G-d was with Yosef, and *he* was a *man* of good fortune" ; the success was ascribed to Yosef. When Yosef was jailed, however, the verse states: "and that which he did *G-d favored* with good fortune" ; whenever Yosef would do something, his success was so astounding that G-d's hand was immediately discernible.

Why was it that when Yosef was merely a slave his luck was of a lower order, yet when he underwent the further degradation of becoming a prisoner his luck became greater?

The prerequisite for supernatural success is self-abnegation, as the verse states:[7] "To this one I will look — to one who is poor and of crushed spirit." The less cognizant a person is of his own ego, the more G-d will be with him, and the more will G-d's might be perceived in his actions.

Herein lies the basic difference between slavery and incarceration. While a slave is wholly subjugated to his master, he still retains a sense of dignity and self; he is able to accomplish meaningful work, and so on.

A prisoner, however, is nothing more than a number, and cannot develop or even employ his talents; a prisoner loses all sense of self-esteem.

Yosef's slavery enabled him to achieve an appropriately profound state of humility. In turn, "G-d was with Yosef and he was a man of good fortune... and G-d made it so that all he did was favored with good fortune in his hand."

---

6. *Bereishis* 39:2.
7. *Yeshayahu* 66:2.

Nonetheless, since Yosef the slave still retained a sense of self, his success was limited to such divine good fortune as was clothed in, and thus necessarily bounded by, "his hand" and actions.

Yosef's incarceration, however, created a state of utter nullification before G-d, to the degree that he lost all feeling of personal ego. The success he then enjoyed was therefore entirely superhuman — "and that which he would do *G-d would favor* with good fortune."

Yes, Yosef's success even now remained based upon his actions, but since Yosef exhibited total self-abnegation, his actions in no way impeded his luck. Thus, the rewards were no longer limited by the hand of a limited being, but were divinely boundless.

Compiled from *Likkutei Sichos*, Vol. XXV, pp. 213-216.

Mikeitz   מקץ

Fighting Famine

The Torah portion of *Mikeitz* relates how Yosef distributed food to the starving people of the "entire earth" during a time of famine.[1] He was able to do so because in the preceding years of plenty, "he placed food in the cities; the food growing around each city he placed inside it."[2]

At first glance we may conclude that he placed food inside the city next to which it grew. But this conclusion raises the following difficulties:

Why does the verse have to emphasize that Yosef placed the food in the nearest city; would we think he had transported it to a more distant one?! Moreover, why does the Torah find it necessary to tell us where he placed the food?

Rashi[3] answers by explaining that "the food growing around each city he placed inside it" means the following: "Each kind of soil is best suited for certain types of produce, therefore earth from the area [where the produce was grown] was placed together with the produce, keeping the food from rotting."

Thus, "he placed inside it" refers not to placing food inside the city next to which it grew, but rather to preserving the food by placing soil from the area in which it grew together with the produce itself — "inside it."

There is a lesson in this *Rashi*:

A Jew's principal "produce" consists of the Torah he learns and the *mitzvos* he performs. When a Jew amasses a huge amount of "produce," he must know that in order for it

---

1. *Bereishis* 41:57.
2. Ibid. verse 48.
3. Ibid.

to be "preserved," he must surround it with "*earth* from that place."

"Earth" symbolizes self-abnegation, as we say at the conclusion of the *Amidah*:[4] "Let my soul be [so humble that it is] as earth to all." This feeling of humility and self-efface-ment makes possible the actions of the next verse: "Open my heart to Your Torah, and let my soul eagerly pursue Your commandments."

There is an additional lesson alluded to by *Rashi*: the "earth" must be from the place in which the produce grew. This means to say that a person's humility must be "in place."

Being so humble as to be defenseless before the blan-dishments of one's evil inclination, or being so servile that one is stepped upon by all — not least by one's own evil inclination — is described as misplaced humility.

In this regard, a person must be "fierce as a leopard and courageous as a lion" — a statement found at the very be-ginning of the *Shulchan Aruch*, the Code of Jewish Law, and thus crucial to its fulfillment.

With regard to Torah and *mitzvos* as well, if one is so meek that he avoids leaving his familiar surroundings to spread Torah learning for fear that the outside world may have an undue influence on him, his humility too is entirely out of place.

On the other hand, being humbled by the fact that the Torah is *G-d's* Word, and as such so completely transcends comprehension that in order for a created being to succeed in his studies he must constantly be aware of the Giver of Torah — that is humility that is "in place."

Here the Torah teaches us yet another vital lesson:

Yosef sustained the "entire earth" during the time of famine. This means that in a time of *spiritual* famine — a pe-riod of ignorance of Torah and things Jewish — it is incum-bent upon each and every Jew (every Jew being spiritually

---

4. This text is originally found in *Berachos* 17a.

termed "Yosef")[5] to provide even those outside his immediate surroundings with spiritual sustenance.

Here *Rashi* teaches us that the spiritual food which one gives a fellow Jew must be of a permanent nature ("keeping the food from rotting"); he must see to it that the lessons will sustain the recipient all the days of his life.

Based on *Likkutei Sichos* Vol. XXV, pp. 220-226.

---

5. *Tehillim* 80:2, and commentary of *Rashi* and *Metzudas Dovid* ibid.; see also *Likkutei Sichos XXV*, p. 252ff.

Chanukah חנוכה

"This is Chanukah"

The final day of Chanukah is customarily called *Zos Chanukah*, "This is Chanukah."[1] The simple reason for this name is that the Torah reading for the last day of Chanukah is "*Zos chanukas hamizbeiach*," "This is the dedication of the altar."[2]

However, since Jewish custom is itself Torah,[3] the saying is to be understood as meaning that this day, as the name implies, "is Chanukah," i.e., the last day of Chanukah contains what Chanukah is all about.

Why is the eighth day of Chanukah so significant?

We find[4] that *Bais Shamai* and *Bais Hillel* differed with regard to the manner of kindling the Chanukah lights. *Bais Shamai* maintained that the lights should be lit in descending order — on the first night, eight lights are lit, on the second night seven, and so on until the final night, when only one light is lit.

Bais Hillel, however, maintains that the lights are lit in ascending order — on the first night one is lit, on the second two, etc., until on the final night all eight lights are lit. The Halacha favors *Bais Hillel*.

The reason for the disagreement is as follows:[5] *Bais Shamai* is of the opinion that we look at matters as they are in their potential state. Thus, on the first day of Chanukah

---

1. See *Maamar Boruch Sh'Asah Nissim, Or HaTorah, Bereishis* Vol. V, p. 957 and onward, conclusion of ch. 4.
2. *Bamidbar* 7:84,88.
3. See *Tosafos* titled *Nifsal, Menachos* 20b; *MaHaril*, quoted in *Ramah, Yoreh Deah* 376:4
4. *Shabbos* 21b.
5. See also *Likkutei Sichos VI*, p. 73ff.

eight lights are lit, for this day encompasses, in potential, all the days of Chanukah that will follow.

Bais Hillel, however, maintains that we look at things as they exist in actuality. Therefore, the number of lights lit is in accord with the actual number of days of Chanukah — the first day only one light is lit, for in actuality it is but the first day of the festival, and from that day on an additional light is lit each day.

Our Sages relate[6] that Chanukah is an acronym for "Eight lights are to be lit, and the law is in accordance with the opinion of *Bais Hillel*." That the name of the holiday itself is said to emphasize the opinion of *Bais Hillel* clearly indicates that on Chanukah particular emphasis is placed on the actual rather than on the potential.

Why?

The argument as to whether one should lean towards potentiality or actuality is in truth a dispute regarding Torah and *mitzvos*. G-d gave the Jewish people His Torah and *mitzvos*. Torah and *mitzvos* therefore reflect aspects of both the Giver and the recipient. We thus find that Torah is not subject to impurity even when studied by an impure individual, for it remains G-d's Torah.[7] On the other hand, a Torah master may forego his own honor, for the Torah is considered to be his property.[8]

As a result, there are two ways in which Torah is found within this world: reflecting the perspective of the Giver, or reflecting the framework of the receiver, the Jewish people.

Bais Shamai holds the former view. They therefore say that matters of Torah and *mitzvos* should always be viewed in their potential state, since from the perspective of the Giver, the actual exists with and within the potential.

Bais Hillel, however, is of the opinion that the most important consideration is that Torah and *mitzvos* affect the Jew as an imperfect created being. Therefore, until a matter

6. *Avudraham, Seder Hadlokas Neir Chanukah.*
7. See *Berachos* 22a.
8. *Kiddushin* 32a.

has reached fulfillment, nothing has been accomplished — we must look at matters of Torah and *mitzvos* as they exist in actuality.

If this is so regarding all other aspects of Torah and *mitzvos*, how much more so with regard to Chanukah, for Chanukah is particularly connected with the recipient. This is because Chanukah differs from all other Torah festivals in that it is of human, Rabbinic origin. Thus, Chanukah in particular reflects Torah and *mitzvos* from the perspective of the recipient — the aspect of the actual rather than the potential.

It is for this reason that it is only on the final day of Chanukah — when all eight days have been actualized — that we say: "This is Chanukah."

Compiled from *Likkutei Sichos*, Vol. XXV, pp. 243-250.

Vayigash ויגש

Completing the Count

In the Torah portion of *Vayigash* we read how Yaakov and his family descended to Egypt. We are informed that "The number of individuals in Yaakov's household who came to Egypt was 70."[1] But when we add up the actual number of Yaakov's descendants listed as going to Egypt, we find only 69.

Many Torah commentators,[2] as well as one opinion in the *Midrash*,[3] explain that Yaakov was included in the count — thus making the total 70. According to *Pirkei d'Rebbe Eliezer*,[4] and yet another opinion in the *Midrash*,[5] "G-d entered among them."

What is the reason for the difference in opinion?

Our Sages tell us[6] that "The Patriarchs are truly the [Divine] chariot," for "all their limbs were completely holy and detached from mundane matters, and throughout their lives they served as nothing but a vehicle for the Divine Will."[7] Because of their lofty state, the Divine Presence was openly revealed to them.[8]

Moreover, because of the lofty spiritual level which they attained, they merited that all their progeny also enjoy some measure of their spirituality.[9] This finds expression, for ex-

---

1. *Bereishis* 46:27.
2. *Iben Ezra* ibid.; verse 23; *Rashbam* ibid., verses 15, 26; *Raboseinu Ba'alei HaTosafos* ibid., verse 27; *Ralbag* ibid., verse 23; *Abarbanel* ibid.; *et al.*
3. *Bereishis Rabbah* 94:9.
4. Ch. 39.
5. *Bereishis Rabbah* ibid.
6. *Bereishis Rabbah* 47:6; 82:6.
7. *Tanya* ch. 23.
8. *Torah Or*, 24a.
9. *Tanya* ibid.

ample, in the pure and simple faith of today's Jew in G-d and His limitless abilities.[10]

In order for such an exalted state to be drawn down to each and every Jew, an intermediate state was necessary, a bridge to span the gap between the lofty heights of the Patriarchs and the much lower level of some of their descendants.

Yaakov's direct descendants — the 12 tribes and the 70 souls of his household — served this purpose perfectly, in that they were neither on the exalted level of the Patriarchs, nor on a lowly spiritual level.

At the same time, in order that the exalted state of the Patriarchs be drawn down to each and every Jew in subsequent generations, it was necessary for Yaakov's immediate descendants to find themselves in Egypt, a land where G-dliness is concealed, and for them to overcome the spiritual difficulties of that land and *reveal* their faith in G-d.

Indeed, the Jewish people were up to the task. During the Egyptian exile "the Jews believed"[11] that G-d would redeem them; notwithstanding the seemingly insurmountable barriers that stood in the way of liberation, the people had a pure and simple faith that obstacles simply did not exist for G-d.

This is at the core of the saying of our Sages:[12] "Our forefathers were redeemed from Egypt only in the merit of their faith." Rather than faith being merely a means to an end, that faith and its revelation *was* the end — the ultimate purpose of the exile.

What was it that gave the Jews in Egypt the strength to withstand the spiritual degradation of that country? Herein enter the two abovementioned opinions as to who counted for the 70th soul.

---

10. See *Likkutei Sichos XVI*, end of p. 53ff.
11. *Shmos* 4:31.
12. *Mechiltah, Beshallach* 14:31; *Yalkut Shimoni*, ibid. *Remez* 240.

According to the first opinion, it was Yaakov's spirituality that enabled the Jews to overcome the spiritual difficulties of Egypt.

The second opinion holds that Yaakov was too far removed from spiritual exile; had his level been maintained by his descendants, they would not have been subject to spiritual exile. Were this to be so, the purpose of the exile could not have been accomplished.

The second opinion therefore maintains that G-d Himself was included in the count. G-d is so transcendent that He can be with His people even in exile, thus empowering them to overcome the spiritual concealment of Egypt, but at the same time remaining separate and apart — not felt by them.[13]

This made it possible for the Jewish people to actually experience spiritual exile and yet accomplish the purpose of that exile by revealing their abiding faith in G-d.

Based on *Likkutei Sichos* Volume XX, pp. 218-223.

---

13. See *Likkutei Sichos IX*, p. 194.

Tears and Deeds

The Torah portion *Vayigash*, in describing the poignant reunion of Yosef and Binyamin, relates:[1] "And he [Yosef] fell on the neck of his brother Binyamin and he wept, and Binyamin wept on his [Yosef's] neck."

The *Gemara* comments:[2] "Yosef wept for the two Holy Temples that were destined to be in the territory of Binyamin and were fated to be destroyed; Binyamin wept for the Tabernacle of Shiloh that was destined to be in the territory of Yosef and fated to be destroyed."

---

1. *Bereishis* 45:14.
2. *Megilah* 16b.

Why did Yosef lament the fate of the Temples in Ben-yamin's territory and Binyamin bemoan the destiny of the Tabernacle in Yosef's territory; wouldn't it have been more appropriate for each to cry about the destruction of their own Temples or Tabernacle? After all, a person loves him-self more than all others.[3]

Moreover, a person's own life takes precedence over the life of another. This is why, if one possesses only enough water for the survival of one person, so that by giving it to or sharing it with his fellow traveler he himself will surely die, he should keep it for himself, for "your own life takes prece-dence over the life of your friend."[4]

The *Zohar*[5] comments on the verse,[6] "And he [Yosef] fell on his [Yaakov's] neck and wept," that Yosef wept about the destruction of the Holy Temples and the final exile. Why did only Yosef weep and not Yaakov?

Our Sages note[7] that Yaakov did not weep because he was in the middle of reciting the *Shema*. But how could Yaakov have been so unmoved by the destruction of the Temples and the final exile as to be able to recite the *Shema* with devotion?

A person weeps mainly in order to feel better. Thus we observe that when one cries because something troubles him, the crying in no way changes the situation; one does, however, feel better about things after a good cry.

Understandably, if a person is able to solve the problem that is causing him so much pain, then rather than crying he should extricate himself from his difficult circumstances — "Better a single action than a thousand sighs."[8]

When an individual witnesses the spiritual destruction of a friend — a destruction of that individual's Holy Temple, since every Jew is a Temple to G-d — he feels for him and

---

3. *Sanhedrin* 9b.
4. *Bava Metzia* 62a.
5. *I*, 211a.
6. *Bereishis* 46:29.
7. See *Rashi* ibid.
8. *HaYom Yom* p. 35.

cries. As a friend he can try to assist his comrade by gently admonishing him and praying for his welfare. In the final analysis, however, the rebuilding of his friend's spiritual state depends on the friend himself.

When an individual has done all he can to help his friend, and observes that his friend's spiritual state is still in disrepair, then he will cry for him.

However, when a person sees that his *own* "Holy Temple" is devastated, he cannot merely sigh and shed tears; he must set about rebuilding through repentance and spiritual service.

Moreover, at times crying can actually hinder the rebuilding of his spiritual status, as he may think to himself that he has already accomplished something by crying about it.

Yosef and Binyamin thus both wept about the destruction of their brother's Temples and Tabernacle; with regard to their own Temples and Tabernacle they were doing all they could to avert the tragedy, for even after a heavenly decree has been issued, it is possible — through profound spiritual service — to nullify it.[9]

Yaakov, too, did not cry over the destruction of the Tabernacle and Temples, for as the father of all the Jewish people, both the Tabernacle as well as the Temples were in his "territory." He therefore occupied himself in attempting to preserve them by reciting the *Shema*.

Compiled from *Likkutei Sichos*, Vol. X, pp. 146-149.

---

9. *Rosh HaShanah* 16b.

Vayechi   ויחי

"Be strong, be strong, and let us strengthen one another."

The first of the five books of the Torah concludes with the portion of *Vayechi*. It is customary[1] that when the Torah reader concludes a book of the Torah, the entire congregation exclaims: "Be strong, be strong, and let us strengthen one another [in the Torah]." This pronouncement thus reinforces the Torah as a whole.

However, since this proclamation comes at the conclusion of a particular book, portion, and verse of the Torah, it also follows that it is particularly germane to that specific book, portion and verse.

The concluding verse[2] of *Bereishis* reads: "Yosef died at the age of 110 years; he was embalmed and placed in a coffin in Egypt."

This gives rise to a most perplexing matter. How is it possible to gain strength — "Be strong, be strong, and let us strengthen one another" — from: a) Yosef's *demise*, and b) from his interment in *Egypt*, a land known as "the abomination of the earth"?[3] Yosef's father, Yaakov, had begged that he not be buried in Egypt.[4]

It is obvious that before Jews enter a state of exile, they are in need of fortification and encouragement. Once they are strengthened in this manner they are able to overcome the trials and tribulations of exile and remain steadfast in

---

1. *Avudraham, Seder Hotza'as Sefer Torah;* Responsa *MaHaram Mintz* sec. 85; *Aruch HaShulchan, Orach Chayim* 139:15: *Keser Shem Tov* (Gagin), 1:38.
2. 50:26.
3. *Bereishis* 42:9; ibid., verse 12; See also *Koheles Rabbah,* conclusion of 1:4.
4. Ibid. 47:29.

their faith, Torah study, performance of *mitzvos*, and general service to G-d.

Thus it follows that before the opening verse of the second book of the Torah — "These are the names of the Jewish people who came to Egypt" — describing the descent of the Jews into exile and servitude,[5] it was necessary for the Jewish people to receive the strength needed to withstand the ordeal.

Indeed, the contents of *Bereishis* serve this purpose well, for its main theme is the story of the Patriarchs, whose service and personalities provide inspiration and encouragement to their progeny at all times.

Among the encouraging narratives of *Bereishis* are the promises made by G-d to the Patriarchs that the Jews would leave exile in a more exalted state than when they entered it — "they will then leave [exile] with great wealth."[6]

Moreover, the further one advances in the book of *Bereishis*, the more strength one finds being given to the Jews, who would eventually be exiled in Egypt. This encouragement reaches its high point in the concluding portion of *Vayechi,* wherein Yaakov blesses his children, drawing down sufficient strength for each tribe and its progeny that they will be able to withstand the test of exile.

Within the final portion of *Vayechi* itself, Yosef brings the blessings and words of encouragement closer to home by assuring the Jews that "G-d will surely remember you and bring you out of this land, to the land that He swore to Avraham, Yitzchak and Yaakov."[7]

The greatest degree of strength and fortitude for Jews about to enter exile, however, comes in the very last verse of the portion: "Yosef died... he was embalmed and placed in a coffin in Egypt."

---

5. See *Shmos Rabbah* 1:4; *Torah Or,* beginning of *Shmos.*
6. *Bereishis* 15:14.
7. Ibid. 50:24.

The fact that Yosef's coffin remained with the Jewish people in Egypt enabled them to have the courage not only to withstand the exile, but to utilize it for good. This was similar to — and derived its strength from — Yosef, who while in Egypt achieved a standing such that "without you no man shall lift a hand or foot in all Egypt."[8]

Based on Likkutei Sichos Vol. XXV, pp. 474-479.

_____

8. Ibid. 41:44.

Yaakov Lives

The Torah portion _Vayechi_ begins by saying:[1] "And Yaakov lived." Why does it begin in this manner when the entire portion deals with Yaakov's demise and the events surrounding it? Additionally, since the title of a Torah portion relates to the entire portion,[2] why the title "And he lived," if the whole portion speaks of dying?

The true meaning of life is eternal. This is why true life exists only in relation to G-d, as the verse states:[3] "G-d, the L-rd is Truth, He is the Living G-d."

Truth is not subject to change; if something is genuinely True it will remain so forever. Since G-d is Truth, never ceasing and never changing, He is also the true aspect of life.

Created beings, however, are not _true_ entities, for they do not exist in and of themselves; they had to be created, and as such are intrinsically subject to change and decay. Only by cleaving to and uniting with G-d can they be invested with true life.

Indeed, the Jewish people are called "alive"[4] precisely for this reason, as the verse states:[5] "And you who cleave to the

_____

1. _Bereishis_ 47:28.
2. See _Likkutei Sichos V_, p. 57ff.
3. _Yermiyahu_ 10:10.

L-rd your G-d are all alive today" — the Jewish people are alive in an eternal manner only because of their unity with G-d.

However, in order for this dimension of "life" to be *perceived* in a physical world, it is necessary to encounter obstacles to one's attachment to G-d and nevertheless remain steadfast and whole in the performance of Torah and *mitzvos*. Only then is one's true "life" fully revealed, for it is then obvious that nothing can stand in one's path and affect one's unity with G-d.

The connection of "And Yaakov lived" to the entire portion, as well as the reason for the whole portion being titled "And he lived" — although its main theme is Yaakov's demise — will be understood accordingly:

During all of Yaakov's years before his descent into Egypt it was not clearly seen that his existence was one of true "life," a life of "And you who cleave... are all alive." For the principle of "Do not be sure of yourself until the day you die"[6] applies even to the very righteous.[7] Thus Yaakov's degree of attachment to G-d throughout his life was not sufficient proof of "life."

Even the fact that Yaakov's conduct caused his children and grandchildren to be righteous as well does not prove that he was truly "alive," for Yaakov and his entire family lived in the Holy Land; and one could not be sure about their conduct in a coarser country.

Only when Yaakov approached the time of his death, having meanwhile descended uncorrupted with his family to Egypt, was it *revealed* that his entire life, although externally filled with pain and suffering, was true life — "And Yaakov **lived**."

---

4. See *Avos d'Rebbe Nassan* conclusion of ch. 34: "Ten are called 'alive,' G-d, Torah, Jews...."
5. *Devarim* 4:4.
6. *Avos* 2:4; *Berachos* 29a.
7. See *Berachos* ibid.; *Zohar III*, 285a.

This also explains why the portion is titled "And he lived," notwithstanding the fact that it describes Yaakov's demise and the events that transpired afterwards:

The *Gemara* states:[8] "Our father Yaakov did not die; as his progeny lives on, he too lives on." Since the true aspect of life is eternal, Yaakov's existence can only be judged after observing its perpetual effect.

This effect is perceived when one realizes that not only did Yaakov's own soul continue to cleave to G-d, but that his children pursue the true life led by their father.

The above provides an additional reason for the Torah portion being titled "And he lived." The title not only emphasizes that even after Yaakov's passing it is still possible to say that he lives, but that it is *specifically* after Yaakov's demise that one can say he lives on.

Compiled from *Likkutei Sichos*, Vol. XV, pp. 427-430.

---

8. *Taanis* 5b.

ספר שמות

Shmos

Shmos   שמות

Children — Large and Small

The first time the Jewish people are referred to as "G-d's children" is in the Torah portion of *Shmos*, where the verse states: "Israel is My son, My firstborn."[1] The term "firstborn," as *Rashi* explains,[2] denotes maturity.

In many other instances, however, we find that Jews are considered G-d's children because of their extreme youthfulness. Thus we find the verse,[3] "For Israel is but a lad and [therefore] I love him." This is further explained by our Sages, who offer the parable of a king who had many children, but loved the youngest most of all.[4]

Since the love for a young child is more palpable than the love for an older one, why does the verse in *Shmos* imply that Jews are *older* children?

What, exactly, causes a parent to manifest a greater degree of love for a young child than for an older one?

An older child, who has already matured intellectually and emotionally, will not always be loved by his parents merely because he is their child. The parents may also come to love the older child because of his wisdom or fine character. This kind of love is grounded in logic.

The love of a parent for a very young child, however, is an *elemental* love — one that transcends reason — since an extremely young child does not display any particular qualities for which he should be loved; the love that ema-

---

1. *Shmos* 4:22.
2. Ibid.
3. *Hosheah* 11:1; See at length *Or HaTorah, Beshallach* p. 382ff; *Ki Na'ar Yisrael, 5666, Sefer HaMa'amarim 5678* p. 159ff.
4. *Devarim Rabbah* 5:7.

nates from parents to young children derives entirely from the fact that the parents and the child are essentially one.

The love for a grown child, although also an essential love, is intermingled with feelings that have a basis in logic. This logical foundation *conceals* the elemental love between parent and child.

Just as this is so regarding the love of human parents, so too with regard to G-d's love for His children, the Jewish people. Here too, there exist two manners and degrees:

When Jews serve G-d and thus reveal their sterling qualities, His ever-present love for us is mingled with a love dictated by logic — similar to the love felt by parents for an older child.

However, G-d also shows His elemental love for the Jewish people — a love that springs from the fact that every Jew is "truly a part of G-d above."[5] This love — similar to that felt by parents for a very small child — does not depend at all on the quality of the Jews' spiritual service.

This elemental love is revealed when Jews serve G-d in the manner of a small child; when they feel small and humble in G-d's presence, and obey Him as a small child obeys his parents — out of a sense of inherent loyalty, even when they fail to understand G-d's reasoning.

This, however, does not mean to imply that when Jews serve G-d intellectually and emotionally His intrinsic love for them is not revealed, for a Jew's intellectual and spiritual state is intricately connected to his degree of self-nullification.

A Jew realizes the necessity of intellectual toil to understand Torah, and that his emotions must be permeated with enjoyment of Torah and *mitzvos*. This realization is a direct result of the fact that such enjoyment is *G-d's desire*.[6]

The reason the verse states "Israel is My son, My *firstborn*" will be understood accordingly:

---

5. *Tanya*, beginning of ch. 2.
6. Cf. *Tanya* ch. 38 (p. 50b and onward).

When seeking to indicate G-d's essential love for the Jewish people *in and of itself,* the metaphor used is that of a very small child, for in that instance the elemental love is felt *naturally.*

When, however, one seeks to convey the essential qualities of the Jewish people, then the term "Israel is My son, My *firstborn*" is used, for it indicates that the Jews' essentially childlike nature permeates even their intellect and emotions.

Based on *Likkutei Sichos* Vol. XXI, pp. 20-26.

Counting by Name

The Torah portion *Shmos* begins by saying:[1] "And these are the names of the children of Israel who came to Egypt...." *Rashi* comments:[2] "Although He counted them by name while they were alive, He counted them again after their passing in order to make known (and demonstrate) his love for them; for they are likened to the stars, which He takes out and brings in by their numbers and names...."

If *Rashi* simply desired to prove that something loved is counted by number as well as by name, he would have simply stated that they are "like the stars which He takes out and brings in by number and name." *Rashi's* statement, "for they are *likened* to the stars," serves to imply that because the children of Israel possess the same quality as the stars, they are therefore counted in a like manner.

What is this "star" quality?

Although love of something is evinced through counting as well as through naming, counting and calling by name emphasize two different aspects of that which is being counted or called:

Counting emphasizes the **commonalty** of things — wholly disparate entities cannot be included in the same

---

1. *Shmos* 1:1.
2. Ibid.

count. A name, on the other hand, emphasizes the **individuality** of each thing.

Rashi indicates this when he states "for they are *likened* to the stars," for stars possess both these aspects. On the one hand, they all share the fact of star-hood, and are counted precisely because each star is important. On the other hand, each star possesses unique qualities, for which reason each has it own name.

Each Jew, who is "likened to the stars," shares the essential quality of Jewishness, and is "truly part of G-d above."[3] In addition, each possesses qualities unique to the individual.

G-d's love for the Jewish people thus finds expression in two ways: By counting them He manifests His love for their essential Jewishness, and by calling each by name He demonstrates His love for the unique qualities of each and every one.

However, when G-d desired to show love for individual Jews, He could have done so in any number of ways. Why did He specifically choose to count them by name?

G-d's intrinsic love for the Jewish people serves as the template for all parental love.[4] With human parents also, we find that mentioning a child's name arouses a degree of love that cannot be elicited by other means, such as by giving the child a gift, showering him with words of love, or even hugging and kissing him.

Giving a child a gift or loving words depends on the child's age: If a parent gives his grown son or daughter a gift fit for a very young child, then rather than it being seen as an expression of love it may be taken in the opposite way. Words of love, too, must be geared to the individual child's level.

Since gifts and loving talk must be tailored to the age and comprehension of each child, it is clear that love manifested through these vehicles is limited. It thus cannot be an

---

3. *Tanya* ch. 2,
4. See discourses titled *Atta Echad 5702, 5729.*

elemental love for the **essence** of the child, since elemental love is not limited by the child's intellect, maturity, etc.

Even hugs and kisses, which can be given to both younger and older children, are limited, for they can only be bestowed when the recipient is close at hand. Essential love is not limited by time or space.

The only evocation of love that is truly unlimited is the mentioning of a child's name: it matters not whether the child is young or old, near or far, bright or dim, etc.

Thus, when G-d desired to show His essential love for the Jewish people, He "counted them by **name.**"

Compiled from Likkutei Sichos, Vol. VI, pp. 1-10.

Va'eira   ואירא

The Matzos and Four Cups of Wine

At the beginning of the Torah portion *Va'eira*, four expressions are used with regard to the redemption from
Egypt: "I will release you... I will save you... I will liberate
you... I will take you...."[1] Our Sages note[2] that the four cups
of wine which we drink during the Pesach *Seder* correspond
to these four expressions.

Accordingly, the following question arises: Bearing in
mind that we eat matzah on Pesach "because our ancestors
were liberated from Egypt,"[3] why do we not eat four matzos,
just as we drink four cups of wine?[4] Why do we take only
three matzos to the Seder?

Evidently, there must be two aspects to the exodus from
Egypt, one that is composed of *three* details and one that is
made up of *four*. What are these two aspects?

At the time the Jewish people departed from Egypt they
were not yet spiritually worthy of redemption.[5] In fact, had
they remained one more moment in Egypt, they would have
become forever mired in impurity.

Notwithstanding their state of depravity, G-d in His infinite kindness revealed Himself to them and redeemed
them.

This is why the *completion* of the exodus came about only
when the Jews received the Torah,[6] for complete liberation

---

1. *Shmos* 6:6-7.
2. *Yerushalmi, Pesachim* 10:1; *Bereishis Rabbah* 88:5; *Shmos Rabbah* 6:4.
3. Text of the *Haggadah*.
4. See *Mordechai, Pesachim* — "*Tosefes m'Arvei Pesachim*"; *Matei Moshe* section
   607.
5. See *Tzror Hamor, Bo* 12:40. See also *Zohar Chadash* beginning of the portion
   Yisro.
6. See *Shmos* 3:12.

from Egypt required that the newborn nation rid itself of Egyptian impurity.

This was accomplished as the Jews prepared themselves in the days between the exodus and the receiving of the Torah;[7] they achieved such heights that by the time the Torah was given they could justifiably be called a "holy nation."[8]

The difference between the symbolism of "matzah" and "wine" will be understood accordingly:

Matzah emphasizes the aspect of the exodus that came about as a result of G-d's redemption from the impurity of Egypt. It is for this reason that matzah is called "impoverished bread"[9] — bread that lacks taste — for it is a remembrance of spiritual impoverishment.

"Taste" refers to[10] something a person can appreciate in some way. Since the liberation from Egypt originated from *Above* rather than from the spiritual preparation of the Jewish people, it is understandable that it lacked "taste" — the Jews were compelled to leave.

Wine, however, has taste and is enjoyable. It is a "remembrance of the liberation and *freedom*"[11] ultimately achieved by the Jews, i.e., it was through *their own service* that they were redeemed from the evil of Egypt.

The reason for three matzos vis-à-vis four cups of wine now becomes clear:

There is a difference between the first three expressions of liberation and the fourth, in that the first three — "I will release you... I will save you... I will liberate you" — are aspects of redemption that took place immediately upon the departure from Egypt; they came from Above.

The fourth expression — "I will take you unto Me as a Nation" — however, depended on the Jewish people; they

---

7. See *Zohar Chadash* ibid.; *Ran* conclusion of *Pesachim*; See also *Likkutei Sichos* XXII, p. 114.
8. *Shmos* 19:6.
9. *Devarim* 16:3.
10. See *Likkutei Sichos XVI* p. 124ff and sources cited there.
11. *Shulchan Aruch Admur HaZakein, Orach Chayim* 472:14.

had to become worthy of being called G-d's nation. This was accomplished when they received the Torah.

Thus, matzah is equated with the number three, corresponding to the first three expressions of liberation, inasmuch as matzah commemorates the redemption as it came from Above.

The cups of wine, however, allude to the liberation accomplished by and within the Jewish people. The cups are therefore equated with the number four, for they denote the fourth expression of redemption — "I will take you unto Me as a Nation."

Based on Likkutei Sichos Vol. XXVI, pp. 43-46.

Believers and Sons of Believers

At the beginning of the Torah portion *Va'eira* the verse states:[1] "And the L-rd [*Elokim*, the Name symbolic of strict justice] spoke to Moshe and said to him: 'I am G-d.'"

Rashi comments: "G-d spoke sternly to Moshe because he [Moshe] was severe in speaking and saying [to G-d]: 'Why have you dealt badly with this nation?'"

Moreover, *Rashi*,[2] quoting the *Midrash* on the verse[3] "And I revealed Myself to Avraham, Yitzchak and Yaakov..." writes that G-d said to Moshe: "Alas for those who have passed on and whose likes are not to be found. I mourn the passing of the Patriarchs.... They did not question My actions as you question My actions."

How is it possible to say that Moshe, the "select of mankind,"[4] questioned G-d's actions, and to compare him unfavorably with the Patriarchs?

---

1. *Shmos* 6:2.
2. Ibid. verse 9.
3. Ibid. verse 3.
4. *Pirush HaMishnayos* of the *Rambam*, chapter of *Cheilek*, in the Seventh Principle.

Rashi comments on the statement "And I revealed My-self" and says: "To the Patriarchs." Many commentators on *Rashi* ask: what does *Rashi* add? The verse itself goes on to say that G-d appeared "to Avraham, Yitzchak and Yaakov"?

By stating "To the Patriarchs," *Rashi* is in effect saying that the clear and unequivocal revelation of G-dliness to Avraham, Yitzchak and Yaakov — for which reason they did not question G-d's actions — stemmed from the very fact that they were the **Patriarchs** of the Jewish people.[5] In other words, such revelations were granted these three in order that they **bequeath** them[6] to their descendants, for "A father bequeaths his son... wisdom."[7]

Accordingly, the question becomes even greater: Since every Jew enjoys the revelation of G-dliness as an inheritance from the Patriarchs, how was it possible for Moshe to be critical of G-d's actions?

Our Sages tell us that the exodus from Egypt came about in the merit of and as a reward for the Jews' belief in G-d.[8] This means that the revelation within the Jewish people of this essential aspect of their Jewishness made them worthy of redemption.

Even in the midst of the most severe Egyptian oppression, the Jews were called "believers, the children of believers."[9] But this inherited, almost unconscious belief — this "baseline belief" — was not yet fully developed and revealed within them. In order to be redeemed in their own merit, it was necessary that the Jews' natural belief in and unity with G-d be consciously recognized — that it become wholly **theirs**.

This is what Moshe was able to accomplish, for herein lay the difference between him and the Patriarchs: As bequeathed by the Patriarchs, the essential hallmarks of Jew-

---

5. See *Likkutei Sichos III*, p. 855ff.
6. See *Torah Or, Va'eira*.
7. *Ediyos* 2:9.
8. *Mechiltah, Beshallach* 14:31; *Yalkut* ibid., *Remez* 240.
9. *Shmos* 4:31; *Shabbos* 97a. See also commentary of *Rashi* on *Shmos* 4:2.

ishness are something every Jew has as a natural consequence of being a child of Avraham, Yitzchak and Yaakov.[10]

Moshe, however, in addition to being one of the "Seven
Shepherds that draws down vitality and G-dliness to all
Jewish souls," is also the "sum of them all, and is called the
Faithful Shepherd."[11] Moshe causes the faith possessed by
every Jew to permeate all aspects of his being.

Moshe's question: "Why have you dealt badly?" and
G-d's response: "I have revealed Myself to the Patriarchs"
will be understood accordingly:

Since the time for the Jews' liberation from Egypt was
fast approaching, and Moshe was acting as G-d's emissary
to redeem them, it was necessary that the people's inherited
belief in G-d come to permeate them completely.

Moshe's question "Why have you dealt badly?" elicited
G-d's revelatory response — va'eira — which brought the
Jews to so believe in G-d that faith penetrated every fibre of
their being. Even the lower levels of their intellect — the
levels that give rise to doubts — would now be permeated
with unquestioning belief in G-d.

The redemption came about as a result of Moshe's question and G-d's response.

Compiled from *Likkutei Sichos*, Vol. XVI, pp. 47-55.

---

10. See *Tanya* chs. 18-19.
11. *Tanya* ch. 42.

Bo בא

Sanctifying Time

In the Torah portion *Bo* we read that, "G-d said to Moshe and Aharon in Egypt: 'This month shall be the head month to you; it shall be the first month of the year.'"[1] We learn from here that it is a *mitzvah* to "sanctify months, set leap years, and establish the festivals of the year according to the determined sanctification."[2]

Our Sages note[3] that the entire Torah might have begun with this commandment, "for it is the *first mitzvah* that the Jewish people[4] were commanded."[5]

The very fact that of all 613 commandments the Torah chose to begin with this one indicates that this *mitzvah* contains an element fundamental to all the rest.

What is so special about this commandment?

The primary function of the *mitzvos* is to enable man to permeate the world with goodness and holiness. Thus all *mitzvos* involve the transformation of physical objects into *mitzvah*-objects, entities of holiness.

This, too, is the overall theme of the commandment to sanctify the new month: The court sanctifies[6] a certain day and declares it to be *Rosh Chodesh*, the beginning of the month — not an ordinary working day,[7] and one which establishes when the holidays shall be celebrated.

---

1. *Shmos* 12:1-2.
2. *Chinuch*, beginning of Mitzvah 4.
3. See *Tanchuma* (Buber) *Bereishis* 11; *Yalkut Shimoni, Shmos* 12:2 (*Remez 187*).
4. "As opposed to *Milah* and *Gid HaNashaeh*... that were commanded to individuals, and were not considered commands so long as *all* Jews were not so commanded." (Commentary of *Reb Eliyahu Mizrachi* on *Rashi* cited in fn. 5.)
5. *Rashi, Bereishis* 1:1.
6. See *Shmos Rabbah* 15:24.
7. *Yechezkel* 46:1.

In addition to the above, this commandment is inherently first in theme and content: Although the world is a composite of both space and time,[8] and time is bound up with space,[9] nevertheless, time precedes space. For all of Creation, including space, implies an aspect of change — present conditions are compared to the past, i.e., to conditions *prior* to creation.

Thus, before anything was created, including space, there already existed an entity subject to change — time. Therefore the starting point of all creation is time.

This is true in terms of man's experience as well. First comes the actual day, and only then can man make an impact on that day by transforming physical objects.

Sanctification of the new month is thus the first commandment, for sanctity is first imbedded in time — the beginning of existence — and only then comes man's interaction with physical objects — the aspect of space.

There is yet another all-encompassing aspect to this *mitzvah*: All of creation was brought about in order to be sanctified through the Jewish people's performance of Torah and *mitzvos*.[10] This is a theme that affects all of creation at all times and in all places.

A Jew's service consists of actualizing and revealing the ultimate purpose within all things. When a Jew performs a *mitzvah* with a particular object, he thereby *fulfills* the object's reason for being, and the object becomes a *mitzvah*-object.

For example, when a Jew transforms an animal's hide into parchment for a *Sefer Torah, tefillin,* or *mezuzos,* that animal's hide attains the purpose for which it was created — the hide has now become imbued with holiness.

Since time, too, is created, it is readily understandable that it is meant to fulfill the same purpose as the rest of creation.

---

8. *Shaar HaYichud VeHaEmunah* ch. 7 (82a).
9. *Likkutei Torah, Berachah* 98a.
10. See *Rashi, Bereishis* ibid.

Herein lies the additional significance of this most important command: Through the Jewish people's *sanctification* of months — *Rosh Chodesh* and festivals — they reveal that the true purpose of time is to be sanctified.

For in reality the sanctification of any one month affects not only the establishment of *Rosh Chodesh* and the festivals in that month, but alters the entire time continuum, so that all of time becomes permeated with the realization that it is to be filled with goodness, holiness, and *mitzvos*.

Based on Likkutei Sichos Vol. XXVI, pp. 59-65.

Remembering the Exodus and the Shabbos

The *Rambam* writes[1] that "On the night of the fifteenth of Nissan it is a positive command of the Torah to relate the miracles and wonders that transpired with our forefathers in Egypt, for it is written:[2] 'Remember this day on which you went out of Egypt,' [and the meaning of 'remember' here is] similar to that which is written[3] 'Remember the day of Shabbos.'"

Why does the *Rambam* find it necessary to liken the manner in which we remember the Exodus to the way in which we remember the Shabbos? Why doesn't the verse "Remember this day on which you went out of Egypt" stand alone?

At the beginning of the laws of Shabbos the *Rambam* states: "Resting from labor on the seventh day is a positive command, for it is written,[4] 'On the seventh day you shall rest.' Whoever performs labor at that time negates a positive command and transgresses a prohibitive commandment."

---

1. *Hilchos Chametz U'Matzah* beg. of ch. 7.
2. *Shmos* 13:3.
3. *Shmos* 20:8.
4. Ibid. 23:12.

Thus Shabbos involves both the positive aspect of rest and the negative aspect of not performing labor.

The fact that the *Rambam* begins the laws of Shabbos with the positive command, notwithstanding the fact that most of the laws of Shabbos deal with prohibitions of various forms of labor, indicates that the main aspect of Shabbos observance lies in this positive aspect.

Both the negative and positive aspects of Shabbos derive from two sections in the Torah: In the section describing Creation the verse states:[5] "He *rested* on the seventh day *from all His labor* which He had done. And G-d blessed the seventh day and made it holy, *for on it He rested from all His labor...*" — emphasizing that on this day there was both rest and cessation from labor.

In the section describing G-d's giving of the Torah, where the Jews are told: "Remember the day of Shabbos," the verse goes on to state:[6] "For [in] six days the L-rd made the heavens, the earth, the sea, and all that is in them, *and rested on the seventh day.*"

In other words, here we are told that Shabbos is unique not only in that G-d ceased on it from the labor of the Six Days of Creation, but more importantly, that Shabbos is G-d's day of rest.

Thus, the more important part of "Remembering the day of Shabbos" is the positive sense of rest rather than the mere negation of labor, as our Sages state[7] that after the completion of the Six Days of Creation the world was lacking rest and tranquillity. Only when Shabbos began did rest and tranquillity arrive. Or as the *Rambam* expresses it:[8] "'Remember it' — a remembrance of praise and sanctification."

---

5. *Bereishis* 2:2-3.
6. *Shmos* 20:11.
7. Commentary of *Rashi, on Bereishis* 2:2 and on *Megillah* 9a. (See also *Bereishis Rabbah* 10:9).
8. Beginning of ch. 29 of *Hilchos Shabbos.*

With regard to the exodus from Egypt as well, we find two aspects:[9] the release of the Jewish people from servitude, and the fact that we became a free, independent people.

This is similar to the condition achieved by every freed slave: His master's dominion over him ceases; as a free man he becomes wholly his own person.

By connecting the tale of the Exodus on the fifteenth of Nissan to remembrance of the Shabbos, the *Rambam* is indicating that with regard to relating the events of the Exodus too, the main aspect is the positive step of becoming free.

For just as remembering the Shabbos involves not so much the negation of labor as the positive theme of rest, so too the obligation to relate the tale of the Exodus involves not so much the recalling of our release from slavery as the recounting of how we became free men.

Thus the *Rambam* goes on to say in the following law that even when one relates the tale of the Exodus to a son who is a minor or simpleton he should say: "On this night G-d redeemed us and took us out **to freedom**," thereby emphasizing that G-d enabled us to become free.

Consequently, the *Rambam* goes on to say[10] that "An individual is obligated to conduct himself as if he himself had just gone out of Egypt" — "as if you yourself were enslaved, and **you went out to freedom and were redeemed.**"

One should conduct himself on this night as a free man.

Compiled from *Likkutei Sichos*, Vol. XXI, pp. 68-73.

---

9.   See also *Likkutei Sichos, XII*, p. 47.
10.   *Halachah* 6-7.

Beshallach   בשלח

The Manna — Enhancing Belief & Trust in G-d

The Torah portion of *Beshallach* recounts the story of the heavenly food that nurtured the Jewish people in the desert for 40 years, until they arrived at the border of Canaan.

The *Tur* states[1] that it is beneficial to recite the passage about the manna daily. The salutary effect of this repetition is twofold:

a) It strengthens belief[2] in G-d, helping man realize that all his sustenance derives from Providence. This was clearly evident with the manna: human activity had absolutely no effect on the amount G-d deemed fit to provide each individual — "the one who had taken more did not have any extra, and the one who had taken less did not have too little."[3]

b) It helps strengthen man's trust[4] in G-d. Not only is a person prompted to recognize that his subsistence derives from G-d, but equally important, man comes to *rely* on G-d, trusting that He will provide. The daily collection of manna amply developed this aspect of trust, for G-d provided it on a constant and ongoing basis. Thus Jews were able to become aware of the fact that every living thing relies completely on G-d for its food.

Although belief in G-d and trust in Him seem to be similar, they are two different traits, each possessing qualities that the other lacks. What are the major differences between these two attributes?

---

1. *Orach Chayim* 1; also in *Shulchan Aruch* ibid. sub-section 5.
2. See commentary of *Beis Yosef* on *Tur* ibid.; *Shulchan Aruch Admur HaZakein, Me'hadura Kamma* 1:8.
3. *Shmos* 16:18.
4. *Shulchan Aruch Admur HaZakein, Me'hadura Tenyana* 1:8.

Belief is a constant — it is the nature of the Divine soul to express an innate belief in G-d. For example, the absolute confidence that one's sustenance will be provided by G-d is found within every believer at all times; it makes no sense to say a man believes this only while actually earning his livelihood.

But while belief is unceasing, it is peripheral, and does not necessarily translate into action. Thus the *Gemara*[5] informs us that it is possible for a thief to pray that his thievery will be successful; the purity of his faith is not affected by the impurity of his deeds.

In contrast, man's trust in G-d is aroused only in times of need.[6] Yet although man's trust is not in the same constant state of revelation as is his belief, when trust is aroused it penetrates every fiber of his being.

This will be better understood by offering a more acute example:

When a person finds himself — Heaven forfend — in a life-threatening situation and sees no way of surviving by natural means, he will not despair, for he trusts that G-d will help him, since He is the Master of nature and able to change it at will.[7]

The ability to put one's trust in G-d, to be confident that He will rescue one from extreme difficulties — "natural" physical reality notwithstanding — indicates that such trust completely permeates a person.

Moreover, this very trust serves as the vessel that draws down Divine assistance and blessing:

When a Jew displays absolute trust in G-d and is confident that G-d will release him from his dire straits — although this seems to fly in the face of reason — this causes G-d to act toward this individual in a like manner; G-d helps that person by freeing him in a supernatural manner.

---

5. *Berachos* 63a.
6. See *Nesivos Olam* of the *Meharal*, beginning of *Nesiv HaBetachon*.
7. See *Rabbeinu Yonah*, quoted in *Kad HaKemach* entry *Betachon*. See also *Likkutei Sichos III*, p. 833.

This also explains how it is possible for man to possess such absolute trust in G-d: Since we know that G-d responds to man measure for measure,[8] we are able to feel certain[9] that by placing our implicit trust in G-d, He will surely help us in our time of need.

Based on Likkutei Sichos XXVI, pp. 95-97.

---

8. See *Mishnah Sotah* (8b).
9. See *Chovas HaLevavos* introduction to *Shaar HaBetachon*.

Waging War Against Amalek

At the conclusion of the portion *Beshallach*,[1] the Torah relates that Moshe appointed Yehoshua to lead the Jews against the attacking Amalekites. During the entire battle Moshe's hands were raised in prayer that the Jews be victorious. As long as Moshe's hands were raised, the Jews prevailed.

The Torah goes on to say that when Moshe's arms grew weary, a stone was taken and placed under him. *Rashi*[2] comments: "Because he was sluggish in performing the commandment [of leading the Jews in battle] and appointed another in his stead, his hands became heavy."

Why does the Torah tell us that Moshe's hands grew heavy as a result of his slothful attitude — something entirely uncomplimentary — when the Torah does not even speak directly of the stigma of an unclean animal? It seems inappropriate for the Torah to speak badly of Moshe, the "select of mankind."

Herein lies an invaluable lesson to all Jews in all places and times with regard to their spiritual battle with the Amalekites of every generation.

---

1. *Shmos* 17:8-13.
2. Ibid., verse 12.

Amalek was only able to affect the Jews who straggled so far behind spiritually that as a result of their sins they were evicted from the Jewish encampment and the Clouds of Glory.[3] Those who remained within the camp were not at all affected by the Amalekites.

In our times as well, most Jews find themselves spiritually within the "Jewish camp," within the framework and protection of the "Clouds of Glory" of Torah and *mitzvos*, which protect them from all ill winds[4] — especially from Amalek's frigid attitude toward Torah and *mitzvos*.[5]

There are, however, Jews who for whatever reasons find themselves "on the outside" — their lifestyle is not yet wholly in keeping with Torah. Amalek — whose numerical equivalent is "doubt"[6] — is therefore able to attack them by causing them to doubt G-d's limitless ability, and by making them "cool" towards matters of holiness.

It is therefore possible that a Jew who finds himself "within the encampment" should question his relationship with those outside, reasoning that since they have no connection with him, he doesn't want anything to do with them.

Such an individual might well think that leaving his warm nest of Torah and *mitzvos* to search for Jews lost in the wasteland of doubt is out of the question.

Herein is the lesson provided by the first war the Jews had to wage after their exodus from Egypt, their battle with Amalek:

When Amalek starts up with a Jew who is "outside the encampment," even if his being there is a result of his own misdeeds, the Jews "within the camp" must leave it in order to protect their weaker brother. In fact, only G-d-fearing Jews have the ability to vanquish Amalek. Thus we find that

---

3. See *Devarim* 25:18 and commentary of *Rashi* there.
4. See *Mechiltah, Beshallach* on verse 13:21.
5. See *Torah Or*, 85a and onward, *Ma'amar V'Hayah Ka'asher Yarim 5680* ch. 3.
6. *Sefer HaMa'amarim 5679* p. 294; *5709* pp. 40, 65.

it was Yehoshua, an individual "who never left the tent"[7] of Torah, who was placed in charge of the battle.

The Torah goes further: Even Moshe, who essentially led the whole war — it was he who appointed Yehoshua as his emissary to lead the battle, and it was Moshe who spiritually led the fight by praying for the welfare of the Jewish people — should have participated in the actual battle. His failure to do so was considered slothfulness.

Herein is a lesson for even the greatest: Spiritual participation in the ongoing battle against Amalek is not enough. Merely praying for the welfare of those attacked by Amalek, or sending one's emissary, is neither adequate nor acceptable; *the person himself* must do whatever is necessary to keep his fellow Jews from the clutches of Amalek.

Compiled from *Likkutei Sichos*, Vol. XXI, pp. 89-99.

---

7. *Shmos* 33:11.

Yisro   יתרו

Achieving Unity in Mind, Heart and Deed

We read in the Torah portion *Yisro* that "In the third month after the Exodus of the children of Israel from the land of Egypt, on that day, they came to the wilderness of Sinai... and Israel encamped there before the mountain."[1]

The *Mechilta* comments:[2] "Everywhere else it is written 'They traveled... they encamped' [in the plural]. That is to say 'they traveled' with dissenting opinions and 'they encamped' with dissenting opinions. Here, however, [it is written] 'and Israel encamped,' [in the singular, for] all were equally of one heart."

The *Mechilta* thus informs us that although it is entirely natural for the members of a multitude to have dissenting opinions, when the Jews encamped in preparation to receive the Torah, all were "of one heart."

This was a result of the Torah's ability to bring complete peace and unity, as the *Rambam* states:[3] "The entire Torah was given in order to bring peace into the world." Therefore the Jews' encampment before Mt. Sinai brought complete unity; they stopped bickering.

What property does Torah possess that enables it to bring about such peace and unity that all are "of one heart"? In fact, the argument could be made that Torah fosters dissonance, for it is replete with dissenting and disparate opinions with regard to various points of Jewish law, etc.

And while it is true that once a definitive judgment is rendered all parties must act strictly in accordance with the

---

1. *Shmos* 19:1-2.
2. Ibid.
3. Conclusion of *Hilchos Chanukah*, quoting *Sifrei, Naso* 6:26. See also *Likkutei Sichos XVIII*, p. 349ff.

halacha, it would seem that private intellectual disagreement must remain.

How then can Torah be said to cause all Jews to be "of *one heart*," which implies that it unites Jews not only in action but also in understanding and feeling?

The Torah stresses that the Jewish people's encampment "with one heart" took place during "the *third* month after the Exodus." Evidently the people's unity resulted not only from their location "opposite the mount," but also from the fact that this took place during the third month.

What is so special about three, and how does it foster unity; if anything, unity seems more directly related to the number one.

The difference between the numbers one, two and three are as follows: "One" stresses that from the very outset there exists but one thing; "two" is indicative of divisiveness — the antitheses of unity. "Three," however, sees a uniting of disparate entities — making "one" out of "two."

This aspect of "three" is similar to the statement of our Sages[4] that "When two Biblical passages contradict each other, the meaning can be determined by a *third* Biblical text, which reconciles them."

We see here the remarkable quality of the "third." Without the third verse the two verses indeed contradict each other. Then the third reconciles the seemingly irreconcilable. Moreover, it does so not by "taking sides," i.e., agreeing with one verse and disagreeing with the other, but by showing that the first two verses are actually in consonance.

Since Torah is inextricably bound up with the concept of "three," as our Sages state:[5] "Blessed is G-d who gave the three-part Torah to the three-part Nation... in the third month," it is understandable that Torah as a whole has characteristics similar to those of the number three.

This results in the fact that even when Torah law is seemingly arrived at not through a reconciling view, but by

4. *Sifra*, Introduction.
5. *Shabbos* 88a; *Tanchuma, Shmos* 10.

agreeing with one opinion and disagreeing with another, those initially opposed agree not only with the adjudication but also with the logic that resulted in the verdict — all are peacefully united "with one heart."

Based on *Likkutei Sichos* Vol. XXI, pp. 108-112.

Obligation and Subservience

The Ten Commandments begin with the verse,[1] "I am G-d your L-rd who brought you out of the land of Egypt, from the place of slavery." In commenting on the words, "who brought you out of the land of Egypt," *Rashi* notes:[2] "Taking you out of Egypt is sufficient reason for you to be subservient to Me."

What difficulty does *Rashi* seek to resolve with his remark?

Some commentators[3] on *Rashi* explain that the difficulty lies in the verse's stating "I am G-d your L-rd who brought you out of the land of Egypt" rather than "I am G-d your L-rd who created heaven and earth." *Rashi* thus explains, they say, that the Exodus was mentioned rather than creation since it was because G-d brought the Jews out of slavery that they became His servants and He became their G-d.

This explanation, however, is somewhat lacking: In the simple context of the verse there is absolutely no reason why it should conclude with the statement "who created heaven and earth," inasmuch as the latter part of the verse gives the reason for G-d becoming "*your* L-rd" — the G-d of the Jewish people.

This being so, it stands to reason that the explanation should be germane to the relationship between G-d and the Jews rather than to that between G-d and the universe.

1. *Shmos* 20:2.
2. *Ibid.*
3. See *Gur Aryei* and *Devek Tov ibid.*

And so the explanation of why the Exodus is given as the reason for G-d becoming the G-d of the Jewish people is obvious — G-d's liberation of the Jews from slavery is what made it possible for Him to give us His Torah and *mitzvos* on Sinai.

Moreover, the fact that G-d took the Jews out of Egypt in order for them to serve Him was already mentioned several times in the Torah;[4] in none of those places did *Rashi* find it necessary to explain that this "is sufficient reason for you to be subservient to Me." What difficulty is there in this particular verse?

The difficulty which *Rashi* addresses is related to this very issue: Since the Jews were already well aware that the ultimate goal of the Exodus was the receipt of the Torah and submission to G-d, what was the need to mention yet again that G-d's declaration: "I am G-d your L-rd" is the consequence of His being the One "who brought you out of the land of Egypt"?

Rashi therefore explains that "who brought you out of the land of Egypt" is neither a reason nor an explanation for "I am G-d your L-rd.," Rather, it is a wholly distinct matter — "Taking you out of Egypt is sufficient reason for you to be *subservient* to Me."

"I am G-d your L-rd" implies the acceptance of G-d's reign.[5] The Jews accepted G-d as their king and ruler, and thereby obligated themselves to obey all His commands. G-d then added an additional matter — merely accepting G-d as king does not suffice; Jews must be wholly subservient to Him.

Accepting a king's dominion does not preclude the possibility of a private life; it only means doing what the king commands and avoiding those things which the king prohibits. However, being "*subservient* to Me" means a Jew has no personal freedom; *all* his actions and possessions are subservient to G-d.

---

4. *Shmos* 3:12, 6:6-7, 19:4-6.
5. See *Mechiltah, Shmos* 20:3; *Rashi, Vayikra* 18:2; *Ramban, Shmos* 20:2.

Performing Torah and *mitzvos* is unlike heeding the commands of a flesh-and-blood king, since it is done in a state of complete subservience. Every moment of a Jew's life involves some aspect of Torah and *mitzvos*.

Based on *Likkutei Sichos* Vol. XXVI pp. 124-128.

Mishpatim   משפטים

Productive Use of Time

The Talmud relates[1] that the great Sage R. Yochanan ben
Zakkai wept before his death, saying: "There are two paths
stretching before me, one to *Gan Eden* [Heaven] and one to
Gehinom. I know not on which I shall be led."

It goes without saying that R. Yochanan ben Zakkai was
concerned as to whether he had attained a sufficient level of
holiness to enter *Gan Eden*. Why did he voice his apprehen-
sion only on his deathbed? His spiritual status should have
been an ongoing concern.

Every Jew is entrusted with a unique Divine mission that
he is to accomplish during his lifetime. He is allotted a specific time in which to accomplish that task — not one day
more and not one day less.[2]

When a Jew fails to make use of a day, an hour, or even a
moment, in pursuit of his mission, he not only fails to
achieve his fullest spiritual potential, but more importantly,
he has failed — during those moments — to accomplish his
entrusted task.

R. Yochanan ben Zakkai spent every moment of his life
totally immersed in his mission, so much so that he simply
did not have time to pause and contemplate his own spiritual level. It was only at the *conclusion* of his mission — just
prior to his demise — that he was able to ponder his own
status.

The importance of absolute dedication to one's mission
is also alluded to in the Torah portion of *Mishpatim*, wherein
Scripture states:[3] "You will serve G-d... No woman will mis-

---

1. *Berachos* 28b.
2. See *Zohar I* 224a.
3. *Shmos* 23:25-26.

carry or remain childless in your land; I will make you live out full lives."

In spiritual terms, the above verses mean that[4] when performed with proper intent, Divine service leads to ever greater spiritual heights — it "bears children." When, however, a person is self-satisfied in his service, it fails to produce the desired results — he "miscarries" and is spiritually "barren."

One can guard against this by "living out a full life." I.e., a person should realize that he is granted a specific number of years. Every moment wasted on something other than his appointed task constitutes an act of rebellion against G-d, who entrusted him with his sacred mission.

When a person realizes this, he will gladly sacrifice all sense of ego, and concentrate solely on completing his assignment. Eventually he will become so absorbed that he will even forget that it is *he* who is fulfilling it; the mission in general and the task at hand will fill his mind completely.

When someone else inquires about such a Jew's spiritual state, he will respond: "How can I possibly think about myself when I have been granted only a limited number of days in which to fulfill my purpose in life? I must constantly be on guard to assure that not one precious moment is lost; I simply do not have time to think about my spiritual achievements!"

When a Jew attains this level of self-abnegation, G-d blesses him with "a full life"; even if there were days in which he did not fulfill his mission, or worse yet, acted in a counterproductive manner, G-d promises him that the missing days will be made up. Ultimately, all his days become whole.

Based on Likkutei Sichos Vol. XVI pp. 271-274

---

4. See discourses titled *Lo Si'hyeh Mishakeilah* in *Torah Or, Toras Chayim* and *Or HaTorah.*

A Tale of Two Portions

At the conclusion of *Mishpatim* — after almost an entire Torah portion that addresses matters not directly related to *Mattan Torah*, the giving of the Torah — Moshe is told: "Go up to G-d."[1] *Rashi* explains[2] that this took place on the fourth of *Sivan*, prior to *Mattan Torah*.

Most of the preparations for *Mattan Torah* are described at length in the portion of *Yisro*. The fact that additional details are provided in *Mishpatim* indicates that a purpose must be served by describing *Mattan Torah* in two portions. What is that purpose?

Mattan Torah accomplished two things: a) G-d gave the Torah — its commandments and laws — to the Jewish people; b) G-d thereby entered into a "covenant of observance" with the Jews — "And you shall keep My covenant."[3] Jews thus became His servants, as the verse states:[4] "You shall serve the L-rd upon this mountain," and as *Rashi* notes,[5] the Jewish people then became subjugated to G-d.

Herein lies the difference regarding the preparations for *Mattan Torah* as described in *Yisro* and the preparations described in *Mishpatim*:

Yisro deals mainly with G-d's giving of the Ten Commandments. That is why the tale of the Jewish people's preparation as related in *Yisro* deals with the *commands* that G-d gave them *to prepare* for *Mattan Torah*.

Mishpatim, however, deals with the covenant and servitude to G-d that *resulted* from *Mattan Torah*. This came about through the events described in this portion,[6] namely, the Jewish people's *acceptance* of the Torah by prefacing "We shall do" to "We shall hear" and writing the "Book of the Covenant."

---

1. *Shmos* 24:1.
2. Commentary of *Rashi* ibid.
3. Ibid. 19:3.
4. Ibid. 3:12.
5. Ibid. 20:2.
6. Ibid. 24:3ff.

There is an even more profound reason for the details relating to *Mattan Torah* to be given in two separate portions: The *Midrash* notes[7] that at the time of *Mattan Torah*, two things were accomplished: "Those Above descended below" — "G-d descended on Mt. Sinai,"[8]; and "Those below ascended Above" — "And to Moshe He said: 'Ascend to G-d.'"[9] Man ascended to G-dliness.

The first portion speaks mainly about *Mattan Torah* from the perspective of those "Above"— "G-d descended," "And G-d spoke." *Mishpatim*, however, addresses the event from the perspective of those "below" — "Ascend to G-d," "We shall do and we shall hear," etc.

The difference between these two aspects of *Mattan Torah* is this: The tremendous degree of Divine revelation that descended from Above at the time of *Mattan Torah* was temporary; the ascent of the Jewish people, however, — becoming G-d's servants and thereby becoming spiritually elevated — was permanent.

The reason why the second aspect of *Mattan Torah* endured was because it came about as a result of man's own service. It therefore became permanently embedded within the Jewish people's psyche.

Accordingly, we are able to understand why the command of building the Tabernacle — mentioned in the next portion of *Terumah* — follows the second aspect of *Mattan Torah*. For the special quality of Divine revelation that resulted from the construction of the *Mishkan* mirrored the service of man:[10]

The revelation of G-dliness within the *Mishkan* came about through the accomplishment of the Jewish people — "You *shall make* for Me a *Mishkan*."[11] Just as the Jewish people's service at *Mattan Torah* resulted in their permanent

---

7. *Shmos Rabbah* 12:3; *Tanchuma, Va'eira* 15.
8. *Shmos* 19:20.
9. Ibid. 24:1.
10. See *Likkutei Sichos XXI* p. 150ff.
11. *Shmos* 25:8.

spiritual elevation, so did the Divine revelation that resulted from the making of the *Mishkan* permanently sanctify its physical structure.

Based on Likkutei Sichos Vol. XXVI, pp. 153-159.

The Jewish Indentured Servant

The Torah portion *Mishpatim* immediately follows *Yisro*, the section that describes G-d's giving of the Torah, which took place shortly after the Exodus and the crossing of the Sea of Reeds. It follows that G-d would relate in *Mishpatim* the commands that were most germane to the Jewish people at that time.

In fulfillment of His promise to Avraham that the Jews would leave Egypt with great wealth,[1] G-d saw to it that the former slaves left that country laden with gold and silver.[2] Then, at the crossing of the sea, the Jews received even more booty;[3] each and every Jew was rich.

Nevertheless, *Mishpatim* begins[4] with the laws of an indentured servant — a Jew whose impoverished state obliges him to sell himself into servitude,[5] or one who lacks the means to make restitution for a theft and is therefore sold into slavery by the court.[6]

Why does the portion begin with these laws when all Jews were then wealthy?

The indentured slave was to serve for only six years, or until the Sabbatical year, at which time he was to be freed. But "If the servant declares, 'I love my master... I do not

---

1. *Bereishis* 15:14.
2. See *Shmos* 12:35-36.
3. See *Rashi ibid.* 15:22.
4. *Shmos* 21:2.
5. See *Vayikra* 25:39.
6. See *Shmos* 22:2.

want to go free'... his master shall pierce his ear with an awl and the servant shall serve until the Jubilee Year."[7]

Our Sages comment:[8] "Why was the ear chosen for piercing rather than another organ? Because it was the ear that heard on Mt. Sinai, 'For unto Me are the Children of Israel servants, they are My servants,'[9] yet it threw off the heavenly yoke and replaced it with the yoke of man, so the verse says: 'let the ear be pierced, for it did not comply with what it heard.'"

With other commandments, we do not find any stress put on the connection between the reward for observance and the manner of that observance. For example, honoring one's parents is rewarded with longevity.[10] There is no obvious connection between the reward and the fulfillment of that command.

The same is true with regard to the punishments for sin — lashes, excision and the like. The nature of the punishments has no obvious connection to the sins which beget them.

With regard to the indentured servant, however, our Sages clearly indicate how the punishment is in keeping with the crime — the ear heard from Mt. Sinai and did not comply, therefore it is pierced.

The reason why the portion which follows the giving of the Torah describes the law of the indentured servant is thus readily understandable, for the punishment of piercing the ear is directly connected to what the ear heard on Sinai.

The connection becomes even more apparent in light of the fact that the entire purpose of giving the Torah was to purify and elevate the physical world through the performance of *mitzvos*. Therefore, the first commandment in *Mishpatim* clearly demonstrates how Torah affects the physical world.

---

7. *Ibid.* 21:5-6.
8. *Tosefta, Bava Kama* Ch. 6.
9. *Vayikra* 25:55.
10. *Shmos* 20:12.

This is particularly true according to the Chassidic explanation of the phrase "Jewish indentured servant," viz., one who transforms "servitude" to his animal soul and physical desires into "Jewish" spiritual service.

Such a transformation demonstrates the effect of Torah in this world — to so change one's animalistic tendencies and the world at large that they are able to enter the domain of holiness.

Practiced by every Jew in every walk of life, such transformations will become so widespread that the individual and everything related to him will become a veritable dwelling for G-d.

Based on *Likkutei Sichos* Vol. XVI, pp. 251-257.

Terumah   תרומה

Constructing the Mishkan — A Common Task

The Torah portion of *Terumah* tells how the Jewish people were commanded to erect the Tabernacle, the *Mishkan*, so that G-d may "dwell among them." It also tells how the Jews went about fulfilling this command by donating the necessary items.

There are three opinions offered by our Sages regarding the time at which this took place:

One opinion[1] is that both the command to build the *Mishkan* and the Jews' donations occurred soon after the Torah was given, and *prior* to the sin of the Golden Calf.

A second opinion holds that both the command and the bringing of gifts took place after G-d forgave the Jewish people on *Yom Kippur* for the sin of the Golden Calf, "so that all the nations would know that they [the Jewish people] were forgiven for the sin of the Calf."[2]

The third opinion is that G-d's command came to Moshe before the sin of the Golden Calf, but that he passed it on to the people only after *Yom Kippur*.[3]

The Talmud informs us[4] that although there may be divergent opinions among our Sages, "All are equally the words of the living G-d."

Thus, it is understood that although the construction of the *Mishkan* and the bringing of donations had to have happened in accordance with only one of these three schedules, all three opinions are true as they relate to the spiritual *Mishkan* within the heart of every Jew.

---

1. *Zohar II* 224a.
2. *Tanchuma, Terumah* 8. See also commentary of *Rashi, Shmos* 31:18, 33:11.
3. *Zohar II* 195a; *Ramban* beginning of Torah portion of *Vayakhel*.
4. *Eruvin* 13b and places cited there.

In what regard are they all true?

Following G-d's giving of the Torah, and before the sin of the Golden Calf, the Jewish people were on the level of *tzaddikim*, the truly righteous. Then they committed the sin of the Golden Calf. When they were forgiven on *Yom Kippur*, they attained the level of *ba'alei teshuvah*, penitents.

Herein lies the difference between the abovementioned opinions: According to the opinion that the command to build the *Mishkan* and the giving of donations occurred soon after the giving of the Torah and prior to the sin of the Golden Calf, the *Mishkan* was constructed by *tzaddikim*.

According to the opinion that the command to construct the *Mishkan* came on *Yom Kippur*, its erection was the work of penitents.

According to the opinion that the sin of the Golden Calf took place between the time of the command to make the *Mishkan* and its actual construction, even the wicked — those who sinned with the Golden Calf — were able to participate in the construction of a Sanctuary for G-d.

The lesson is as follows: A Jew on the lofty plane of a *tzaddik* may mistakenly think that having attained so high a level he should involve himself with purely spiritual matters, and that making a physical dwelling place for G-d should be left to those still struggling with the corporeal world.

Herein comes the lesson of the first opinion: The command to construct the Sanctuary was given to *tzaddikim*. Since the *tzaddik* still exists within this physical world, failing to elevate the mundane by transforming it into a *Mishkan* can lead to a spiritual downfall.

We may think that this manner of service applies only to a *tzaddik*, who never had to confront and vanquish evil. The penitent, however, has achieved this victory, and may think that he need not occupy himself any longer with physical service. We therefore have the second opinion, which informs us that the command to construct the Sanctuary was given to penitents.

Then we have the third opinion: It teaches us that repentance is not a prerequisite to doing good deeds. Even something as sacred as a Sanctuary for G-d may be built by sinners who have not yet repented.

Begin doing good at once, secure in the knowledge that repentance will surely follow!

Based on *Likkutei Sichos* Vol. VI, pp. 153-156.

Three Forms of Terumah — Three Forms of Spiritual Service

In the Torah portion *Terumah*, the Jews are commanded to bring *Terumah*, offerings, for use in the *Mishkan*. The command is repeated three times: "They shall take unto Me *Terumah*;" "you shall take My *Terumah*;" "This is the *Terumah* that you shall take."[1]

Our Sages comment[2] that the Torah is referring here to three different offerings: The first reference is to the offering used in constructing the sockets for the *Mishkan*'s beams; the second refers to the donation of silver half-*shekels* for the purchase of communal offerings; the third refers to general offerings for the construction of the *Mishkan*.

Of these three, only the last is described here in detail; the first two are only hinted at, and are described at length in later portions.[3] Since all three *Terumah* offerings were for the sake of the *Mishkan*, why were they not all described here in detail?

The *Mishkan* was built in order to provide a dwelling place for G-d in this world — "And you shall build for Me a Sanctuary so that I may dwell in your midst."[4]

---

1. *Shmos* 25:2-3.
2. *Yerushalmi, Shekalim* 1:5.
3. The first *Terumah* in *Pekudei*, 38:25ff; the second *Terumah* in *Sisa*, 30:13ff.
4. *Shmos* 25:8.

The building of a *Mishkan* foreshadows the transformation of the entire world into a dwelling place for G-d. This is accomplished through Torah, Divine service, and deeds of kindness — the "three pillars" upon which the world stands.[5]

Since the transformation of the world into a *Mishkan* is connected to the building of the physical *Mishkan*, it can be understood that these three pillars played a part in the construction of the *Mishkan* as well.

Torah is the root and foundation of all spiritual service. Every level and manner of serving G-d through *mitzvos* and good deeds is rooted in and based upon Torah, for every aspect of Judaism has its foundation and beginning in Torah.

In the construction of the *Mishkan*, Torah is alluded to by the *Terumah* for sockets, since they served as the underpinnings of the entire structure, just as Torah serves as the underpinning of all Judaism.

The *Terumah* used for the purchase of communal sacrifices relates to Divine service, for "Divine service" involves sacrificial offerings[6] and prayer — prayer having been substituted for offerings.[7]

The general *Terumah* for the *Mishkan*, which included gold, silver, copper, etc., corresponds to the service of *mitzvos* — all of which are known by the term "deeds of kindness"[8] — for they are performed with physical objects similar to those used in constructing the *Mishkan*. This third manner of service — "deeds of kindness" — possesses a quality lacking in the first two. Torah and prayer relate to an individual's spiritual occupation with himself. Consequently, they are only able to affect the individual; uniting a person with G-d's wisdom.

"Deeds of kindness" — the service of *mitzvos* — however, requires one to be involved with physical matter. Here

---

5. *Avos* 1:2.
6. Commentary of *Rashi* and *Bartenura et al, Avos* ibid.
7. *Berachos* 26b; See also commentary of *Rabbeinu Yonah* to *Avos* ibid.
8. *Likkutei Torah, Re'eh* 23c.

a person is able to transform physical things — by using them in the performance of *mitzvos* — into holy objects. It is specifically through man's transforming of the world into a *Mishkan* that the Divine intent of creation is fulfilled, for "G-d earnestly desired a dwelling place in the nethermost level,"[9] i.e., this lowly physical world.[10] But in order for this manner of service to be proper and complete, man must also possess the attributes of Torah and prayer.

Since all aspects of spiritual service are reflected in the *Mishkan*, the Torah portion details only the general *Terumah* — man's service of *mitzvos* — for that is the ultimate intent.

Based on *Likkutei Sichos* Vol. XVI, pp. 292-297.

---

9. *Tanya* ch. 36, based on *Tanchuma, Naso* 16.
10. Ibid.

The Aron, Kapores and the Keruvim

The Torah portion *Terumah* contains the command to make the *Aron*, (the Ark), the *Kapores* (the lid for the Ark), and the Keruvim (the Cherubs that jutted out from the edges of the lid).[1]

According to *Rashi*, the Ark and its lid were two distinct entities,[2] while *Ramban* maintains that the Ark's covering was part and parcel of the Ark; only when the *Kapores* was upon the Ark could it be called the *Aron*.[3]

Why do they differ?

According to the *Ramban*, the main reason for G-d's desiring a *Mishkan* was to have a place for the indwelling of the Divine Presence.[4] This was accomplished by placing the

---

1. *Shmos* 25:10-22.
2. See *Rashi ibid.* verse 21.
3. See commentary of *Ramban* on verses *ibid.*
4. See *ibid.* 25:1.

"Testimony" within an Ark that had upon it the *Kapores* and the *Keruvim*.

According to *Rashi*, however, the purpose of the *Aron* was for the storage of the Torah,[5] while the *Kapores* had a different function. "I shall make Myself known to you and I shall speak to you from above the *Kapores*, from between the two *Keruvim*."[6]

This leads to yet another disagreement between *Rashi* and the *Ramban*: According to *Rashi*, the *Keruvim* were part of the *Kapores*, which was, as mentioned previously, wholly distinct from the *Aron*, while according to *Ramban* the *Keruvim* together with the *Kapores* and *Aron* served one purpose — they were a place where the Divine Presence resided.[7]

In light of the above, the reason for yet another difference between *Rashi* and the *Ramban* becomes clear: According to *Rashi*, the *Keruvim* looked like human infants,[8] while according to the *Ramban* they resembled the Divine Chariot seen by Yechezkel.[9]

Since according to *Ramban* the *Keruvim* served as a residence for the Divine Presence, its form was symbolic of that Presence — the Divine Chariot. According to *Rashi*, however, who maintains that the *Kapores* and *Keruvim* were wholly distinct from the Ark, they resembled human infants, thereby emphasizing G-d's love for the Jewish people, as the verse states: "For Israel is but a lad, and therefore I love him."[10]

Thus, according to *Rashi* the *Aron* with its "Testimony" denoted the Torah, while the *Kapores* and the *Keruvim*, serving as the place where G-d made His will known, emphasized G-d's love for the Jewish people.

On a more esoteric level, the difference between the two sages lies in the following:

---

5. See commentary of *Rashi ibid.* verse 16.
6. Ibid. verse 22 and see commentary of *Rashi*.
7. Commentary of *Ramban ibid.* verse 22.
8. *Rashi ibid.* verse 18.
9. *Ramban ibid.* verse 21.
10. *Hosheiah* 11:1.

The *Aron*, containing as it did the "Testimony," is symbolic of Torah. Thus the *Ramban* notes[11] that all the Jews took part in making the Ark "so that they all merit Torah."[12]

It thus follows that according to the *Ramban*, who maintains that the *Kapores* and *Keruvim* were one with the *Aron*, the phrase "I shall make Myself known to you... and speak to you from above the *Kapores* between the *Keruvim*" relates entirely to the Torah, while according to *Rashi* the *Aron* related to Torah while the *Kapores* and *Keruvim* related to G-d's love for the Jews.

The reason for this difference between *Ramban* and *Rashi* is as follows: *Ramban* speaks in a **revealed** manner about esoteric matters of Torah. His commentary therefore deals with things as they are seen to exist. In this state, "Jews are bound to Torah and Torah is bound to G-d"[13] — only through Torah can the Jewish people be bound to G-d.

The commentary of *Rashi*, however, speaks of the **simple** meaning of the verses, and as such addresses the essential aspect of the Jew — wholly one with G-d's simplicity.[14] This direct connection of a Jew with G-d transcends the connection achieved through Torah.[15]

Accordingly, *Rashi* states that the *Keruvim*, which indicated G-d's love for the Jewish people, were in the shape of infants, for the essential love of a father for his child is not dependent on anything; it stems from the simple fact that father and child are one. And it was this love that was revealed by the shape of the *Keruvim*.

Based on *Likkutei Sichos* Vol. XXVI, pp. 175-181.

---

11. *Shmos* 25:10.
12. *Shmos Rabbah* 34:2. See also *Rabbeinu Bachya* and *Abarbanel* on the verse *ibid.*
13. See *Zohar III* 73a.
14. See *Likkutei Dibburim III*, 491b.
15. *Bereishis Rabbah* 1:4; *Tanna d'Vei Eliyahu Rabbah* ch. 14. See also *Likkutei Torah, Shir HaShirim* 19:b-c; *Hemshech 5666, ma'amar* titled *Vayidabeir... b'Midbar Sinai.*

Tetzaveh   תצוה

Ephod, Breastplate & Robe —
Three Unique Vestments

In the Torah portion of *Tetzaveh* the priestly vestments
are described at length. Among the garments worn by the
High Priest were the *ephod*, the breastplate, and the *me'il*, the
robe. After the commands concerning the making of each,
the verse tells us what purpose each served:

With regard to the *ephod* the verse states:[1] "Place the two
stones on the shoulder pieces of the *ephod* as remembrance
stones for the children of Israel; Aharon shall carry their
names on his two shoulders before G-d as a remembrance."

At the conclusion of the command of the breastplate the
verse states:[2] "Aharon will thus carry the names of the children of Israel on the decision breastplate over his heart
when he enters the Sanctuary; it shall be a constant remembrance before G-d."

Concerning the robe the verse states:[3] "Aharon shall
wear it when he performs the service; the sound [of the
bells] shall be heard when he enters the Sanctuary before
G-d, and when he leaves...."

Thus, each vestment accomplished its purpose — remembrance, etc. — by the very fact that Aharon entered the
Sanctuary while wearing it. This was not the case with the
other vestments worn while performing the service — they
accomplished nothing in and of themselves.[4]

When the High Priest entered the Sanctuary garbed in
the eight vestments and performed the divine service, two

1. *Shmos* 28:12.
2. Ibid. verse 29.
3. Ibid. verse 35.
4. See ibid. verses 41 and 45.

things were thus accomplished: The *entry* itself accomplished remembrance, etc., by his being garbed in the three special vestments. Then there was that which was accomplished through his actual *service*, this being dependent on his wearing all his vestments.

The High Priest served as an emissary[5] of the Jewish people. His task was to unite the Jews with G-d. Thus, the High Priest's *entry* and *service* correspond to accomplishments of the Jewish people.

A Jew's unification with G-d is twofold: a) through his service of Torah and *mitzvos*; b) as a result of his intrinsic relationship, for he is considered G-d's child or servant even prior to his service.

These two things are alluded to in the High Priest's service: First comes his *entry* into the Sanctuary, indicative of the Jews' remembrance before G-d (independent of their service). Only then begins the *service* of the High Priest, symbolic of the spiritual service of each and every Jew.

The reason why the entry of the High Priest was connected to the three abovementioned garments will be understood accordingly, for these garments hint at the various categories of Jews:

The gemstones on the shoulder straps of the ephod and in the breastplate were inscribed with the names of the Tribes of Israel — the Jewish people. This refers to the loftier kind of Jew, within whom may be found the "revealed and inscribed" Judaism.

The robe, on the other hand, descending as it did close to the ground, alludes to a less lofty category of Jew. The fringe of the robe featured bells and pomegranates, for "Even the 'emptiest' Jew is as full of *mitzvos* as a pomegranate [is full of seeds]."[6]

The "remembrance before G-d" was accomplished by the High Priest's entry wearing all three vestments; should even one category of Jew be missing, the priest's action lacks

---

5. See *Nedarim* 35b.
6. See *Eruvin* 19a; conclusion of Tractate *Chagigah*.

significance. For the unity of the Jews with G-d defies division — it encompasses all Jews equally.

Based on *Likkutei Sichos* Vol. XXI, pp. 185-188.

The Two Altars

At the conclusion of the portion *Tetzaveh*[1] the Torah commands that an altar be built and placed within the Tabernacle for the sole purpose of offering incense. This Interior Altar supplemented the Exterior Altar (placed in the courtyard of the *Mishkan*), upon which all other offerings, libations, etc., were brought.

Why were two altars necessary, one in the courtyard and limited to offerings, the other within the *Mishkan* itself and limited to incense; why would one altar not suffice?

Chassidus explains[2] that the two altars corresponded to two levels of Divine revelation: the Interior Altar to the internal revelation that transcends creation, the Exterior Altar to the more overt and less revelatory level of G-dliness that descends within creation.

The External Altar — corresponding as it did to the more external level of G-dliness — was thus in a less sacred section of the *Mishkan*, while the Interior Altar — corresponding as it did to the more internal level of G-dliness — was found within the more sacred portion.

In terms of man's spiritual service, we find two general categories as well: a) that of refining and separating good from evil and elevating the good to holiness — a form of service known as *birurim*; b) a higher level, where one does not have to combat evil, rather one strives to achieve a greater degree of unity with G-d.

The Exterior Altar, corresponding as it did to the G-dliness found within creation — with creation containing

1. *Shmos* 30:1ff.
2. *Toras Chayim, Shmos* 443a and onward; *Derech Mitzvosecha* 86b.

aspects of both good and evil — was limited to the less superior form of service, that of elevating the physical through
sacrificial offerings: the service of *birurim*.

The Interior Altar, on the other hand — corresponding to
G-dliness as it transcends evil — was for the spiritually superior service of incense, or *ketores*, etymologically related to
kotar, or cleaving[3] — achieving a greater degree of cleaving
to G-d.

Parallels to the two altars are also to be found within all
Jews, for the *Mishkan* as a whole is found within the heart of
every Jew, as our Rabbis comment[4] on the verse,[5] "They shall
make for Me a Sanctuary and I will dwell in them" — "It
does not say 'I will dwell in it' rather, 'I will dwell in them'
— in the 'heart' of each and every Jew."

Here, too, the Interior and Exterior Altar correspond to
the internal and external levels of the Jewish heart:[6] the external level of a Jew's service — the external level of his
heart — is occupied in the service of *birurim*, while the internal level is occupied in achieving a greater degree of cleaving to G-d.

Simply stated, a Jew is supposed to occupy himself not
only in the study of Torah and the performance of *mitzvos*,
but also in permissible things such as eating, drinking and
the like. However, this is not to say that such mundane matters are indulged in for their own sake; the intent should be
to use the activity for a sacred purpose[7] — "All one's actions
should be for the sake of Heaven."[8]

A person may mistakenly be led to think that since his
involvement with the physical is entirely for a spiritual pur-

---

3. Similar to the saying in Zohar III, p. 288a: "with one perfect union have I
   cleaved to you."
4. See *Likkutei Sichos III*, and places cited there. See also *Toras Chayim* ibid.
5. *Shmos* 25:9.
6. *Toras Chayim* and *Derech Mitzvosecha* ibid. See also *Likkutei Torah, Sukkos* 78b;
   Shemini Atzeres 86d et al.
7. See *Likkutei Sichos III*, pp. 907, 932.
8. *Avos* 2:12.

pose, he may therefore involve not only the heart's external level, but its internal level as well.

But since these are, after all, *physical* actions, one should employ only the external aspect of the heart in performing them; the internal and more profound level — one's Interior Altar — should be reserved for matters of a purely holy nature.

However, in order to achieve this superior form of service, a person must first employ his Exterior Altar in the service of *birurim*, imbuing all his physical thoughts, words and deeds with sacred purpose. Only then can he utilize his Interior Altar to achieve a greater degree of cleaving to G-d.

Based on *Likkutei Sichos*, Vol. VI, pp. 185-187.

| Tetzaveh | תצוה |
| Zayin Adar | ז' אדר |

Moshe's Demise

During most years, the seventh of Adar — the day of *Moshe Rabbeinu's* demise — occurs in close proximity to the reading of *Tetzaveh*. Our Sages note[1] that there is an allusion to Moshe's demise in *Tetzaveh*, in that this is the only Torah portion (from the time of Moshe's birth until the Book of *Devarim*[2]), in which he is not mentioned by name.

This must be understood. Only Moshe's *name* is not mentioned in this portion; there are, however, a multitude of passages that relate to him, beginning with the first verse of the portion:[3] "And you [i.e., Moshe] shall command...."

Moreover, not mentioning the name of a dying *tzaddik* seems to nullify the very meaning of his demise; the passing of a *tzaddik* in no way affects his good name and deeds — they live on forever — only the body passes from this world.

How, then, can we say that Moshe's demise is alluded to in a portion that does not mention his name?

In addition, the commands directed to Moshe in *Tetzaveh* are given directly — "And you shall command," "And you shall do," "And you shall take" — whereas in many other Torah portions Moshe is referred to only elliptically: "And to Moshe He said...,"[4] etc., as if Moshe were not present!

---

1. *Ma'or Einayim, Tetzaveh.* See also *Likkutei Sichos XVI*, p. 342 fn. 5 and sources cited there.
2. See commentaries of *Rosh* and *Tur* on portion *Tetzaveh.*
3. *Shmos* 27:20.
4. *Ibid.* 24:1.

The *Zohar* states[5] that "A *tzaddik* that has passed on is found in all worlds [including this physical world] to an [*infinitely*] greater degree than when he was alive."[6]

The Alter Rebbe explains[7] that the reason why a dead *tzaddik* is found in all worlds to an infinitely greater degree than a living one is twofold: While the *tzaddik* was alive his life-force was clothed in a physical body, so only a glimmer could be perceived. However, after his demise this limitation ends and it is possible to receive from his essence.

In addition, the demise of a *tzaddik* involves the elevation of his spirit and soul to its First Root and Source; this elevation is then reflected in all worlds, including this physical plane.[8]

The reason why Moshe's demise is alluded to by not mentioning his name in the Torah portion *Tetzaveh* will be understood accordingly:

A person's name has little to do with his essence; a name is needed only so that other people can call on him; a person as he exists for himself needs no name.[9]

The pronoun "you," however, relates to the essence of a person — when one turns to another and says "you," one is referring to the entire individual.

So too with regard to Moshe. The name "Moshe" was given to him quite some time after his birth; until then he had gotten by quite well without a name. Moreover, this name was not even given to him by his parents, but by Pharaoh's daughter, "For I drew him — *mashe* — from the water."[10]

Herein lies the allusion to Moshe's demise. At the time of Moshe's passing he ascended to a level far loftier than can be encompassed by a name. Thus at the time of his demise, he is not referred to by name.

---

5. III 71b. See also *Iggeres HaKodesh* 27 and its exposition.
6. See *Iggeres HaKodesh ibid.*
7. *Ibid.*
8. See also *Siddur im Dach, Sha'ar HaLag B'Omer* p. 304b-c.
9. See *Torah Or* beginning of portion *Terumah*. See also *Likkutei Torah, Behar* 41c.
10. *Shmos* 2:10.

Nevertheless, he continued to lead with his entire essence even at the moment of death. Moshe is therefore indeed to be found in the portion *Tetzaveh*, and moreover, he is
addressed there in a manner that relates to his essence,[11] for
his demise caused that essence to permeate all worlds to an
even greater degree than when he was alive.

Based on *Likkutei Sichos* Vol. XXVI, pp. 204-206.

---

11.   See commentary of *Klei Yakar*, beginning of portion *Tetzaveh*. See also *Likkutei
Sichos XXI* pp. 174, 177ff.

Ki Sisa   כי תשא

The Golden Calf — Entree to Repentance

The Talmud relates[1] that the Jewish people were incapable of committing the sin of the Golden Calf on their own, for they had mastered their evil inclination.[2] Rather, the sin was "a decree of the King, so as to provide an opening to penitents. For a sinner might think that repentance is of no avail. He is therefore shown that G-d accepted the penance of even those who committed the heinous sin of the Golden Calf."[3]

"So as to provide an opening to penitents" refers not only to later generations; it also afforded the Jews of that time the opportunity of achieving repentance.[4]

Repentance is not a manner of service that a sinless person can choose. Quite the contrary: "He who says, 'I shall sin and then repent' is not afforded the *opportunity* to repent."[5] It is only after a person has sinned that he is provided with the opportunity to repent.

Nonetheless, the service of repentance is so great that it contains certain merits which are lacking even in the service of the truly righteous, as our Sages say:[6] "The level attained by penitents cannot be achieved by the completely righteous."

In order for the Jews who experienced the giving of the Torah, and consequently became truly righteous, to also experience repentance, it was necessary that there be a "decree of the King." Only this enabled the evil inclination to gain

---

1. *Avodah Zarah* 4b and commentary of *Rashi*.
2. *Rashi*, ibid.
3. Ibid.
4. See also *Likkutei Sichos IX* p. 240 and fn. 28 ibid.
5. *Mishnah* conclusion of Tractate *Yoma*.
6. *Berachos* 34b; *Rambam, Hilchos Teshuvah* 7:4. See *Likkutei Sichos* ibid. fn. 29.

temporary dominance over them; they could then experience the tremendous elevation of penitence.

One of the qualities of repentance that is lacking in the service of the completely righteous arises from the fact that a righteous individual is only capable of elevating those sparks of holiness that lie within permissible matters. His approach to evil is one of negation; it is impossible for him to transform it into holiness.

However, a sinner can, through complete repentance, effect the transformation of misdeeds into merits.[7] Thus, he not only negates evil, but is able to elevate the holiness that was trapped within it.

This difference between the service of a completely righteous individual and the service of a penitent results not only from the fact that the righteous individual simply lacks sins to transform; it is also related to the difference between their methods of divine service.

The service of the truly righteous individual is that of revealing G-dliness within the world. Since evil as it exists within the world conceals and opposes G-dliness, the righteous individual negates it.

However, the service of the penitent elevates the physical world into the realm of the holy. He is thus cognizant of the world not as something that opposes G-dliness, but rather as it is looked upon from Above.

The same is true regarding evil: Penitents realize that G-d's ultimate intent is not merely the negation of evil, but the transformation of it — through repentance — into good, thereby elevating the divine spark concealed within.

G-d's giving of the Torah revealed G-dliness in a manner that transcended the corporeal world; a Jew's repentance engages the corporeal world and transforms it into G-dliness.

Based on *Likkutei Sichos* Vol. XVI pp. 412-414.

---

7. *Yoma* 86b.

Breaking The Luchos —
A Break for the Jewish People

The *Midrash* on the portion of *Sisa* relates[1] that Moshe was distressed that as a result of the sin of the Golden Calf he had to break the *Luchos*, the Tablets upon which were inscribed the Ten Commandments.

G-d told him, continues the *Midrash*, that he need not be overly upset, for the first *Luchos* contained only the Ten Commandments, while the tablets that were to be given as a result of the shattering of the first *Luchos* would also possess, "Laws, *Midrash* and *Aggados*" — the Oral Torah.

The *Midrash* thus reveals that only by breaking the first *Luchos* could the "Laws, *Midrash* and *Aggados*" be received; if they could have been received without the loss of the first *Luchos*, Moshe's anguish would have been justified.

Why, indeed, was it necessary for the first *Luchos* to be broken in order for G-d to give the "Laws, *Midrash* and *Aggados*"; could He not have done so without having Moshe shatter the Tablets?

The study of Torah is wholly unlike other intellectual disciplines, whose mastery requires only a keen mind and an inquisitive intellect. To be successful in the study of G-d's Torah, humility and self-effacement are necessary.

We find this concept expressed in the prayer *Elokai Netzor*, at the conclusion of the *Amidah*:[2] "Let my soul be [so humble that it is] as earth to all. Open my heart to Your Torah..."; i.e., only with humility and self-abnegation can one succeed in the study of Torah.

This is because the Torah is *G-d's* wisdom; just as He is infinite and thus completely beyond the intellectual grasp of any created being, so too is His Torah.[3] And though G-d condensed His wisdom in the Torah as given to us so that even mortals can grasp it, Torah remains G-d's wisdom.

---

1. *Shmos Rabbah* 46:1.
2. The text is originally found in *Berachos* 17a.
3. See *Rambam, Hilchos Teshuvah* conclusion of ch. 5; *Tanya I*, ch. 2, *Tanya II*, ch. 7.

Thus, for a person to truly comprehend the Torah he must first achieve total self-nullification, thereby assuring that his "being" will not hinder him from becoming attached to G-d's being, which in turn enables him to comprehend G-d's wisdom.

One of the things that helps us realize that even as Torah exists below it remains G-d's wisdom is its limitlessness — "Its measure is longer than the earth and broader than the sea."[4] This infinite quality is specifically revealed in "Laws, Midrash and Aggados" — the Oral Torah.[5]

The Written Torah is strictly delineated; it may contain only the number of words that comprise its 24 books. With regard to the Oral Torah, however, we are told to "increase it,"[6] i.e., we are charged to come up with new and novel Torah thoughts, etc. It is notably this part of Torah that knows no bounds.

This is why the Oral Torah could be given only after the breaking of the Luchos.

At the time G-d gave the Torah to the Jewish people, He clearly declared that He had "chosen us from among all nations"[7] and "lifted us up from among all tongues."[8] Understandably, when Jews were in such an exalted state it was entirely unnatural for them to experience such utter humility that they felt "like dust to all."

For while it is true that the Divine revelation at Sinai caused the Jews to be humbled, they had just been "chosen" and "uplifted." Moreover, the humility they did experience resulted from the tremendous revelation from Above; they did not feel insignificant in and of themselves.

---

4. *Iyov* 11:9.
5. See *Shulchan Aruch Admur HaZakein, Hilchos Talmud Torah* 1:5.
6. *Zohar I* 12:b. See also *Shulchan Aruch Admur HaZakein, Hilchos Talmud Torah* 2:2; *Iggeres HaKodesh* 145a.
7. Text of Blessing preceding *Krias Shema*; and as explained in *Shulchan Aruch Admur HaZakein, Orach Chayim* conclusion of ch. 64 (gleaned from the *Ramoh*) that this refers to *Mattan Torah*.
8. Text of Festival *Amidah* and *Kiddush*.

Moshe's breaking of the *Luchos* before their eyes, however, made them completely heartbroken and abjectly humble. It was this utter state of self-nullification that enabled them to receive the infinite Oral Torah that accompanied the second *Luchos*.

Based on *Likkutei Sichos*, Vol. XXVI, pp. 249-252.

Vayakhel-Pekudei   ויקהל-פקודי

"In All Their Journeys"

The book of *Shmos* concludes with the words "in all their journeys." The theme of the book is the story of how, as the *Midrash* says:[1] "the Jewish people departed from darkness to light." It stands to reason that the theme of Shmos should find expression in the words "in all their journeys," inasmuch as "everything follows the conclusion."[2] What connection is there between "in all their journeys," and "departing from darkness to light"?

The above-quoted *Midrash* must also be understood: *Shmos* begins by relating how the Jews *entered* Egypt, not how they left it. Why then does the *Midrash* describe the book as one whose theme is "departing from darkness to light"?

The simple meaning of "in all their journeys" refers not to the actual journeys, but to the encampments between journeys.[3] The term journey is used, explains *Rashi*,[4] "because they repeatedly journeyed on from their resting places."

This, too, must be understood: The *Gemara*[5] says that every stop made by the Jews in the desert was considered the final one, since it was G-d who commanded them to stop. This being so, how is it possible to consider these stops as part of their journey?

We must perforce say that the stops are called journeys because each one — serving as it did as a stepping stone to

---

1. *Bereishis Rabbah* 3:5.
2. *Berachos* 12a.
3. See *Shmos* 40:35.
4. Ibid. verse 38.
5. *Eruvin* 55b.

the journey that followed — possessed not only permanence but also foreshadowed the future journey. Since each stop facilitated the ensuing journey, therefore in an internal and concealed manner the stops themselves became *part* of that journey.

The *Alter Rebbe* explains the verse[6] "These are the *journeys* of the Jewish people who left Egypt..." in the following manner:[7] Although physically the Jews left Egypt by dint of their first journey from Ramses to Sukkos, the plural "journeys" is used by Scripture to indicate that as long as the Jews had not yet reached the Promised Land they were still "in Egypt" — the word Egypt being etymologically related to "straits and limitations." Thus, *every* journey on the way to the Promised Land was a "journey from Egypt."

We can now understand that the difference between the "journeys" and the "stops" was the difference between exile and liberation; While the Jews were actually coming closer to Eretz Yisrael they were in the process of leaving Egypt — liberation; while they encamped, their journey to the Promised Land was "put on hold" — a partial return to the state of exile.

Still and all, the verse also deems the "stops" to be part of the "journeys," for the whole purpose of exile is the subsequent revelation of redemption.

The use of the phrase "in all their journeys" to describe the stops thus makes it clear that as even as the Jewish people began their descent into Egypt — described in the opening of *Shmos* — they were beginning their *liberation* from exile.

The whole book then is one of "departing from darkness into light."

Based on *Likkutei Sichos* Vol. VI pp. 235-239.

---

6. *Bamidbar* 33:1.
7. *Likkutei Torah, Masei* 88c and onward.

Vayakhel   ויקהל

Offerings for the Mishkan —
The Superior Quality of the Jewish Woman

With regard to the general offerings for the construction of the *Mishkan*, the Tabernacle, the Torah tells us in *Vayakhel* that "any person inclined to give an offering"[1] could do so. This of course included both men and women. In fact, the Torah goes on to relate[2] that "the men accompanied the women," which our Sages[3] interpret to mean that, in giving, the men were subservient to the women.

This being so, why is it that in the earlier portion of *Terumah*, when discussing the donation of these gifts, the Torah says:[4] "from any *man* whose heart moves him to give" — an expression that seems to exclude women?

One of the aspects in the relationship between men and women is that of giver and recipient. This is why the union between G-d and the Jewish people is likened to that between groom and bride.

This is also why the Written Torah is called the "moral exhortations of your *father*,"[5] while the Oral Torah is called "the Torah of your *mother*."[6]

The difference between the Written and Oral Torah is that the Written Torah was transmitted entirely from the

---

1. *Shmos* 35:5.
2. Ibid. verse 22.
3. *Ramban* ibid. See also *Ibn Ezra* and *Rabbeinu Bachye* ibid.
4. *Shmos* 25:2.
5. *Mishlei* 1:8.
6. Ibid. *Iggeres HaKodesh* 29, quoting the *Zohar; Torah Or, Vayakhel* 88c; *Likkutei Torah, Shemini Atzeres* 85b.

Giver Above, while the revelation[7] of the Oral Torah is through the Jewish people — the recipient, the woman.

This aspect filters down to physical man and woman as well, and is observed within the Jewish people; women are more spiritually receptive than men. We therefore observe that women need not be exhorted as often as men regarding their observance of Judaism, the reason being that their faith is instinctively more revealed and their fear and awe of G-d is greater than men's.[8]

We find this to be so as well with regard to the Torah's first commandment, to "be fruitful and multiply"[9] — a command incumbent on men but not women. Why are women not so commanded?

The reason is that a man must be commanded to "be fruitful and multiply," for his innate nature might not otherwise move him to reproduce.

A woman, however, is not in need of this command, for feeling as she does that her mission is to establish future generations, she does so of her own volition.

This is also one of the reasons why, in preparing the Jews to receive the Torah, G-d instructed Moshe to inform the women about the forthcoming event in a gentle tone, while the men were to be told in a harsh manner.[10] Even a gentle tone sufficed to prepare the women; their character was such that they strongly desired to receive it. The men, however, had to be told in a harsher fashion, as they were not as receptive to the idea of having to follow all the commandments.

This difference also came into play regarding the gifts for the *Mishkan*: Jewish women excelled in the offerings that had no established criteria as to amount, obligation, etc.

---

7. Although this, too, was given on Sinai, for "All the *mitzvos* given to Moshe were given with their commentary" — *Rambam*, beginning of his introduction to *Yad HaChazakah*.
8. See *Or HaTorah, Tehillim* p. 432; ibid. *Nach II*, p. 927.
9. *Bereishis* 1:28.
10. *Shmos* 19:3 and *Mechiltah* ibid.

These gifts came strictly because the donors were moved to give. In this aspect the women were clearly superior.

The earlier portion of *Terumah*, however, concentrates on the two offerings which the Jews were obliged to bring because *G-d had so commanded*. That was not the place to emphasize the unique qualities of women in relation to free-will gifts.

It is specifically in the portion of *Vayakhel*, where the Torah emphasizes the eagerness with which the Jews gave their voluntary gifts, that it is most germane to stress the superior quality of the Jewish women.

Based on *Likkutei Sichos*, Vol. XXVI, pp. 266-268.

Pekudei   פקודי

An Eternal Resting Place

The *Zohar* on the portion *Pekudei*[1] speaks of the *Mishkan*, the *Beis HaMikdash*, and the placing of the Ark in the *Beis HaMikdash's* Holy of Holies. When the Ark was placed there, says one opinion in the *Zohar*, the Ark said:[2] "This is my eternal resting place; here I shall dwell, for I desire it."

According to another opinion, this verse was recited by the Jewish people when the *Beis HaMikdash* was completed and the Ark was placed in the Holy of Holies. There is yet a third opinion, namely, that "G-d recites this verse regarding the Jewish people when they obey His will."

Since all three opinions are mentioned in the *Zohar* in conjunction with its discussion of the *Mishkan*, *Beis HaMikdash*, and the placing of the Ark, it follows that all three opinions relate in some way to the *Mishkan* and *Beis HaMikdash*.

How does the final opinion relate to the *Zohar's* earlier discussion regarding the *Mishkan*, etc., when according to this interpretation the verse is speaking of G-d eternally dwelling within the Jewish people? Moreover, why the difference of opinion as to who recites this verse?

The difference between these three views stems from different attitudes regarding the primary purpose of the *Mishkan* and *Beis HaMikdash*:

The first opinion maintains that the principal purpose of, and desire for, the *Mishkan* was in order that there be a resting place for the Divine Presence, as it dwelled within the Ark.[3] Thus it says that the Ark recited this verse.

---

1. 222b.
2. *Tehillim* 132:14.
3. See *Ramban* beginning of portion *Terumah*.

The second comment holds that the main purpose of the *Mishkan* and *Beis HaMikdash* was to give the Jewish people an established place in which to serve G-d.[4] This was accomplished upon the completion of the *Mishkan* and *Beis HaMikdash* and the placement of the Ark in the Holy of Holies. It therefore holds that the Jewish people recited the verse.

The third opinion contends that the chief purpose of the *Mishkan* and *Beis HaMikdash* was that the Divine Presence reside among the Jewish people[5] — G-d's "resting place" is dependent upon the Jewish people. Thus it was G-d who recited this verse regarding the Jewish people.

The three views, however, are in basic agreement; all three considerations are of primary importance for the *Mishkan* and *Beis HaMikdash*; they merely refer to different time periods.

The structures involved represent several distinct phases: the *Mishkan*, the first and second *Beis HaMikdash*, and the future *Beis HaMikdash*.

The *Mishkan* first and foremost allowed for the dwelling of the Divine Presence within the Ark. Moreover, the permanent "resting place" of the Ark was primarily in the *Mishkan*, for the second *Beis HaMikdash* was without the Ark[6] while the first *Beis HaMikdash* was partially deprived of it.[7] The first opinion thus refers to the time of the *Mishkan*.

The full meaning of "a resting place," however, cannot be applied to the *Mishkan*, for it moved from place to place. Both the first and second *Beis HaMikdash* were stationary. The Jewish people could therefore realize their dream of a permanent place for the service to G-d only in relation to the *Beis HaMikdash*, and not the *Mishkan*.

---

4. See *Rambam,* beginning of *Hilchos Beis HaBechirah* and *Sefer HaMitzvos,* Positive Command 20.
5. See *Shmos Rabbah* ch. 33:1, 34:3; *Tanchuma* (Buber), *Bechukosai* 5, *Naso* 19.
6. *Yoma* 21b.
7. *Divrei HaYomim II* 35:3; *Yoma* 52b.

But both the first and second *Beis HaMikdash* were destroyed because of the iniquities of the Jewish people. Thus, in terms of "G-d reciting this verse regarding the Jewish people when they obey His will," this could not apply to the first and second *Beis HaMikdash*.

It is only with regard to the third (and everlasting) *Beis HaMikdash* that G-d recites the verse. For then the Jews will fully obey His will, and the Divine Presence will wholly unite with, and reside within them. G-d will thus be able to say of the Jews: "This is My eternal resting place; here I shall dwell, for I desire it."

Based on *Likkutei Sichos* Vol. XXI, pp. 260-263.

ספר ויקרא

Vayikra

Vayikra   ויקרא

The Wood Offering

In the commentary of *Toras Kohanim* on the Torah portion of *Vayikra*, our Sages note that a gift of wood for use upon the altar may constitute a valid sacrificial offering.[1] How can a mere adjunct to the actual offerings constitute a valid offering in itself?

The *Ramban* explains the significance of offerings in the following manner:[2] The person who brings an animal sacrifice must realize that all those things being done to the animal should by right have been done to him. It is only because of G-d's mercy that an animal is substituted.

Thus, the intent of one bringing an animal sacrifice should be to offer *himself* to G-d. This also serves to explain why every sacrifice had to be consumed together with the wood of the altar:

There are various types of sacrifices, each possessing its own laws as to the manner in which it is to be offered. According to the *Ramban*, we may understand the differences in the laws according to the effect the particular offering has upon the individual who brings it. This depends, of course, on the reason the offering is brought — whether it is an expiation offering, a free-will offering, etc.

On the other hand, the essence of every sacrifice is the offering of the person *himself*; the person must be prepared to dedicate himself entirely to G-d. It is only then that each form of offering fulfills its purpose.

That all offerings share this attribute is symbolized by the wood that is consumed together with every sacrifice: the

---

1. *Vayikra* 2:1.
2. *Vayikra* 1:9.

wood provides the constant subtext of every offering — that the person offers himself to G-d.

The Torah tells us that "Man is a tree of the field."[3] Man's offering of himself to G-d is thus expressed by means of wood. One of the differences between man's "general offering" that finds expression in the consumption of wood upon the altar, and the "particular offering" of man's individual powers (symbolized by the various sacrifices) is the following:

When a person offers a particular part of himself, he cannot free himself entirely of his ego, for his self-abnegation and devotion to G-d refer only to this particular part of himself. The remaining components in every personality conceal and hinder a person's selfless devotion to G-d.

When a person realizes that, regardless of the particular nature of his sacrifice, *he is offering himself totally to G-d*, there is nothing left within him to act as a barrier. The person then can dedicate himself in a manner that transcends intellect or emotion — even holy intellect and emotion.[4]

Based on *Likkutei Sichos* Vol. XXII pp. 7-12.

---

3. *Devorim* 20:19. See also *Ta'anis* 7a.
4. See *Sefer HaMa'amarim* 5659 p. 23ff; *Likkutei Sichos* XX p. 176ff.

The Additional Fifth

At the conclusion of the Torah portion *Vayikra* we learn[1] that if a person commits a robbery, withholds funds, etc., and denies it by swearing falsely, he must — when seeking to atone for his crime — make restitution of the principal plus an additional 20%

Our Rabbis explain[2] that the reason for the additional fifth is "because the money went for naught while in his

---

1. *Vayikra* 5:21-24.
2. *Klei Yakar* ibid.

possession": Money is used to earn money. In seeking to make restitution, the thief must therefore return not only the principal but a sum sufficient to make up for this loss of potential profit.

We find, however, in *Tanya*[3] that when an individual acts badly toward another, the individual who was wronged should not be angered at the person who wronged him, for the damage that he suffered had been foreordained; the harm would have been done in any case, even if not committed by that particular agent.

Although the perpetrator is subject to punishment for his crime, for he could have chosen not to harm the other,[4] (and the Heavenly decree would have come about in another manner, since "G-d has many messengers,") this reckoning applies only to the person who caused the damage, and does not involve the injured party.

Indeed, if this damage had not been preordained, then the person would not have suffered at all, even if a wrong-doer *wanted* to harm him: Man's free choice applies only to those acts that relate to himself; no individual can damage another without Divine consent.

Accordingly, the following question arises: The very fact that the thief stole a sum for a certain period indicates that this loss was preordained. Thus, even if the theft had not occurred, the victim would in any case be lacking the money for this period. This being so, why does the thief have to add a fifth when he makes restitution?

In truth, the same question applies even to the principal: Since Heaven decreed that the victim would lose the use of this money, and since this decree would have been realized even without the theft, why does the thief have to return the money to the *victim* at all? Why not give it to charity or the like?

The answer is obvious: The fact that the person had this money stolen from him does not necessarily indicate that he

---

3. *Igeres HaKodesh XXV.*
4. See *Rambam, Hilchos Teshuvah* conclusion of ch. 6.

was to lose it permanently. Whether it was decreed that the person lose the money temporarily of permanently only becomes clear upon its return; if the thief gives back the money, then it is obvious that the loss was to be only temporary; if the stolen goods are never returned, we will then know that the decree was for a permanent loss.

Since we cannot know the nature of the decree, clearly the thief has no right to keep the money (or even delay its return) with the specious argument that by doing so he proves that the victim was meant to suffer a permanent loss. In the same way, it is wrong to hurt another person and justify this action with the argument that the victim was meant to suffer.

The same is true with regard to the additional fifth: Since adding this fifth means that the victim suffers no monetary loss, it is entirely possible that the victim was to lose this additional fifth only until the time of its return.

The above discussion contains an invaluable lesson in interpersonal relationships: When someone acts badly towards another, he may be tempted to think that since the person was destined to suffer anyway, he need not ask his forgiveness.

The answer is that by asking forgiveness, one lessens the other's pain. A person does not have the right to inflict even greater pain by not asking forgiveness, for there is no proof that the other person was decreed to suffer that much. One must do all he can to lessen the pain of others.

Based of *Likkutei Sichos*, Vol. VII, pp. 9-16.

Tzav   צו

"Speak," "Say," and "Command" — Three Types of Mitzvos

When G-d told Moshe to relay various *mitzvos* to the Jewish people, He used the expressions: "*speak* to the children of Israel," "*say* to the children of Israel" or "*command* the children of Israel."[1]

All commandments, even those conveyed with the expressions "speak" or "say," are termed *mitzvos*, rooted in the word *tzavei* — "command." Thus, all are considered commands and decrees. Nevertheless, the use of the expression "command" concerning specific *mitzvos* indicates that the idea of command plays a larger role with these than it does with *mitzvos* introduced with the terms "speak" or "say."

This is why our Sages state in *Toras Kohanim*, at the beginning of the Torah portion of *Tzav* ("Command"), that "command" indicates an "urging on with alacrity, both now as well as for coming generations."

Chassidus explains[2] that the word *mitzvah* — commandment — derives from the expression *tzavsa v'chibur*, "cleaving and attachment," for the underlying purpose of all *mitzvos* is that through them one becomes bound and "attached" to G-d.

We thus understand that although binding and attachment applies to all *mitzvos*, a greater degree of attachment is achieved through those *mitzvos* relayed to us with the expression "*tzav* — command," for this expression more clearly indicates attachment.

The difference between "speak," "say," and "command" is that when one is merely spoken to, or is merely told to do

---

1. See *Rashi*, beginning of *Vayikra*; See also *Toras Kohanim* ibid.
2. *Likkutei Torah, Bechukosai* 45c, *et al.*

something, he is entirely free to do as he wishes. This is not the case when one is *commanded* to do something. The issuing of a command presupposes that the one doing the commanding has some degree of dominance over the individual being commanded. For example, an army officer can command a subordinate; he cannot issue commands to one of the same rank as himself — he can "speak" to him, but cannot "command" him.

Thus, a person is less free to ignore *mitzvos* conveyed with the term "command" than he is to ignore those relayed with the words "speak" or "say"; in the former instance, it is as if the person were coerced to obey.

Accordingly, "speak" and "say" *mitzvos* — obedience to which is left up to the hearer — accomplish most of their "cleaving and attachment" when a Jew actually fulfills them.

Not so with *mitzvos* conveyed with the word "command": Since there is a greater certainty that the person will fulfill them, their "cleaving and attachment" is fully accomplished at the moment the command is issued.

While "command" *mitzvos* achieve "cleaving and attachment" at an earlier stage than do other *mitzvos*, all *mitzvos* accomplish this sooner or later. How so?

The previous Lubavitcher Rebbe offers the following parable:[3] An intellectual giant whose whole life revolves around knowledge will ignore a person who has nothing to do with matters of intellect — the simpleton is not negated; he simply does not exist in the genius's world. The simpleton, too, will feel himself to be nonexistent in comparison to the prodigy.

However, when the wise man commands the simple one to do something for him, suddenly the simple person exists to the wise man. As well, the simple person becomes aware of his own importance.

Based on *Likkutei Sichos* Vol. VII pp. 30-34.

---

3. *HaTamim I*, p. 25ff.

Day People Vs Night People

In the opening verse of the portion *Tzav* we read that "The burnt-offering shall remain on the firewood on the altar all night until morning."[1] *Rashi* comments:[2] "This teaches us that the fat and the limbs may be burned the entire night."

Although the priests were to endeavor to do the burning by day — this being the most appropriate time[3] — they could also do it throughout the night, in order to obey the command "Do not allow the fat of My offering to remain... until morning."[4]

The *Ramban* states[5] that the offering of an animal upon the altar was able to achieve atonement for a sinner because the person realizes that everything transpiring with the animal should have been happening with him, were it not that G-d in His kindness permitted the substitution.

It is thus understandable that all aspects of an offering, including the burning of fat and limbs, find corollaries in terms of man's spiritual service.

How does "burning the fat" apply to our spiritual lives?

Fat is indicative of pleasure.[6] The lesson here is: "All fat is to be offered to G-d"[7] — all of a Jew's pleasure and satisfaction should be offered to G-d.

This is why the main purpose of burning the fat is achieved by day. "Day" and "night" symbolize man's spiritual states: day is the condition in which one's soul shines within its body; night refers to a person who lacks this spiritual illumination.

The "day person" feels G-dliness not only while engaged in Torah study and *mitzvah* performance, but the whole day

---

1. *Vayikra* 6:1.
2. Ibid.
3. *Menachos* 72a; *Rambam, Hilchos Ma'aseh HaKarbanos* 4:3.
4. *Shmos* 23:18.
5. Commentary on *Vayikra* 1:9.
6. See *Gittin* 56b.
7. *Vayikra* 3:16.

through — even while engaged in mundane affairs. For this individual is sensitive to the G-dliness that permeates the world. He is thus able to serve G-d even while engaged in mundane actions — "In *all your ways* you shall know Him."[8]

The "night person" lacks this spiritual sensitivity and illumination. Thus, this person must struggle while engaged in mundane affairs to see that such actions are done "for the sake of heaven" and not for selfish pleasure. It goes without saying that unlike the "day person," the "night person's" mundane actions are not elevated to holiness.

Moreover, the "night person" must be on guard even while engaged in the study of Torah and the performance of *mitzvos*: Since Torah is clothed in human intellect and *mitzvos* are garbed in the physical world, a person who lacks spiritual illumination must toil mightily to be sure that his Torah study is done purely for the sake of Torah, and not for the intellectual pleasure it causes. And so too with his performance of *mitzvos*.

Thus, while each kind of individual sacrifices his pleasure to G-d, "day people" do so in a positive manner — their entire delight in even mundane affairs is that of G-dliness. "Night people," however, cannot truly say that their entire pleasure is G-dly. Their spiritual toil lies mostly in subduing their baser instincts, and in seeing to it that whatever they do should at least be "for the sake of heaven." Thus, their primary manner of service is the negation and suppression of evil.

This is why "offering the fat to G-d" — dedicating one's pleasure to holiness — is achieved principally by those on the level of "day," while the burning of fat by night reflects the forestalling of transgression through the negation and subdual of evil.

Although lacking the spiritual intensity of a soul unencumbered by the body, the service of the average soul — struggling to elevate the body and the world — contains

---

8. *Mishlei* 3:6.

elements superior to the soul's service prior to its incarnation.

Based on *Likkutei Sichos*, Vol. III, pp. 948-952.

Pesach   פסח

Passover —
Season of our Freedom & Festival of Matzos

The festival of Passover is commonly referred to in our prayers as the "Season of our Freedom" and the "Festival of Matzos." These names relate to aspects of Passover that are germane at all times and in all places.

The other names of this holiday — "Passover" and the "springtime festival" — apply only to distinct times and places: The name "Passover" is related to the Passover offering, which could be brought only when the Holy Temple stood; "springtime festival" refers only to the Northern Hemisphere, for in the Southern Hemisphere Pesach occurs in the fall.

Understandably, the festival's message for the entire year[1] can best be gleaned from those titles that apply at all times and in all places. The term "Season of our Freedom" alludes to more than just the Jews' freedom from enslavement in Egypt thousands of years ago: it invokes the true freedom of each and every Jew in all times and places.

The ultimate purpose of the Exodus finds expression in the verse:[2] "Upon your taking out the nation from Egypt they shall serve G-d on this mountain," i.e., the experience of receiving the Torah at Sinai. For the Jewish people could not be truly free of the physical bondage of Egypt until they were spiritually free as well.[3]

---

1. See *Likkutei Torah, Berachah* 98b.
2. *Shmos* 3:12.
3. See *Avos* 6:2; See also *Shmos Rabbah* 41:7; *Vayikra Rabbah* 18:3; *Zohar II* 113b and onward.

Spiritual enslavement — the Hebrew word for Egypt being etymologically related to "straits and limitations"[4] — can come about from without as well as from within: A person may be enslaved to the mores of his society, or he may be a slave to his own passions. True freedom from this kind of enslavement can be achieved only through Torah and *mitzvos* — "serving G-d on this mountain."

But what specifically is the freedom seeker to do? Herein comes the lesson of the festival's other name — the "Festival of Matzos."

The "Festival of Matzos" consists of two parts: the obligation to eat matzah and the prohibition of eating *chametz*, leavened products. The obligation to eat matzah is limited to a specific amount at a specified time — a quantity the size of an olive must be eaten on the first night of Passover.[5] However, the prohibition against *chametz* knows different limits; the tiniest particle of *chametz* is forbidden throughout the holiday.[6]

The natural differences between *chametz* and matzah, and the consequent differences between eating matzah and refraining from *chametz* provide a valuable lesson in the quest for spiritual freedom.[7]

Leavened dough rises continually. Matzah is the very antithesis thereof — the dough is not permitted to rise at all.

Our Rabbis explain[8] that *chametz* is symbolic of haughtiness and conceit — traits so deleterious that they are at the root of all negative traits. This is one of the reasons why

---

4. See *Torah Or, Yisro* 71c and onward.
5. *Tur* and *Shulchan Aruch* and *Shulchan Aruch Admur HaZakein, Orach Chayim* 475. [The size of one "olive" in Halachah is 28 grams, or 1 ounce.]
6. *Pesachim* 30a; *Rambam, Hilchos Chametz u'Matzah* 1:5; *Tur* and *Shulchan Aruch* and *Shulchan Aruch Admur HaZakein, Orach Chayim* beginning of section 447; *Shulchan Aruch Admur HaZakein, Orach Chayim* beginning of sections 431 and 445.
7. See *Likkutei Torah, Tzav* first *ma'amar* titled *Sheishes Yamim*, ch. 3; *Likkutei Torah, Shir HaShirim* 14d and onward, *et al.*
8. See places cited in previous footnote.

even the minutest amount of *chametz* is forbidden — haughtiness and conceit must be *completely* nullified.[9]

Ridding oneself of the traits represented by *chametz* and performing the *mitzvah* of eating matzah enable the Jew to overcome his own faults and the blandishments of the mundane world. He is then able to free himself from spiritual exile, and enjoy this freedom throughout the year.

Based on Likkutei Sichos Vol. XXII pp. 266-270.

---

9. See *Rambam, Hilchos Deos* 4:3; commentary of R. Yonah on *Avos* 4:4.

The First and Final Redemption

The last day of Passover, known as *Acharon Shel Pesach*, concludes the theme of liberation and redemption from exile. While the first night of Passover commemorates the redemption from exile in Egypt, the final day celebrates the future Redemption, which G-d will bring about through Moshiach.[1]

The connection between the first and the last redemptions is also gleaned from the verse:[2] "As in the days when you left Egypt, I shall show you wonders [during the final Redemption]."

Our Rabbis ask:[3] Why does the verse say "As in the *days* when you left Egypt," when the Exodus took place on *one* day, as the verse states:[4] "Remember this day on which you left Egypt."

On the day the Jewish slaves left Egypt they achieved the status of free people.[5] This transition, however, is an ongoing experience that requires constant meditation on the

---

1. See *Sefer HaSichos* 5700 p. 72.
2. *Michah* 7:15.
3. *Zohar III* 176a; *ma'amar* titled *Kimei Tzeischa* 5708.
4. *Shmos* 13:3.
5. *Gevuras HaShem* ch. 61.

concepts of slavery and freedom. A person's ruminations must have a salutary effect on his daily conduct.

This is why spiritual redemption from all straits and limitations that constitute spiritual Egyptian exile is an ongoing process, notwithstanding the fact that the Jews' physical Exodus took only one day.

This is expressed by our Sages when they state:[6] "In each and every generation and on each and every day, every man is obligated to see himself as if he had gone out from Egypt on that very day." Man's viewing the Exodus from Egypt as a continuous process will lead to daily improvement in conduct as well — as befits a free man.

Both the first and the final redemption involve the liberation of all the Jewish people. Just as the Exodus encompassed the entire nation and resulted from the Jews' collective service, so will the future Redemption liberate all Jews from exile, and it too will result from our collective efforts.

This collective liberation and effort came about during the Exodus as a result of the effort of each Jew, who first liberated himself from his own spiritual exile. And so with the final liberation: the efforts of each and every Jew in redeeming himself from spiritual exile will result in the collective redemption of all Jews from the final exile.

In practical terms, the lesson from the above is that each and every Jew is entrusted by G-d with a unique mission that he, and only he, is capable of accomplishing. He cannot rely on someone else to fulfill that mission for him, for the other individual is entrusted with his *own* mission.

On the other hand, each person must also realize that he is part of a collective — the Jewish nation. His mission is thus of vital importance not only to himself but to all the Jewish people. Fulfilling his mission as an individual thus helps the Jewish people fulfill their mission as a collective whole. Ultimately, each Jew's personal redemption from

---

6. *Pesachim* 116b, *Tanya* ch. 47.

spiritual exile leads to the collective redemption of all Jews
from the final exile.

Based on Likkutei Sichos Vol. XXII pp. 258-263.

Vaulting, Bounding and Leaping

The name of the holiday *Pesach*, or Passover, derives
from the Hebrew words meaning "and G-d will leap over."[1]
Rashi[2] explains further: "The festival is called *Pesach* because
of [G-d's] leaping.... Therefore perform all its aspects in a
manner of bounding and leaping."

What is the particular relationship between the holiday
that celebrates the Exodus, and bounding and leaping?

The Jewish people lived in Egypt for many generations,
eventually descending to a state of slavery. Some became so
mired in slavery that when the time came for their liberation
they did not want to leave Egypt![3]

During the period that the Jews were in Egypt, the country was considered to be the most culturally advanced of its
time in terms of knowledge, art, technology and philosophy[4]
— the things people commonly refer to when they speak of
"culture" and "civilization." But in terms of morality and
ethics, Egypt was the most depraved, degenerate and im-
moral of lands,[5] so much so that it was known as the
"abomination of the earth."[6]

It was from a land such that the Jewish people had to attain complete physical and spiritual freedom, so that soon
afterward they would be able to lift themselves to the
heights necessary for receiving G-d's Torah. For the main
purpose of the Exodus was the receipt of Torah, as G-d told

---

1. *Shmos* 12:23.
2. Ibid. 12:11.
3. See *Shmos Rabbah* 14:3; *Tanchuma, Va'eira* 14.
4. See commentaries of our Sages on *I Melachim* 5:10.
5. See *Toras Kohanim, Acharei* 18:3.
6. *Bereishis* 42:12.

Moshe: "When you will take the nation out of Egypt, they shall serve G-d upon this mountain [of Sinai]."[7] Indeed, *Rashi* notes[8] that it was in merit of their eventual service to G-d at Sinai that the Jewish people were redeemed from exile.

Receiving the Torah from G-d involved the acceptance of all its decrees, beginning with the Ten Commandments, the first of which was: "I am the L-rd your G-d, you shall have no other gods," and the last of which was: "You shall not covet... anything that belongs to your fellow man."[9] These themes of G-d's absolute unity and the highest degree of ethics and morality in terms of man's relationship with his fellows stood in stark contrast to the depravity of Egyptian "culture" and "civilization."

Clearly, departing from such an abject state and achieving true inner freedom to the extent of accepting Torah and *mitzvos* before fully comprehending them[10] required the mighty leap of "*Pesach* — in a manner of bounding and leaping."

All this began while the Jews were still in Egypt, when G-d told them about the Passover service, including the instruction that the entire service be done "in a manner of bounding and leaping."

This vaulting manner of service culminated on the first night of *Pesach*, when G-d Himself leapt over the bonds and fetters of exile, revealed Himself to the Jewish people while they were still in Egypt, released them from their captivity and established that from then on their inner state would be one of spiritual freedom.

This Passover theme of vaulting and leaping is fundamental to Jews and Judaism at all times and in all places, and is to be carried through the rest of the year.

---

7. *Shmos* 3:12.
8. Ibid.
9. Ibid. 20:2-14.
10. See ibid. 24:7; *Shabbos* 88a.

We find ourselves exiled in a physical world, with a pre-ponderance of our time required for physical acts such as eating, drinking, sleeping, earning a living, etc. The time remaining for spiritual affairs such as Torah study, prayer and the performance of *mitzvos* is thus severely restricted.

Nevertheless, *Pesach* tells us that as Jews we are expected and empowered to "leap over" all physical and corporeal limitations to attain true spiritual freedom the whole year through.

Based on *Likkutei Sichos* Vol. XII, pp. 160-164.

Shemini   שמיני

Two Brothers — Two Worlds

The Torah portion of *Shemini* relates[1] how Aharon's elder sons, Nadav and Avihu, were consumed by a heavenly fire when they brought an unauthorized offering on the Altar. As a result, Aharon's remaining sons, as well as Aharon himself, felt it was improper to eat the sin offering presented at that time. This sacrifice is also brought every *Rosh Chodesh*. They did, however, eat the special one-time sin offerings.

When Moshe discovered their abstention "He was angry with Aharon's surviving sons...." and said to them: ""Why did you not eat the [*Rosh Chodesh*] sin offering...?" Aharon explained that since this was a *regular* offering and such a terrible tragedy had befallen them that day, it would have been inappropriate for them to eat it. "When Moshe heard this, he approved."

Moshe understood that there was no difference between regular and one-time offerings, while Aharon and his two surviving sons felt that there was.

Why did they differ?

Furthermore, since Moshe originally maintained that no difference existed between regular and one-time offerings, what caused him to change his mind when he heard Aharon's response; seemingly Aharon supplied no innovative reasoning?

The difference between Moshe and Aharon is expressed by our Sages thusly:[2] "Kindness — that is Aharon... Truth — that is Moshe." Truth is not subject to change — at all times

---

1. *Vayikra* Ch. 10; See also commentary of *Rashi*.
2. *Shmos Rabbah* 5:10.

and in all places it remains the same.[3] Kindness, however, must consider the circumstances of the recipient. Since no two people and no two circumstances are ever entirely alike, it follows that there are differences in the beneficence radiated by the attribute of kindness.

Moshe's logic, resulting as it did from the viewpoint of Truth, dictated that whenever an issue was in doubt, there should be no change from one time and circumstance to the other. He therefore saw no difference between regular and one-time offerings.

Aharon's trait of kindness resulted in his being "...a lover of peace, a pursuer of peace, a lover of creatures, [a person] who drew them close to the Torah."[4] I.e., Aharon's devotion to his fellow Jew was such that he dedicated himself even to those individual who could only be described as "creatures." Aharon saw to it that even such people should have their needs met according to their level and status.

He therefore said there was a difference between "*sacred* one-time offerings" and "*sacred* regular offerings." From the perspective of the beneficiaries who are in need of the kindness resulting from a sacred offering, it is impossible to expect that sanctity will come in the same manner and degree for all people at all times.

Moshe, however, influenced the Jewish people by causing holiness to descend upon them from Above, so that it was felt below with the same intensity with which it was felt Above.[5] Relating to the Jewish people in this manner caused him to feel that the same degree of sanctity could be showered upon all Jews at all times and in all places.

Aharon then explained to Moshe that while Moshe's intentions were surely the best and the noblest, Jews in this physical world differ from each other, as do their spiritual levels; it would prove nigh impossible for them to all be permeated with the same degree of sanctity.

---

3. See *Tanya* Ch. 13; *Likkutei Torah, Masei* 93b, *et al.*
4. *Avos* 1:12.
5. *Likkutei Torah, Bamidbar* 2d and onward, *et al.*

When Moshe perceived Aharon's reasoning he readily agreed.

Based on *Likkutei Sichos* Vol. XVII pp. 113-114.

"When In Doubt...."

The Torah portion *Shemini* concludes:[1] "To distinguish between the unclean and the clean...." *Rashi* explains[2] this to mean: to distinguish between a kosher animal that had only half its windpipe severed during ritual slaughter, (thus rendering it non-kosher, or ritually unclean), and an animal that had the majority of its windpipe severed (thus rendering it kosher, or ritually clean).

Thus, the conclusion of *Shemini* informs us that such an infinitesimal difference more than suffices to bring about a distinction between *tameh* and *tahor*, unclean and clean.

The title of a Torah portion applies to all its verses.[3] In fact, because "The beginning is embedded in the end and the end in the beginning,"[4] the title is particularly reflected in a portion's conclusion.

This being so, we must understand the connection between the conclusion of the portion which deals with the concept of clean and unclean and the title *Shemini*, "Eighth" — the day that followed the seven days of the Tabernacle's consecration.

Especially so since "eight" signifies a concept that far transcends the numbers one through seven, for as the *Keli Yakar* explains,[5] all aspects of creation fall within the cycle of "seven" — the "Seven Days of Creation" — while "eight" is

---

1. *Vayikra* 11:47.
2. Ibid. *Toras Kohanim* ibid.
3. See *Likkutei Sichos VII*, p. 25 fn. 40.
4. *Sefer Yetzirah* 1:7.
5. Beginning of Torah portion *Shemini*; see also *Rabbeinu Bachya, loc. cit.*; Responsa of the *Rashba* I-9.

"unique to G-d Himself." Indeed, this is why this eighth day "received ten crowns."[6]

As further elucidated by our Sages,[7] the cycle of "seven" includes not only those things encompassed by creation, but also the degree of G-dliness vested within creation. "Eight," however, alludes to a level of G-dliness that transcends creation.

Since *Shemini* relates to so lofty a level, concerning which the verse states:[8] "Evil does not dwell with You," how does the "unclean" enter the picture?

The difference between unclean and clean dealt with at the conclusion of *Shemini* is minuscule: sever exactly half the windpipe and the animal is non-kosher; anything more than that and the animal is kosher.

In such a situation it is easy to err and think that unclean is clean. In order to be able to determine an unclean state and cast it aside one needs the ability which emanates from the exalted level of *Shemini*:

When an individual is aware of only the limited degree of G-dliness that descends within creation, then when in doubt concerning a fine point he may easily err. The person's evil inclination may say to him that since he has the opportunity of elevating the divine spark found in the doubtfully kosher object, what right does he have to cast it aside?

The evil inclination may well go on to say there is no need to worry about the object or animal being non-kosher in such an instance, for usually when an animal is slaughtered the slaughter is properly performed and the animal is kosher. Is it right that such a minute doubt should cause one to cast aside an animal and miss elevating the divine spark found within it?

---

6. *Seder Olam Rabbah* ch. 7; quoted by *Rashi* beginning of Torah portion *Shemini*.
7. See *Maamarim* titled *Vaye'hi Bayom HaShemini* of the years 5704 and 5705. See also *Likkutei Sichos III*, p. 974.
8. *Tehillim* 5:5.

However, when a Jew is sensitive to the G-dliness that transcends creation, he will be loath to deviate from the Divine Will in even the slightest way. Moreover, this desire to be holy is so powerful that it will transcend the intellect. It enables a Jew to rise above all blandishments of the evil inclination, for a Jew's essential desire to be one with G-d is far stronger than any doubts generated by his evil inclination.

Thus it is specifically the qualities of *Shemini* that enable a person "to distinguish between the unclean and the clean."

Based on *Likkutei Sichos*, Vol. VII, pp. 65-73.

Tazria-Metzora   תזריע-מצרע

Circumcision — Always a Timely Act

The Torah portion *Tazria* opens by saying:[1] "When a woman conceives and gives birth to a boy.... On the eighth day, [the child]... shall be circumcised." This is so only if the infant is healthy; if the child is not completely well, *milah* (the ritual of circumcision) is delayed until he is fully recovered.

The *Rambam* explains why only a healthy child is circumcised:[2] "A threat to life sets everything else aside; it is possible to circumcise later on, but it is impossible to return a Jewish soul [to its body after its passing]."

The *Rambam's* exposition — "it is possible..." — indicates that he is providing two reasons:

"The threat to life sets everything else aside" means that even if the *mitzvah* of circumcision can *never* be performed because of "a threat to life," it is to be forever forfeited, since "a threat to life sets everything else aside."

The second reason — "it is possible to circumcise later on" — suggests that when *milah* is delayed because of ill-health, nothing is really lost. We thus understand that performing the *mitzvah* of *milah* at a later date affects the previous days as well, so much so that, retrospectively, it is equal to circumcision on the eighth day.

How can an action so affect the past?

We must also understand the following: At the conclusion of the second reason of "it is possible to circumcise later on" the *Rambam* adds: "but it is impossible to ever return a Jewish soul." Seemingly, these words are more closely re-

---

1. *Vayikra* 12:2-3.
2. *Hilchos Milah* 1:18.

lated to the first reason of "A threat to life sets everything else aside"?

Chassidus explains[3] that *milah* allows the drawing down of a Divine illumination far greater than man's service alone could accomplish; the illumination reflects an "arousal from Above." So long as a person is uncircumcised, his state acts as a barrier to this light. *Milah* removes this barrier.

The same is true regarding the "entry of the holy soul" accomplished through circumcision:[4] The ritual draws down a level of soul that transcends intellect.[5] This, too, cannot be realized through man's service alone — it forms an essential part of every male Jew, and is merely *revealed* through *milah.*

Since circumcision merely exposes a pre-existing spiritual state, it is able to affect the past as well. If *milah* is never performed, then the spiritual state remains concealed. But once *milah* is performed and the pre-existing state is revealed, it influences the past as well.

Accordingly, the *Rambam* states: "but it is impossible to ever return a Jewish soul" after both reasons, in order to explain how *milah* performed "later on" is considered as if it were done on time.

A Jew's connection with G-d transcends all bounds, and is always whole. "It is impossible to ever return a Jewish soul" thus means that the bond with G-d can never be "returned," i.e., severed.

This being so, all that is required is for this bond to be revealed. This is accomplished by *milah* even "later on" — even then, its effect is the same as that of *milah* performed in its proper time.

Based on *Likkutei Sichos* Vol. III pp. 979-983.

---

3. *Likkutei Torah, Tazria* 21a; *Derech Mitzvosecha* 9b.
4. *Shulchan Aruch Admur HaZakein Me'hadura Basra* 4:2.
5. See *Basi LeGani 5713.*

Tazria   תזריע

The Purpose of Punishment

The titles given to Torah portions do more than distinguish one from another; they reflect the theme and overall content of each.[1]

What possible connection is there then between the title of *Tazria* ("Conceive") and the contents of this portion, which deal mainly with the leprous-like affliction of *tzora'as* — unknown nowadays — that resulted from evil gossip, *Lashon HaRah*.

Not only does the title *Tazria* seem to have no connection with *tzora'as*, they are seemingly antithetical:

Tazria, "Conceive," refers to birth and new life, as the verse states:[2] "When a woman conceives and gives birth...," while *tzora'as* indicates the very opposite, as our Sages state:[3] "One afflicted with *tzora'as* is considered as if dead."

The concept of Reward and Punishment is one of the foundations of Jewish faith. The *Rambam* states it thusly:[4] "The eleventh fundament is that G-d rewards those who obey the Torah's commandments and punishes those who transgress them...."

Since the Torah is replete with verses that indicate that G-d is compassionate and merciful, it follows that His punishments are not for the sake of revenge[5] — Heaven forbid — but are for the sinners benefit.[6]

---

1. See previous essay. See also sources cited in *Likkutei Sichos XXI*, p. 250 fns. 1-2.
2. *Vayikra* 12:1.
3. *Nedarim* 64b.
4. Commentary to the *Mishnah*, Introduction to Chapter *Cheilek*.
5. See *Berachos* 5a.
6. See *Kuzari* II-45; *Ikrim* IIII-38.

However, it is not patently obvious that most of the Torah's punishments benefit the individual during his lifetime. This was not the case regarding *tzora'as*; it was clearly revealed that this benefited the person:

The *Rambam* writes:[7] "This alteration [of *tzora'as*] that affects clothing and dwellings.... was not a natural phenomenon. Rather, it was a sign and a wonder that affected the Jewish people in order to keep them from speaking *Lashon HaRah*. For he who speaks *Lashon HaRah* will have the beams of his house altered [by *tzora'as*].

"If he repents, then the house becomes undefiled... If he does not... ultimately the person himself will become afflicted with *tzora'as*, and will have to be separated from others until he ceases occupying himself with evil speech, scoffing and *Lashon HaRah*."

Thus, G-d reordered nature to keep individuals from engaging in *Lashon HaRah*. *Tzora'as* would first afflict a person's home, then his clothing, and finally his person, in order to tell the sinner, gently at first and then more severely, to stop indulging in *Lashon HaRah*.

Even the punishment of the person himself, which required that he "sit alone; outside the camp shall be his dwelling,"[8] was for the purpose of seeing to it that he "cease occupying himself in evil speech, scoffing and *Lashon HaRah*."

The reason why this portion is titled *Tazria* will be understood accordingly: *Tazria*, "Conceive," is the beginning of life. The *tzora'as* itself, as well as the person's dwelling alone, are not so much meant as a punishment, but as a means of rectification and healing, enabling one to begin a new lifestyle free of *Lashon HaRah*.

All aspects of Torah serve as a lesson. *Tzora'as*, then, was clearly for the benefit of the individual. The same is true of

---

7. Conclusion of *Hilchos Tumas Tzora'as*, and similarly in his Commentary on the *Mishnah, Nega'im* 12:5; *Moreh Nevuchim* III-47.
8. *Vayikra* 13:46.

all punishments in the Torah; they are all for the rectification of the sinner, that he return to the proper path in life.

And why is this lesson specifically gleaned from *tzora'as*? Because the suffering of *tzora'as* — being considered as if dead and compelled to exist in absolute solitude — is one of the most severe in the Torah.

If in this instance we can clearly see the benefit — being reborn anew, *Tazria* — then surely this is so with other punishments: they are all part of a sinner's spiritual rehabilitation, thus helping make a new beginning possible.

Based on Likkutei Sichos, Vol. XXII, pp. 70-73.

Metzora   מצרע

Purification of the Metzora —
A Lesson in Repentance

The Torah portion *Metzora* begins by stating: "This shall be the law of the *metzora*: he shall be brought to the *kohen*, the priest."[1] The verse then goes on to say,[2] "The *kohen* shall go out of the camp" and inspect the *metzora*.

Since the *metzora* could not possibly come to the *kohen*, (for until he was declared free of *tzora'as* he was prohibited from entering the Jewish encampment), what are we to make of the verse "he shall be brought to the *kohen*"?

Additionally, why does the Torah use the expression "he shall be brought to the *kohen*," rather than "he shall come to the *kohen*"? The former phrase seems to imply that the *metzora* a) is brought forcibly, or b) that his appearance before the *kohen* is inevitable.

The leprous-like affliction of *tzora'as* was a punishment for speaking *Lashon Hora*, slanderous and evil gossip. As part of the punishment, the *metzora* was to "sit alone; outside the camp."[3]

The *Gemara*[4] explains that since the *metzora's* gossip caused a separation between one person and another, he is punished by being separated from others.

In a more spiritual sense, to cause separation and strife is to oppose holiness, one characteristic of which is unity. This was why the *metzora* was banished from even the lowest of Jewish encampments, for his actions were thoroughly unholy.

---

1. *Vayikra* 14:2.
2. Ibid. verse 3.
3. Ibid. 13:46.
4. *Erachin* 16b.

However, even a person who committed such a dastardly act will eventually atone,[5] for "G-d devises means so that even he who is banished shall not be outcast forever."[6]

The opening verse of our Torah portion thus assures us that even an individual afflicted with *tzora'as* will eventually "be brought to the *kohen* " — he will repent and return to holiness.

And this is so even if the person has absolutely no *desire* to repent, for G-d desires his repentance. Therefore, willingly or unwillingly, he will surely "be brought to the *kohen*."

G-d, however, doesn't want anyone's repentance to be forced upon him from Above; every sinner should *desire* to repent. This is why, after the verse says "he shall be brought to the *kohen*," it goes on to add that "the *kohen* shall go out of the camp":

The first step in achieving repentance for one who has no desire to repent comes about because of a desire from Above. As such, it does not permeate the sinner.

The verse indicates this first step by saying: "he shall be brought to the *kohen*," meaning that the person is transported from his own status and is forcibly brought to a situation that he would not have chosen on his own — repentance is foisted upon him from Above.

Thereafter comes the second stage, wherein "the *kohen* shall go out of the camp." This means to say that the urge to repentance must be framed in the mindset in which the *metzora* finds himself, so that repentance is done willingly.

Moreover, when the purification of the *metzora*, i.e., the act of repentance, comes about in the *same place* in which the *metzora* finds himself — outside the pale of holiness — then the sinner's very iniquities are transformed into merits.

This causes a person to rise to such an exalted level that he can attain a degree of holiness which is impossible for

---

5. See *Hilchos Talmud Torah, l'Rabbeinu HaZakein*, 4:3; conclusion of ch. 39 of *Tanya*.

6. *II Shmuel* 14:14.

those righteous individuals who have never been banished "outside the camp."[7]

Based on *Likkutei Sichos* Volume VII, pp. 100-103.

---

7. See *Rambam, Hilchos Teshuvah* 7:4.

Acharei-Kedoshim   אחרי-קדושים

Holy and Holier

The Torah portions of *Acharei* and *Kedoshim* are uniquely related in terms of content. This is mirrored by the fact that in most years the two are read together.

Acharei begins by describing the service of the *High Priest* in the *Holy of Holies* during *Yom Kippur* — the coming together of the most sacred aspects of space (the Holy of Holies), the holiest moment in time (*Yom Kippur*), and the holiest person (the High Priest).

This holiness is also paramount in the portion of *Kedoshim*, beginning as it does with the verse,[1] "You shall be holy, for I am holy," and stating near the conclusion:[2] "You shall be holy unto Me, for I, the L-rd, am holy."

Moreover, the name of the portion itself, *Kedoshim*, means holy — separate from the mundane.

Indeed, a Jew's sanctity can be so lofty that it bears some comparison with G-d's, as the verse states: "You shall... be holy, for I... am holy."

But how is it possible for corporeal man to reach such heights? The verse addresses itself to this question when it states "for I, the L-rd your G-d, am holy." Since G-d is holy, each and every Jew can and must be holy as well, for all Jews "are truly part of G-d above."[3]

The measure of sanctity which each and every Jew is capable of achieving may best be appreciated when one realizes that the sanctity we are told to aspire to in *Kedoshim* follows that previously achieved in *Acharei*. In that portion, the passing of Nadav and Avihu is described as the result of

---

1. *Vayikra* 19:2.
2. Ibid. 20:26.
3. *Tanya*, beginning of Ch. 2.

their souls' extreme longing for G-d. So great was their love that their bodies could no longer contain their souls, which literally expired.

The portion of *Kedoshim* informs every Jew that he is capable of even greater heights. For the pursuit of holiness is never-ending, one level always following another, the reason being that holiness emanates from G-d, who is truly infinite — "for I am holy."

Herein lies a lesson for each and every Jew: Even a Jew who has achieved a great measure of sanctity may not rest on his laurels; he must constantly strive to attain even greater holiness. Moreover, he must progress boldly, so that each elevation is infinitely higher than the preceding one.

The portions of *Acharei* and *Kedoshim* are generally read on the Sabbaths between Passover and Shavuos, i.e., during the days that are bound up with the Exodus, the receiving of the Torah on Shavuos being the culmination of that Exodus. What connection is there between these Torah portions and the Exodus?

According to the above, the connection is readily discernible: The Exodus was a leaving of physical and spiritual servitude in favor of physical and spiritual freedom. This involves a radical elevation. Man's quest for holiness, expressed in these Torah portions, also entails this quest for radical elevation.

Based on *Likkutei Sichos* Vol. 12, pp. 91-94.

Acharei   אחרי

The Kohen Gadol's Home

In describing the service of the High Priest on *Yom Kippur*, the Torah portion *Acharei* tells us that the *Kohen Gadol* "shall atone for himself and for his home."[1] Our Sages explain[2] that "his home" means his wife.

By stating that the *Kohen Gadol* is to atone for both himself and his wife, the verse implies that the High Priest must be married.

However, the requirement that the *Kohen Gadol* be married is germane only to *Yom Kippur*; during the rest of the year a *Kohen Gadol* may serve even if he is unmarried.

Yom Kippur represents the acme of spiritual service, when the holiest of the Jewish people — the *Kohen Gadol* — served in the most holy place — the Holy of Holies — on the holiest day of the year.

Why was it necessary for the *Kohen Gadol* to be married in order to perform this most sacred service? This is even more puzzling in light of the fact that it was necessary for the *Kohen Gadol* to *separate* from his wife during the week preceding *Yom Kippur*.[3]

The fact that the Torah refers to the *Kohen Gadol*'s wife as "his home" rather than simply "his wife" shows that not only must the *Kohen Gadol* be married, but also that at the time of his service on *Yom Kippur* he must also have a wife that is "his home."

But what superior quality makes a wife one's "home"? Furthermore, what exactly do we mean that the *Kohen Gadol*'s wife was his "home"?

---

1. *Vayikra* 16:6.
2. Opening *Mishnah* of tractate *Yoma*.
3. Ibid.

The great Sage Rabbi Yossi once said:[4] "I have never referred to my spouse as 'my wife,' but rather as 'my home.'" R. Yossi's statement about how he would refer to his wife was one of a number of statements concerning how careful he was to conduct himself in an exemplary fashion. What was so special about his always referring to his wife as "his home"?

In referring to his wife in this manner, R. Yossi sought to indicate his awareness that the ultimate purpose of marriage is to fulfill the commandment "be fruitful and multiply" — to establish a Jewish home filled with children. He therefore saw his spouse not as "his wife" but as "his home."

Rabbi Yossi's conduct differed from the other Rabbis' who would refer to their spouses as their wives. The other Sages would not relate to their spouses only as "their homes," for they realized that to have a wife — even without children to make her "one's home" — is a desirous end in itself.

Thus we find that during the first year of marriage — when there are no children — a husband is exempt from military service so that he may "gladden his wife."[5] So too, a husband is freed from certain obligations during festivals so that he will be able to "gladden his wife."

Clearly, the Torah recognizes the value of the relationship between husband and wife in and of itself.

R. Yossi's degree of sanctity, however, was such that his view of married life centered around the fact that marriage would enable him to have children. Thus, when thinking of his wife he would envision the result of his marriage — a Jewish home replete with children.

On *Yom Kippur* the *Kohen Gadol* was charged with the awesome responsibility of achieving atonement not only on his own behalf and on behalf of his "home," but — most importantly — on behalf of all Israel.[6]

---

4. *Shabbos* 118b.
5. *Devarim* 24:5.
6. *Vayikra* ibid.

Kedoshim   קדושים

Two Forms of Ahavas Yisrael

One of the commandments in the portion of *Kedoshim* is
Ahavas Yisrael — loving one's fellow as one loves oneself.[1]
There are two famous comments regarding this command.
R. Akiva said: "This is an important principal of the Torah."[2]
Hillel noted: "This is the *entire* Torah; the rest is commen-
tary."[3]

Hillel lived many generations before R. Akiva. Since the
statement had already been made that *Ahavas Yisrael* is the
entire Torah, what did R. Akiva seek to accomplish by stating that *Ahavas Yisrael* is "[merely] an important principal of
the Torah"?

There is a statement in the *Midrash* that "G-d's thoughts
about the Jewish people preceded all else,"[4] even coming
before His thoughts about the Torah. I.e., the Jewish people
are spiritually superior even to Torah.

On the other hand, the *Zohar* says[5] "the Jewish people
bind themselves to Torah, and Torah [cleaves] to G-d." This
statement seems to imply that Torah is spiritually superior
to the Jewish people.

How are we to reconcile these seemingly contradictory
statements?

The explanation is as follows:[6] The souls of the Jewish
people *as they exist at their source* are indeed spiritually superior to Torah. However, when Jewish souls descend into

---

1. *Vayikra* 19:18.
2. *Toras Kohanim*, ibid.
3. *Shabbos* 31a.
4. *Bereishis Rabbah* 1:4; *Tanna d'Vei Eliyahu Rabbah* ch. 14.
5. See *Zohar III*, 73a.
6. See *Likkutei Torah, Shir HaShirim* 16:4; *Hemshech 5672*, ch. 76; *Ma'amar Az Yashir* 5700, ch. 3ff.

this world, the Torah is spiritually superior to them; their reunification with G-d can come about only through Torah.

This gives rise to two opposite extremes in the Jewish personality: On the one hand, no matter how much a Jew sins, his Jewishness remains unaltered,[7] for his eternal relationship with G-d transcends his service of Torah and *mitzvos*.

On the other hand, because a Jew's relationship with G-d is so profound, even the greatest sinner is assured of eventually returning to the path of righteousness.

The above also gives rise to opposite extremes with regard to *Ahavas Yisrael*:

The essence of a Jew's love for his fellow Jew derives from the essential unity of all Jews at the eternal root and source of their souls[8] — a bond that transcends the stipulations and strictures of Torah. Keeping in mind this essential unity, all Jews should be loved equally, even those who are distant from G-d and spiritual service, for on the most fundamental level it is impossible to differentiate between a righteous Jew and any other.

However, since a Jew's mortal in this world is bound up with and subservient to Torah, *Ahavas Yisrael* — even of the degree that emanates from the root and source of their souls — is bound up with Torah as well.

This being so, it is self-understood that this love is subject to the laws of the Torah, e.g., one may not compromise Torah for the sake of *Ahavas Yisrael*. Thus the *Mishnah* says:[9] "Love your fellow creature and draw him closer to Torah;" loving one's fellow is to be achieved by raising him to Torah, not by pulling Torah down to his level.

The different expressions of R. Akiva and Hillel regarding *Ahavas Yisrael* will be understood accordingly:

Rabbi Akiva speaks of the practical level of *Ahavas Yisrael* — the level bound by the dictates of Torah. He therefore

---

7. See *Sanhedrin* 44a.
8. See *Tanya* ch. 32.
9. *Avos* 1:12.

cannot possibly say that *Ahavas Yisrael* is the "entire Torah," for if this were so, Torah would be interchangeable with, and could be set aside for, *Ahavas Yisrael*. Rather, *Ahavas Yisrael* is an important principal *of* the Torah, subject to its rules and regulations.

Hillel, however, speaks of *Ahavas Yisrael* in relation to the Jews' source — the level at which every Jew *precedes* Torah. On this level, all of Torah is for the sake of the Jewish people, for it is the observance of Torah that reveals the nation's unique qualities.

Since the essential quality of the Jewish people is revealed in the command of *Ahavas Yisrael*, it thus follows that "This is the entire Torah — the rest is commentary."

Based on *Likkutei Sichos* Vol. XVII, pp. 219-224.

Emor   אמור

Weekdays, Sabbaths & Festivals

At the beginning of the section of *Emor* — in which the
festivals and their laws are enumerated — the verse says:[1]
"Six days shall you work, and the seventh day is a Sabbath
of Sabbaths... you shall perform no labor."

Rashi comments:[2] "What is Sabbath doing among the
festivals? To teach you that whoever desecrates the festivals
is considered as if he desecrated the Sabbath, and whoever
observes the festivals is considered as if he observed the
Sabbath."

Rashi's comment needs to be understood: What is it
about the festivals that makes their observance (by not laboring) or their non-observance (by laboring) tantamount to
observing or desecrating the Sabbath?

Thephrase"six days" refers not only to six individual
days, but to a unit of time that is six days long. Thus, when
the Torah states "Six days shall you work" it implies that
G-d made a distinct period of time during which, and *only*
during which, labor is to be performed. Labor is thus prohibited during any and all times that do not fit in this *weekday* framework of six mundane days.

By prefacing the festival section with "Six days shall you
work," the Torah defines two general time periods with regard to labor: a) six days during which work should be
done; b) *any* other time, during which labor is prohibited.

We thus understand that by implication, "whoever desecrates the festivals is considered as if he desecrated the Sabbath; whoever observes the festivals is considered as if he
observed the Sabbath." For although the punishment for

1. *Vayikra* 23:3.
2. Ibid.

performing labor during the festivals is less severe than that for working on the Sabbath, the general grounds for the prohibition during a festival is the same as on the Sabbath — neither time period is included within the six days during which work is permitted.

Our Sages say in the *Mechilta* that the phrase "Six days shall you work" is a positive commandment. Thus, not only is labor *permitted* during the six weekdays, it is a *mitzvah*. This is in keeping with the verse:[3] "G-d your L-rd will bless you in *all you do*," i.e., each person is to make of himself a natural receptacle for G-d's blessings.

However, this manner of conduct pertains only to the physical body, and to the Jew's soul as it is clothed within his body. Though the body tends to conceal the eternal qualities of the G-dly soul, the Torah commands every Jew to conduct himself according to nature. This is in accord with the sayings of our Sages: "One should not rely on miracles,"[4] "The laws of the land are valid laws,"[5] etc.

But with regard to the soul itself, labor is superfluous; the soul fulfills its purpose while enjoying the spiritual "rest" of Sabbaths and Festivals.

So two opposite aspects are required in the spiritual service of each and every Jew: During the "six days" in which a person is to labor, labor becomes a positive command. But when it comes to the Sabbaths and festivals, a Jew's soul shines forth in all its glory. He must then transcend the body and its needs.

Understandably, while in such a state mundane work is anathema.

Based on *Likkutei Sichos* Vol. XVII pp. 242-246.

---

3. *Devarim* 15:18.
4. See *Pesachim* 64b; *Zohar I* 111b, 112b.
5. *Gittin* 10b.

G-d as Kohen and Kohen Gadol

The Torah portion *Emor* begins with the precept that a *Kohen*, a priest, may not ritually defile himself by coming into contact with a dead body, except in the case of a close relative, such as a son, daughter, etc.[1]

The *Midrash* states[2] that G-d Himself performs all the *mitzvos* that He commanded the Jewish people to perform. Understandably, this also applies to guarding against ritual defilement: Since "G-d is a *Kohen*,"[3] He guards against "defilement" as well.

Thus *Tosefos*[4] explains that G-d was "permitted" to "defile" Himself when He personally buried *Moshe Rabbeinu*, inasmuch as Jews are G-d's children, as it were, and a father who is a *Kohen* may defile himself while burying his child.

G-d, however, is not merely a *Kohen*, but a *Kohen Gadol*, a High Priest.[5] As such, He may not defile himself by coming into contact even with the body of a deceased child.[6] How, then, was G-d able to "defile" Himself by burying *Moshe Rabbeinu*?

Each and every detail of creation has its spiritual counterpart. Thus, the differences within created beings derives from differences in their sources Above.

This is why created beings can serve as a guide to their spiritual source; a thorough understanding of a particular being gives us some understanding of its spiritual counterpart Above.

Nevertheless, the inherent limitations of all created beings do not apply to their source and root Above. Thus, while created beings may serve as an analogy to the realm of the spiritual, they can do so to only a limited extent. Thus we say that just as the sun's rays do not effect any change in the sun itself, so too, creation does not effect any change the Creator.[7] Understandably, this analogy does not apply in its

---

1. *Vayikra* 21:1-4.
2. *Shmos Rabbah* 30:9. See also *Yerushalmi, Rosh HaShanah* 1:3.
3. *Sanhedrin* 39a.
4. Ibid.
5. See *Zohar III*, 17b.
6. See *Vayikra* ibid., verse 11.
7. *Likkutei Torah, Shir HaShirim* 14c, *et al.*

entirety, for the sun — itself a created being — has inherent limitations, while G-d is not bound in any way.[8]

The same is true with regard to the appellations *Kohen* and *Kohen Gadol* as applied to their counterparts Above: While a *Kohen Gadol* of flesh and blood is analogous to the *Kohen Gadol* Above, this is so strictly with regard to the additional measure of priesthood and sanctity that is to be found within a *Kohen Gadol* compared to a regular *Kohen*.

Those attributes of a physical *Kohen Gadol* that are found within him purely because he is encumbered by a physical body do not, of course, apply to the *Kohen Gadol* Above.

The *inherent sanctity* of a *Kohen Gadol* is such that he is separated and removed from any and all impurity.

The fact that he is subject to ritual defilement and impurity — thus the prohibition against defiling himself even for "his father and mother"[9] — stems not from his being a **High** Priest, but from the fact that he is limited by his physicality. Thus, with regard to the level of *Kohen Gadol* as it exists Above, the whole concept of defilement simply does not exist.

This, however, is not so with regard to the spiritual counterpart of a regular *Kohen*, for the fact that a regular *Kohen* can defile himself for a close relative is part and parcel of his priesthood; he is permitted (and *required*)[10] to defile himself for a close relative.

Thus, there is no problem with G-d as High Priest defiling Himself for *Moshe Rabbeinu*, for on His level there simply is no impurity. The only question is, how G-d as spiritual counterpart of the simple *Kohen* could do so. Here the answer is that Jews are His children, and a *Kohen* may defile himself in interring his child.

Based on Likkutei Sichos Vol. VII, pp. 153-156.

---

8.   See *Hemshech 5666*, p. 477.
9.   *Vayikra*, ibid.
10.   *Tur* and *Shulchan Aruch, Yoreh Deah* 373:3.

Behar   בהר

Mitzvos — The General and the Particular

The Torah portion of *Behar* begins by saying:[1] "G-d spoke
to Moshe on Mount Sinai...." It then details the laws of
Shemitah, the Sabbatical year. *Rashi*, quoting *Toras Kohanim*
asks:[2] "What [particularly] has *Shemitah* to do with Mount
Sinai; *all* the commandments were given on Sinai.!" He answers: "Just as the general, specific, and most minutely detailed laws of *Shemitah* were related at Sinai, so too, all [the
mitzvos] were related, generally, specifically and most minutely at Sinai."

This comment is in accord with the opinion of Rabbi
Akiva that "The general as well as the specific laws were
given at Sinai"[3]; it negates the opinion of Rabbi Yishmael,
who maintains that only "the general principles were given
at Sinai," and "the specific laws were related in the Tabernacle."[4]

Why do Rabbis Akiva and Yishmael disagree; what lies
at the root of their argument?

R. Yishmael, who was a High Priest, served G-d in the
priestly manner of "holy of holies"[5] — the service of the
completely righteous *tzaddikim*, while R. Akiva, who descended from proselytes, served in the manner of penitents.[6]

This explains why R. Akiva said concerning the self-sacrificial manner of service known as *mesirus nefesh*,[7] "All my
days I agonized.... when will the opportunity [for actual *me-*

---

1. *Vayikra* 25:1.
2. Ibid.
3. *Chagigah* 6a; *Sotah* 37b; *Zevachim* 115b.
4. Ibid.
5. *I Divrei HaYomim* 23:13.
6. See *Likkutei Sichos,* VI p. 123ff; XI p. 107.
7. *Berachos* 61b.

sirus nefesh] present itself so that I will be able to perform it?"

The service of *tzaddikim* is such that the feeling of *mesirus nefesh* is required only at the beginning of the day, at the time of the recital of the *Shema;* during the rest of the day they go about their service of Torah and *mitzvos* with but a remnant of that emotion.

However, he whose service is in the manner of repentance — a manner of spiritual service that transcends all limitations — will find himself in the state of *mesirus nefesh* "all his days," i.e., the whole day through.

It was this difference in approach to spiritual service that caused R. Yishmael to disagree regarding whether the specific laws were given on Sinai or in the Tabernacle:

The difference between Sinai and the Tabernacle was that the Tabernacle was constructed in a most orderly fashion, with separations between its various parts, with a progression from courtyard to Sanctuary, and within the Sanctuary itself, from the holy to the Holy of Holies. As such, it symbolized orderly and progressive spiritual service.

Sinai, however, was in the desert. It was not a place of order and settlement. It was thus representative of spiritual service that transcends order — transcendent *mesirus nefesh.*

Herein lies the basis of their disagreement: For the service of *tzaddikim* — R. Yishmael — it suffices that the general principles were given at Sinai. I.e., when we speak of *mitzvos* in their general state (i.e. the underlying foundation of all *mitzvos*) we presuppose the state of Sinai — *mesirus nefesh.* However, when we speak of their detailed and specific fulfillment, the orderly manner of service symbolized by the Sanctuary is required.

R. Akiva, however — displaying the service of penitence that transcends orderly progression — maintains that it is possible as well as necessary to experience *mesirus nefesh* — Sinai — even as one goes about performing the specific details of *mitzvos,* and indeed during all of one's activities.

Based on *Likkutei Sichos* Vol. XVII pp. 276-284.

Spiritual Buying and Selling

In this week's Torah portion of *Behar*, the verse states:[1] "When you buy or sell [land] to your neighbor, do not cheat one another." The *Rambam* says[2] that implicit in this verse are the laws of buying and selling.

Among these laws is the principal that "One cannot sell something that has not yet come into existence."[3] Thus, while selling a tree's existing fruit is a simple matter, selling the tree's *future* produce can only be done by selling "the tree itself for its fruit" — the tree already being in existence.[4]

There are thus three different types of acquisition: acquiring the thing itself — a tree, for example; acquiring the produce — the tree's fruit; and acquiring "the tree itself for its fruit."

How are we to understand all this in terms of man's spiritual service?

The overall quality of Divine service is that of selling and acquisition — a Jew so totally binds himself to G-d that his entire being is under G-d's dominion and ownership. This is accomplished when all of one's thoughts, words and deeds are in consonance with G-d's desire.

This form of spiritual acquisition can take place in one of two ways: acquisition of the object itself, or acquisition of [the object's] produce.

In terms of a human being, the "actual" object refers to the person's soul and body and their powers, including intellect, emotions, and the powers of thought, speech and action.

"Produce" alludes to the *results* of man's soul and body and their powers — the actual thoughts, words and deeds that are a direct outgrowth of man's intellect, emotions and other powers.

---

1. *Vayikra* 25:14.
2. *Sefer HaMitzvos, Mitzvas Asei 245.*
3. *Rambam, Hilchos Mechirah,* beginning of ch. 22.
4. *Rambam,* ibid.

"Acquisition of the produce" thus refers to a Jew who dedicates all his thoughts, speech and actions to G-d, being scrupulously observant in assuring that they are all in accordance with G-d's will.

However, in such a person the "object itself," i.e., the essence of his intellect, emotions and other powers, have not become G-d's acquisition. In other words, the person's mind and heart have not been liberated from their capacity to think evil thoughts and harbor sinful desires; the person merely vanquishes these thoughts and desires, preventing them from coming to fruition in thought, word or deed.[5]

"Acquisition of the object itself," however, refers to the service of a truly righteous individual whose intellect, emotions and *very being* have become G-d's acquisition; he has rid himself of all vestiges of evil, so all his desires are holy.

We can now understand in spiritual terms the concept that "One cannot sell something that has not yet come into existence." An individual who is only able to make his thoughts, words and deeds into G-d's acquisition must know that he can guarantee only his present thoughts, words and deeds; he has not gained enough mastery over himself to "sell something that has not yet come into existence."

Thus, when such a person resolves to do something good and holy in the future, that "acquisition" has not yet taken place, for since he must constantly strive against his evil inclination, his future actions may not be in accord with his good resolutions.

However, even such an individual can offer G-d "the tree itself for its fruit," i.e., he can "sell" his fruit — his future good thoughts, etc. — that has yet to come into existence by letting G-d acquire his body itself, similar to the truly righteous individual.

For during prayer even the individual who is merely on the level of "acquisition of the produce" can elevate himself

---

5. See *Tanya* ch. 12.

to the point where his evil will lie dormant,[6] thereby enabling him to offer G-d "the tree itself for its fruit."

Based on *Likkutei Sichos* Vol. XXVII, pp. 176-179.

---

6.   See *Tanya* ibid. and also ch. 13.

Bechukosai   בחקתי

Toiling in Torah

The Torah portion *Bechukosai* opens with the words "If you will follow My statutes (*bechukosai*)...."[1] *Rashi*, quoting *Toras Kohanim*,[2] explains that since the verse goes on to say "and you will observe My commandments," "If you follow My statutes" must therefore mean "that you toil in the study of Torah."

How does the word *bechukosai* (My statutes) — when used in the context of Torah study — express not only the concept of Torah study but also "*toil* in the study of Torah"?

Aside from the generic term *mitzvos*, which applies to all commandments equally, there are specific appellations that apply to the three categories of commandments:

Eidos, or Testimonies, refer to *mitzvos* like Shabbos and *tefillin* that serve as a witness and testimony to events such as Creation and the Exodus. *Mishpatim*, or Rational Commandments, allude to those commandments that could have been arrived at by man on his own.

The third category, *Chukim*, or Statutes, denotes commands that have no basis in logic — they are clearly Divine edicts.

The word *chukim* is rooted in the word *chakikah*,[3] which means to hew out or engrave. What is the connection between suprarational commandments and engraving?

Engraving requires much more effort than simply writing. Suprarational commandments, commands that not only are not understood but often fly in the face of logic, are so much harder to perform than other *mitzvos* that observing

---

1. *Vayikra* 26:3.
2. Ibid.
3. *Likkutei Torah*, beginning of Torah portion *Bechukosai*.

them is likened to the difficulty of engraving as opposed to writing.

We thus understand that when the word *bechukosai* — rooted as it is in *chakikah* — is used with regard to Torah study, it refers to *"toiling* in the study of Torah."

Since the term used to denote toiling in Torah — *chukah* — is the same at that used for suprarational commandments, we are also given to understand that toiling in Torah involves the transcending of rational thought.

This seems difficult to understand: As explained in the *Zohar*,[4] "If you will follow My statutes" addresses itself specifically to toiling in the study of the Oral Torah, during which one must utilize one's intellect. So it is that with regard to the Oral Torah, an individual may not recite the blessing made over Torah study if he fails to comprehend what he is studying. How, then, is this aspect of Torah study related to the suprarational?

In truth, both the actual toil in studying Torah as well as the results of that toil must go beyond the student's rational understanding:

"Toiling in the study of Torah" must necessarily exceed the degree that the person thinks is required; if a person only strives to the degree indicated by his intellect, it is not considered toil, for intellect dictates that a person toil merely to satisfy his intellectual curiosity. Truly toiling in Torah study will lead a person to understand that even those matters that he comprehends intellectually are, in truth, beyond his intellect. For G-d and His Torah are one,[5] and just as a created being's intellect cannot possibly comprehend its Creator, so too, it is incapable of comprehending His wisdom.

This is in accord with the saying concerning knowledge of G-d, that "The ultimate wisdom is that we do not know

---

4. *Bechukosai* (113a); see also *Likkutei Levi Yitzchak*, ibid.; *Divrei David* on *Vayikra* 26:14.
5. *Rambam Hilchos Yesodei HaTorah* 2:10; *Hilchos Teshuvah*, conclusion of ch. 5.

You."[6] And just as this is so with regard to G-d, so too with regard to His Torah, for Torah is utterly united with Him.

Therefore, if a person says he understands Torah completely, it is a clear sign that he hasn't toiled in it; were he to have truly toiled he would have recognized that Torah far transcends his limited intellect. The proper approach to Torah must be *bechukosai* — "toiling."

Based on *Likkutei Sichos* Vol. XVII, pp. 313-320.

---

6. See *Bechinos Olam* 7:2; *Ikarim* 2:30; *Shaloh* 191b.

ספר במדבר

Bamidbar

Bamidbar   במדבר

"Everyone Counts"

In the Torah portion of *Bamidbar* we learn that G-d commanded Moshe to take a census of the entire community by
tribes.[1] G-d also told Moshe that while conducting this census "alongside him there shall be one man for each tribe."[2]

Rashi explains that Moshe was instructed "that when
you count them, there shall be with you the princes of each
individual tribe." Thus, each tribal leader assisted Moshe not
only in counting his own tribe, but in tallying the other
tribes as well.

The general objective of this census — counting the Jews
in order to know their overall number — required that it be
done by someone connected to all Jews equally; Moshe fit
that bill perfectly. Accordingly, it would have sufficed for
Moshe to conduct this count single-handedly, as he had
previous counts.

The singular aspect of this count — that of first counting
each tribe separately — required that the leader of every
tribe take part in the count of his own tribe. But why was it
necessary for the tribal leaders to assist in the count of the
other tribes as well?

At the very beginning of the Torah portion, *Rashi* explains that because the Jewish people were very dear to G-d,
He counted them frequently. By doing so, G-d revealed their
qualities. As the *Shaloh* explains:[3] counting the Jewish people

---

1. *Bamidbar* 1:1-2.
2. Ibid., verse 4.
3. 347a and onward.

gave them importance; it made them "an object worthy of numeration — that cannot become nullified."[4]

The previous counts, in which all Jews were numbered as one entity — revealed the Jews' general qualities and endearedness that transcends individual differences: the essential quality of the Jewish soul, in regard to which all Jews are exactly alike.

The count in the Torah portion of *Bamidbar* was intended to reveal the Jews' individual merits as well. This is why in the latter count each tribe is tallied separately, for each of the 12 tribes had its own distinctive lifestyle, manner of Divine service, etc.

Yet, even while considering the particular qualities of the individual, every Jew remains a part of a single whole. This indicates[5] that there was an aspect in this count in which all were equal — notwithstanding that they were counted according to their particular qualities and merits.

We are thus presented with an anomaly: Although this count was connected with the particular qualities of individual Jews — with the inevitable result of highlighting those disparate qualities and merits — nonetheless, every Jew was counted as equal to all other Jews.

The reason for this is the following: Counting the Jews in order to reveal the particular merits of each — counting according to tribes — not only served to emphasize individual qualities *in and of themselves*, but these qualities taken as a whole comprise one totality — the Jewish people.

It was thus necessary for the tribal leaders to be involved in the census of the other tribes as well, for it was necessary to remind them that their individual tribe constituted part of the Jewish people as a whole.

Based on *Likkutei Sichos* Vol. XXIII pp. 3-7.

---

4. *Beitzah* 3b, and citations *ad loc; Shulchan Aruch, Yoreh Deah* 110:1; *Shulchan Aruch Admur HaZakein, Orach Chayim* 447:20.
5. See *Likkutei Sichos VII* p. 3ff.

A Most Revealing Count

The majority of the Torah portion *Bamidbar* revolves around the census of the Jewish people on the "first day of the second month [*Iyar*] of the second year of the Exodus,"[1] at which time G-d commanded that the nation be counted.

Rashi[2] notes that G-d's love for the Jewish people causes Him to count them at every opportunity. Thus He counted them a) when they departed Egypt; b) after the sin of the Golden Calf and prior to the erection of the *Mishkan*; c) with the erection of the *Mishkan* He counted them yet again, "for the *Mishkan* was erected on the first of *Nissan* and He counted them on the first of *Iyar*" — exactly one month later.

Surely G-d knew how many Jews there were without a census. Why, then, His repeated requests to count them?

Furthermore, while G-d chose to count the Jewish people three times in a little over a year, we do not find Him commanding a subsequent count for the next 38 years. What reason did He have for counting them at these three specific points?

The census of the Jewish people saw all counted equally; the greatest was counted as no more than one, the least significant was counted as no less than one.

As such, it is understandable that G-d's love for the Jewish people — a love that finds expression in His counting them at every opportunity — is not the result of their particular merits (which differ from one Jew to another) but because of their quintessential Jewishness, in which all Jews are equal.

Since the quintessential aspect of a Jews' Jewishness transcends revelation, G-d commanded that the Jewish people be counted — although He surely knew their exact number — in order to reveal this aspect, for "counting" reveals this essential level.

---

1. *Bamidbar* 1:1.
2. Ibid.

When this quality is invoked within a Jew, he will readily give his very life in order not to be sundered from G-d.
More particularly, the revelation of a Jew's essential Jewishness will generally have one of three effects:

a) It is possible that although this quality is revealed
within a Jew, it will not have an ongoing impact on his intellect, emotions, speech and actions.

Thus, while as a rule even the most sinful Jew will face
martyrdom rather than deny G-d's unity,[3] this same person
may very well transgress in other areas, the reason being
that this quality did not influence his intellect, emotions, etc.

b) Alternately, this essential quality may not permeate
and transform him, but rather overpower and overwhelm
him.[4]

c) Finally, the quintessential aspect of the person's Jewishness may so permeate the individual that all his powers
and faculties are transformed and act in tandem with this
essential quality.

Herein lies the reason for the three counts: At the time of
the Exodus, the Jews' simple faith in G-d was revealed.
However, it did not affect their inner powers — the count
affected them only on the most elementary level.[5]

The *Mishkan* was then to be erected in order for G-d to
reveal Himself and reside "within them"[6] — within each
and every Jew.[7] For this to transpire, yet another count was
necessary, so that their essential quality would be revealed
in a manner that affected their inner powers as well.

Yet this revelation too came about as a result of *G-d's*
desire to dwell within them, and as such did not transform
the Jews themselves. Once the *mishkan* was erected and G-d
resided within them as a result of their *own* service, the third

---

3. See *Tanya* ch. 18ff.
4. See *Siddur Im Dach,* beginning of *Sha'ar Lag B'Omer.*
5. Thus the reason for the Jewish people having to flee Egypt in great haste. See
   Tanya ch. 31.
6. *Shmos* 25:8.
7. See *Likkutei Sichos III,* p. 906 and places cited there.

count permitted the Jews' essential quality to permeate and transform their entire being.

Based on *Likkutei Sichos* Vol. VIII, pp. 1-6.

Shavuos   שבועות

Mattan Torah

The festival of *Shavuos* commemorates *Mattan Torah,*
G-d's giving of the Torah to the world. Since, as the *Gemara*
informs us, "Our forefathers in Egypt never ceased studying
Torah,"[1] the Jewish people evidently possessed Torah before
it was formally given on Sinai. What, then, is novel about
Mattan Torah?

The accomplishment of *Mattan Torah* lies in the fact that
"G-d *gave* us His Torah"[2]: Prior to *Mattan Torah*, Torah was
merely "taken" by man according to his inherently limited
intellectual capacity. When G-d *gave* the Torah, however, He
gave it to us utterly and completely, in accordance with His
infinite capacity.

Moreover, this was not simply a one-time event. Rather,
at the time of *Mattan Torah* G-d wholly "incorporated" Himself within Torah. Thus we find that G-d says with regard to
Torah: "I have written and placed [within Torah] My very
'soul' and Essence"[3]; whenever a person studies Torah, G-d
says: "You are actually clutching Me."[4]

This, then, was the novel aspect of G-d's revealing Himself in Torah: *Mattan Torah* achieved something so novel that
Torah as it existed prior to *Mattan Torah* bore absolutely no
comparison to Torah as given at *Mattan Torah*:

Prior to *Mattan Torah*, Torah study was limited to man's
restricted intellect, etc. Understandably, man's achievement
in Torah was limited to what a finite being is capable of understanding of an infinite G-d's wisdom.

---

1. *Yoma* 28b.
2. Text of Blessing of the Torah.
3. *Shabbos* 105b.
4. *Tanchuma, Emor* 17. See also *Shmos Rabbah* 33:1; *Tanya* ch. 47.

However, with the giving of the Torah, Torah study brings a student not only to comprehension of Torah, but to a unity with the Giver of Torah Himself.

While differences existed between Jews in their degree of comprehension of Torah as it existed prior to *Mattan Torah*, these differences did not apply to Jews as they studied Torah as it existed after *Mattan Torah*; the aspect of "You are actually clutching Me" is the same among all Jews who study Torah, whether it be the greatest scholar or the simplest Jew.

Mattan Torah thus brought about not only an extraordinary degree of unity between the Jewish people and G-d, but also among the Jewish people themselves — they were all equal in "clutching" G-d.

This quality of *Mattan Torah* was so potent that when the nation encamped opposite Mt. Sinai, even before the Torah was given, it did so "as one man with one heart."

For the fact that G-d was about to give the Torah to the Jewish people revealed within them the quintessential aspect of their Jewishness, something that resides in all Jewish hearts equally: a faith in G-d that transcends logic; a power that enabled all Jews — through Torah — to equally grasp G-d's essence.

The loftiness of this degree of *Mattan Torah* notwithstanding, Torah is ultimately to be studied and learned with one's intellect. For the purpose of *Mattan Torah* is not only that G-d's Essence be revealed in Torah, but that the student so thoroughly unites himself with Torah that Torah becomes his very reason for existence.

When one understands something with one's own intellect, then that concept is so thoroughly grasped that it becomes part and parcel of one's spiritual being, to the same degree that food becomes transformed into part of one's physical being.[5]

---

5. See *Tanya* ch. 5.

This is the ultimate intent of *Mattan Torah*: To allow man to grasp G-d Himself — a relationship that wholly transcends intellect — yet be able to assimilate the Torah's lessons and have them permeate the human intellect, so that the individual actually becomes one with Torah.

Based on *Likkutei Sichos Rosh Chodesh Sivan*, 5746.

Naso   נשא

Shabbos — "Before and After"

The Torah portion *Naso* is commonly read on the Shabbos following *Shavuos*. Since the festivals are related to the
Torah portions in whose time they fall,[1] it is understandable
that within *Naso* there is an allusion to the special qualities
of this Shabbos.

What is special about this Shabbos; where is it alluded to
in the portion of *Naso*?

Before G-d gave the Torah at *Mattan Torah*, there was a
"rift" between Heaven and earth: "Those who were on high
could not descend below; those who were below could not
ascend on high."[2] *Mattan Torah* healed this rift; Heaven and
earth could then be united. Thus, the *mitzvos* performed before *Mattan Torah* lacked the quality of the *mitzvos* performed afterwards.[3]

The same holds true for the commandment of Shabbos.
Although the Jews observed Shabbos even before *Mattan
Torah*,[4] their observance then could not compare to their ob-
servance once the Torah was given.

Since all past events are "reawakened" at the time of
year during which they first occurred,[5] we understand that
the Shabbos following *Shavuos* is an echo of the *first* Shabbos
after *Shavuos*, to wit: it is the first complete Shabbos observed as a result of *Mattan Torah*.

Before *Mattan Torah*, "on high" had yet to descend
"below," and the performance of *mitzvos* was limited by a

---

1. See *Shaloh, Cheilek Torah She'Biksav*, beginning of the Torah portion *Vayeishev*.
2. *Shmos Rabbah* 12:3; *Tanchuma, Va'eira* 15.
3. See *Likkutei Sichos I* p. 41; *III* p. 757ff; *V* p. 316ff.
4. *Sanhedrin* 56b.
5. See *Ramaz* in *Tikkun Shovavim*, quoted and explained in *Lev David* of the
   Chida, ch. 29.

person's individual capacity. As a result, it was impossible to infuse the objects with which one performed *mitzvos* with the infinity of holiness.

When G-d gave the Torah to the world, the *mitzvos* emanated from His essence. "On High descended below" and man became able to perform *mitzvos* with *G-d-given* power. Consequently, the physical objects used in the performance of *mitzvos* themselves become G-dly — "below ascends on High."

This is particularly germane to Shabbos: The intrinsic quality of Shabbos — even prior to *Mattan Torah* — is loftier than creation, for Shabbos commemorates the *cessation* of creative labor. This is why a Jew is granted on Shabbos "a simple love for G-d that transcends intellect." This love is much loftier than the rational weekday love that grows from *toil* and *labor*.[6]

This higher degree of love transforms a person and his animal soul, so that he ceases to desire those things he desires during the rest of the week.

Thus, Shabbos is intrinsically lofty in two aspects: Shabbos is itself "on high," i.e., Shabbos is illumined by a degree of holiness that cannot be attained through man's service alone; and with regard to "below," on Shabbos even the *animal* soul is transformed.

These inherent qualities notwithstanding — qualities remarkably similar to the achievement of Mattan Torah — there is still no comparison between the sanctity of Shabbos before *Mattan Torah* and the sanctity it achieves afterwards.

This unique quality, mirrored every year in the Shabbos following *Shavuos*, is alluded to in the portion of *Naso*, which states at the outset: "Count Gershon's descendants....[7]"

The name *Gershon* is etymologically related[8] both to the bringing out of produce[9] — in spiritual terms, revealing

---

6. *Torah Or* 87b.
7. *Bamidbar* 4:22.
8. *Likkutei Torah, Naso* 24b, c.
9. "*U'mimeged geresh yerachim*".

one's latent love for G-d — and to the "chasing away" of evil.[10] These two actions bear a remarkable similarity to what transpires on Shabbos.

Based on *Likkutei Sichos* Vol. VIII pp. 49-60.

---

10. *"Vayigarsheihu vayeilech."*

G-d Makes Himself Heard

The Torah portion *Naso* concludes by relating that when Moshe would enter the *Mishkan*, he would hear G-d's voice emanating from between the two *Keruvim*. The portion concludes by stating once again: "Thus would G-d speak to him."[1]

Rashi[2] explains that the verse reiterates "Thus would G-d speak to *him*," to inform us that although Aharon may have been in the *Mishkan* at the time, only Moshe would hear G-d's voice.

This was no ordinary occurrence, for as *Rashi* goes on to say, G-d's voice was as powerful then as it was when it spoke at Sinai. Rather, it was a miracle that in the *Mishkan* only Moshe would hear it.

This gives rise to the following question: Since G-d's voice was so powerful, why did Moshe have to enter the *Mishkan* at all? And if G-d desired that only Moshe hear Him, He could have done so, just as within the *Mishkan* only Moshe heard Him speak.

Rashi concludes by stating that "when the voice reached the entrance of the *Mishkan* it would cease, and would not emanate outside the *Mishkan*." Thus, in order for Moshe to hear G-d speaking, it was necessary that he be within the *Mishkan*.

---

1. *Bamidbar* 7:89.
2. Ibid.

But this, too, must be understood: Since by right the voice should have been heard outside the *Mishkan*, why did it stop at the entrance, thus compelling Moshe to enter in order to hear it?

This will be understood in light of *Rashi*'s explanation that G-d's voice was "the same voice that spoke to him at Sinai."

We find that "the voice that spoke to him at Sinai" also was subject to cessation, albeit not a cessation in space (as was the case with the voice in the *Mishkan*), but a cessation in *time*. For after *Mattan Torah*, "when the ram's horn sounded a long blast,"[3] the "Divine Presence departed and the voice ceased."[4]

The reason for the cessation of the voice is clear: Were it to have continued following *Mattan Torah* it would have precluded Divine service predicated on man's freedom of choice; when G-d's mighty voice in its full glory proclaims "I am G-d your L-rd,"[5] there is no room for choosing anything other than G-d's will.

Just as this is so regarding the cessation of the voice in time, it is true with regard to G-d's voice ceasing in space — at the entrance of the *Mishkan*.

Since this voice was "the [very same] voice that spoke to him at Sinai" — with the same degree of revelation and sanctity — it is understandable that were it to have been drawn down on an ongoing basis outside the *Mishkan*, then the whole world would have automatically been transformed into a *Mishkan*, and once again the ability to freely choose to serve G-d would have been thwarted.

Moreover, "G-d earnestly desired to have a dwelling place [specifically] in the *nethermost* level"[6] — in the crass physical world. It was in such a world that G-d desired that

---

3. *Shmos* 19:13.
4. *Rashi* ibid.
5. Ibid. 20:2.
6. *Tanchuma, Naso* 16.

His voice be drawn down and revealed as *man's* service transformed this world into a dwelling for Him.

Were this world to be constantly inundated by G-d's voice, then it would neither be a lowly world, nor would man be needed to accomplish its transformation, since it would be G-dly in its own right.

There is a lesson here: We should not be satisfied with enclosing ourselves in our own private *Mishkan* of Torah study, where G-d's voice is constantly heard, and neglecting the rest of the world. Rather, man's main service is to let the world outside the *Mishkan* know that which was revealed, thereby transforming the planet into a dwelling place for G-d.

Based on *Likkutei Sichos* Vol. XIII, pp. 20-23.

Behaalos'cha   בהעלתך

Two Passovers — Two Methods of Service

The Torah relates in *Beha'alosecha* that when the Jews brought the Paschal offering in the desert, some individuals could not participate because they were ritually impure. In response to their cry, "Why should we lose the privilege of bringing the offering," G-d said that those who were unable to bring the offering at the appointed time could do so one month later.[1] This "makeup" offering is known as *Pesach Sheni*, in contrast to the regular *Pesach Rishon*.

Among the differences between *Pesach Rishon* and *Pesach Sheni*: a) during *Pesach Rishon*, leavened products are prohibited in the person's domain, on *Pesach Sheni*, however, the person may have such products in his house;[2] b) *Pesach Rishon* extends for the seven days of Passover, while *Pesach Sheni* lasts only one day.[3]

Since *Pesach Sheni* serves as a "makeup" for *Pesach Rishon*, one might think it would be similar in all aspects; why do they differ so radically?

The *Pesach Rishon* offering is in accord with the orderly pattern of Torah — it is brought in its time. *Pesach Sheni* involves an offering that is not. This is akin to the difference between the service of a wholly righteous individual, a *tzaddik*, and a penitent. A *tzaddik* serves G-d in an orderly manner — in harmony with the order of Torah. A penitent, however, having by definition transgressed the orderly pattern of Torah, is afforded the opportunity to make up for that which he is lacking.

---

1. *Bamidbar* 9:6-11.
2. *Mishnah, Pesachim* 95a.
3. *Tosefta, Pesachim* 8:3.

The service of a penitent, however, contains a quality that a *tzaddik's* service lacks. The *tzaddik's* service deals solely with permissible matters; his experience with evil is limited to subduing or negating it. Consequently, the *tzaddik* is unable to transform evil into holiness. A penitent, however, returns to G-d out of love, and is able to transform evil — his past iniquities — into merits.[4]

This explains the differences between *Pesach Rishon* and *Pesach Sheni*: *Pesach Rishon* — the service of the *tzaddik* — has nothing to do with evil. Leavened products — symbolic of evil — are thus not to be found. This is also why *Pesach Rishon* lasts seven days: the orderly and progressive spiritual service of the *tzaddik* consists of "seven days" — a complete cycle.

Pesach Sheni, however — the service of the penitent — can transform evil into holiness; leavened products are thus permitted to exist, for they can be transformed into good. Furthermore, the holiday lasts but one day, for the service of the penitent transcends limitation and division, and this is symbolized by the indivisible "*one* day" — a level that transcends division and orderly progression.

In practical terms, *Pesach Sheni* teaches us:

a) that it is never too late[5] — even an individual whose spiritual impurity resulted from a conscious desire to exist in that state can still rectify his error;

b) that "one day" suffices, or as the *Zohar* puts it:[6] repentance can be accomplished in an instant.

Based on *Likkutei Sichos* Vol. XVIII pp. 118-122.

---

4. *Yoma* 86b.
5. See *HaYom Yom*, 14th of *Iyar; Likkutei Sichos XVIII* p. 126ff.
6. *Zohar I* 129a.

The Most Humble of Men

One of the greatest attributes possessed by Moshe was his humility, as the Torah attests in the portion *Beha'alosecha*: "Moshe was extremely humble, more so than any other person on the face of the earth."[1]

Of all the Jewish people, G-d selected Moshe to lead the Jews out of Egypt. Then G-d chose him, and him alone, to receive the Torah, and learned with him for 40 days and nights.[2]

Moreover, in the portion *Beha'alosecha* the Torah states that Moshe was able to converse with G-d whenever he wished[3]; that he shared his spirit with the 70 elders and lacked not because of it;[4] and that his relationship with the Jewish people was that of a nurse carrying an infant.[5]

How was it possible for an individual who was so great to be so utterly humble. Was Moshe not aware of his stature? Especially so, since knowing one's true station is a prerequisite to proper service of G-d. For a person must serve G-d according to his rank, and in order to do so one must be aware of both his virtues and his faults.

Moshe was indeed aware of his unique position, and that he far surpassed other men. Nevertheless, this did not prevent him from being the most humble of men. For Moshe thought to himself that were another individual to have been blessed with his talents, that person would have developed them to an even greater degree than he had. This was the cause of Moshe's humility.[6]

However, this still remains to be understood: The thing which set Moshe apart from all other people was his prophetic ability, in that G-d revealed Himself to him "face to face, in a vision not containing allegory, so that he saw a

---

1. *Bamidbar* 12:3.
2. *Nedarim* 38a; *Shmos Rabbah* 41:6; commentary of *Rashi, Shmos* 31:18.
3. *Rashi* 9:7, quoting the *Sifrei*.
4. Ibid. 11:17, quoting the *Sifrei*.
5. *Bamidbar* 11:12.
6. See *Sefer HaMa'amarim 5710* p. 236. See also *Zachor 5665*, ch. 8.

true picture of G-d."[7] So great was his spirit of prophecy that the Torah testifies: "There has never again arisen in Israel a prophet like Moshe."[8]

Prophecy is not something that an individual attains by dint of his own spiritual service, rather it is a *revealed* quality granted from above. Thus, it is impossible to say that concerning the attribute of prophecy Moshe thought that another individual would have developed this trait to a greater degree, for prophecy does not depend on the individual.

How was it, then, that Moshe was the most humble of men, when his main attribute — his degree of prophetic vision — could be replicated by nobody else?

We find in the *Gemara*[9] a discussion as to whether humility is a greater or lesser trait than being a G-d-fearing individual. Our Sages explain[10] that there are two levels of humility, one of them superior and the other inferior to the trait of being a G-d-fearing individual:

The inferior level of humility is based upon reason, e.g., humility based upon the thought that had another person been blessed with the same talents, that individual would have developed them to an even greater degree. The superior level of humility is humility that is an integral part of the person's essence. The proof that this latter degree of humility — humility that transcends logic — indeed exists, can be ascertained from the fact that the trait is ascribed to G-d Himself, as our Sages say:[11] "In the very same place that you find G-d's greatness you also find His humility."

Surely, with regard to G-d the humility based upon the assumption that someone else would have done better, etc., simply cannot exist. We must therefore say that there is a degree of humility that surpasses logic.

---

7. *Bamidbar* 12:8.
8. *Devarim* 34:10.
9. *Avodah Zarah* 20:b.
10. *Likkutei Torah, Matos* 81d and onward; *Or HaTorah, Vayeishev* 259b.
11. *Megillah* 31a.

Moshe possessed both degrees of humility: Regarding those qualities that he attained through his own spiritual service, he felt that had another person been granted his talents, that person would have developed them to an even greater degree.

With regard to his humility notwithstanding the fact that only he was granted such an outstanding degree of prophecy, the trait stemmed from Moshe's innate character as "the most humble man upon the face of the earth."

Based on Likkutei Sichos Vol. XIII, pp. 30-37.

Shlach   שלח

A Natural Mistake — The Error of the Spies

The Torah portion of *Shlach* relates how the men sent to spy out Eretz Yisrael returned and reported that the country was unconquerable. The Jewish people, they said, would be unable to enter the land, since "The inhabitants of the land are mighty."[1]

Furthermore, say our Sages,[2] the spies went so far as to say that even G-d would not be able to wrest the land from its inhabitants. Their words caused great consternation among the Jews, who feared that they would be unable to enter *Eretz Yisrael*.

How was it possible for the spies to mislead the Jewish people and convince them that even G-d could not help them, when the Jews themselves had constantly witnessed the miracles performed on their behalf, e.g., G-d provided their daily food and drink in a miraculous manner — manna from heaven and water from Miriam's well.

The Jewish people also experienced supernatural victories over their enemies: when they were pursued by the Egyptians, G-d Himself split the sea for them. They should have understood that just as G-d had performed miracles for them in their war with Egypt, He would also perform miracles for them in their battle for Canaan.

Chassidus explains[3] that the spies did not *want* to enter Eretz Yisrael, preferring to remain in the desert, because they did not want to descend into the realm of the material and occupy themselves with the mundane.

---

1. *Bamidbar* 13:28.
2. *Sotah* 35a.
3. *Likkutei Torah*, beginning of Torah portion of *Shlach*.

While the Jews were in the desert they were cut off from the material world; even their food and drink transcended materiality, and their clothing grew along with them.[4]

However, upon entry into Eretz Yisrael the manna ceased and they were forced to eat physical bread, which involved physical labor such as plowing, sowing, etc. At that time they also ceased receiving their water from Miriam's well. The spies preferred the wholly spiritual lifestyle of the desert.

Despite their lofty idealism, the spies' aspirations were misplaced: The intent of the Jew's creation is to make a dwelling place for G-d within the *nethermost* level by transforming the physical into a vessel for G-dliness. This they could only do in *Eretz Yisrael*, for it was only there that the primary manner of spiritual service consisted of performing *physical mitzvos*.

The change in lifestyle which the Jews would have to undergo in order to enter *Eretz Yisrael* explains the logic underlying the spies' claim that even G-d could not conquer the land for them: They reasoned that the miracles G-d had performed on behalf of the Jewish people while they lived in a supranatural state would not continue should they embark on a lifestyle which deals with the material world in a *natural* manner.

Seemingly, the logic of the spies was impeccable; where did they err?

The spies mistakenly thought that only two kinds of conduct are possible — the natural and the supernatural — and that these are mutually exclusive. In truth, G-d is not bound to these two paths, for He equally transcends both the natural and the supernatural; furthermore, He is quite capable of combining the two.

Therefore, since G-d desired that the Jews provide Him a dwelling place by performing physical *mitzvos* in Eretz Yisrael, the Jews had nothing to fear from the inhabitants; al-

---

4. *Yalkut Shimoni, Devarim* 8:4.

though the world retains its natural characteristics, G-d would guarantee the Jewish people — as they exist in a natural state — success that is truly supernatural.

Based on *Likkutei Sichos* Volume IV, pp. 1041-1044.

Increasing the Might of the Divine Name Adnay

The Torah portion *Shlach* relates[1] that G-d was upset with the Jewish people for believing the report of the spies.[2]

The portion then goes on to relate that Moshe sought to obtain forgiveness for the nation by saying to G-d: "And now G-d, increase the might of Your Divine Name *Adnay*"[3] so that- as the *Midrash* explains[4] — "Your Attribute of Mercy will overwhelm Your Attribute of Justice."

Since Moshe was trying to arouse G-d's Attribute of Mercy, he should have asked G-d to increase the might of the Divine Name *Havayah* (the name that symbolizes Mercy), rather than seeking to increase the power of the name *Adnay* — L-rd — which is related to the Attribute of Justice.

Also, how could the spies and the Jewish people think that G-d could not help them conquer the land, when they had already been the beneficiaries of many miracles?

The spies argued as follows: G-d's supernatural manner of conduct with regard to the Jewish people could only continue while the Jews found themselves in the desert, where their whole manner of existence was beyond the bounds of nature — *manna* from heaven, etc.

They therefore reasoned that the miracles performed on behalf of the Jewish people while they existed in this state could not be expected to continue when the Jews entered

---

1. *Bamidbar* 14:12.
2. *Sota* 35a.
3. Ibid. 14:17.
4. *Bamidbar Rabbah* 16:22.

Eretz Yisrael, where they were to embark on a lifestyle that would deal with the material world in a *natural* manner.

The spies were tragically mistake. Although G-d ordained that the world should exist in a natural manner, He is in no way bound to this manner — He can change the course of nature at will.

Moreover, since Jews are "truly a part of G-d above,"[5] they too are not bound by the limitations of nature, and when necessary can position themselves above and beyond its constraints.

The Divine name *Adnay* — "L-rd of the whole earth" — governs the conduct of nature, as this name and attribute of Kingship is responsible for creating and sustaining the world in a manner whereby the world *appears to be* a wholly separate and independent entity, entirely governed by the laws of nature.[6]

At the same time, the Divine name *Adnay*, "L-rd of the whole earth," indicates that G-d is master of the planet, and as such is able to change nature's rules whenever He so desires.

Thus, when the spies claimed that G-d was limited by the constraints of nature, they were in effect casting aspersions on the Divine name *Adnay*, which refers to G-d's mastery over creation.

Moshe therefore beseeched G-d to increase the might of the Divine Name *Adnay* — that the true power of *Adnay* be revealed — to show that G-d has full and complete control over nature.

The spies' lack of understanding of *Adnay* — G-d's mastery over creation — stemmed in part from their inability to recognize the qualities of the Jewish people — that even though Jews find themselves within the world, they are not shackled by its laws.

The spies mistakenly thought that the Jews' relationship with G-d was limited to their otherworldly actions — pray-

---

5. *Tanya*, beginning of ch. 2.
6. See *Tanya II*, ch. 7.

ing, studying Torah and performing *mitzvos*; while occupied in normal, natural affairs — they thought — there would be no difference between Jew and non-Jew.

Since they failed to realize that the Jewish people exist supernaturally even while functioning in the natural world, they also failed to perceive how a G-dliness that transcends nature exists within nature. By "increasing" — i.e., revealing — the might of the Divine Name *Adnay*, their mistake was rectified.

Based on *Likkutei Sichos* Vol. XVIII, pp. 171-174.

Korach קרח

"It's the Thought that Also Counts"

The Torah portion of *Korach* relates how Korach and a band of 250 men rebelled against Moshe and Aharon. This revolt took place after the incident of the *Meraglim*[1] sent by Moshe to spy out Canaan, and who returned with a pessimistic report regarding the ability of the people to conquer the land.

The elevation of Aharon to the High Priesthood was what touched off Korach's revolt. But this elevation took place at least a year before the incident of the *Meraglim*. Why did Korach wait so long before revolting?

The *Meraglim* contended[2] that it was important for the Jewish people to be separate from the material world. In that way they would not be hindered in cleaving to G-d through the study of Torah. They therefore desired that the Jews remain in the desert, where they would be freer of worldly distractions. Moshe, however, replied that the physical performance of the *mitzvos* is vital, since it is through such performance that Jews make a dwelling place for G-d in this world.

The difference between Torah study and practical *mitzvos* is the following: Comprehension is a fundamental aspect of Torah, in which there are diverse levels. Some people understand more and some less.

This is not so in the case of the *mitzvos*. In this regard, all Jews are equal; the donning of *tefillin* performed by Moshe was exactly the same as the donning performed by the simplest Jew. Moshe and the simple Jew may differ in intensity

1. *Seder Olam Rabbah*, ch. 8; quoted in *Rashbam* and *Tosafos B. Basra* 119a.
2. See previous essay.

of concentration while performing the *mitzvah*, but they did not differ in the physical act.

This is why Korach's rebellion took place only after the incident with the *Meraglim*: Korach was aware that Moshe and Aharon far outdistanced other Jews in comprehension of Torah, for Moshe received the Torah directly from G-d and then proceeded to teach it to Aharon. Korach's complaint "Why are you setting yourselves above G-d's congregation"[3] related to that in which all Jews are equal — the performance of *mitzvos*.

Thus, it was only after the *Meraglim* had expressed the desire to devote themselves exclusively to spiritual service and were informed that the physical performance of *mitzvos* is most important that Korach felt justified in his complaint. For with regard to the physical performance of *mitzvos*, all Jews are indeed equal.

Where did Korach err?

G-d desires not only the physical performance of *mitzvos*, but also the proper spiritual intent. A dwelling place for G-d must provide a home for G-d's *essence*, and His essence must be in a *revealed* state; it must be a *luminous* dwelling. Just as a physical structure must be illuminated in order to be habitable, so too, G-d's dwelling must be made habitable by providing it with illumination.

In order for G-d's dwelling to be illuminated, it is necessary that the *mitzvos* themselves be performed with the proper intent in order to illuminate the person himself and the surrounding world.

Thus, while Moshe's and Aharon's actual performance of *mitzvos* in no way differed from that of the simplest Jew, the intent with which the *mitzvos* were performed varied greatly.

G-d considers the intent as well as the deed.

Based on *Likkutei Sichos* Vol. IV, pp. 1048-1054.

---

3. *Bamidbar* 16:3.

A Lesson in Priesthood

In the Torah portion *Korach* we read how Korach led a band of 250 men in a rebellion against Moshe and Aharon. Underlying their revolt against Aharon's High Priesthood was the charge: "All the people in the community are holy and G-d is in their midst; why are you setting yourselves above G-d's congregation?"[1]

From Moshe's response,[2] "...and you seek priesthood as well," we readily perceive that Korach and his band desired to become priests. This being so, their argument that "All the people...are holy," and nobody can set himself above anybody else seems to contradict their desire to be above others by obtaining priesthood.

The *Kohanim*, the priestly class, differed from the rest of the Jewish people in that the *Kohanim* were wholly dedicated to spiritual matters. This was especially true with regard to the *Kohen Gadol*, the High Priest, who was commanded "not to leave the Sanctuary."[3]

Their apartness from the general populace notwithstanding, the *Kohanim* in general, and the *Kohen Gadol* in particular, imparted their level of sanctity to *all* the Jews. Thus we find that Aharon's service of lighting the Menorah in the Sanctuary imparted sanctity to all Jews, and enabled them to reach Aharon's level of service and love of G-d.[4]

Korach, however, argued that just as *Kohanim* were removed from worldly matters — a quality lacking in the rest of the Jewish people — the rest of the people possessed a quality that the *Kohanim* lacked: the ability to occupy themselves with worldly matters and transform physical objects into vessels for G-dliness.

Moreover, since G-d's main intent is for this nethermost world to be transformed into a dwelling place for Him by elevating it to holiness, Korach maintained that it was spe-

---

1. *Bamidbar* 16:3.
2. Ibid. verse 10.
3. *Vayikra* 21:12.
4. See *Likkutei Torah*, beginning of portion *Beha'alosecha*.

cifically the populace as a whole who were accomplishing this task — not the *Kohanim*, who were separate and aloof from mundane matters.

Since the Jewish people as a whole possessed qualities that *Kohanim* lacked, Korach therefore rebelled against the thought that *Kohanim* in general and Aharon in particular could set themselves apart from the rest of the people because of their ability to impart holiness to them.

Korach and his band's complaint that "All the people...are holy," however, did not contradict their own desire for priesthood, for they desired a manner of priesthood totally removed from the rest of the congregation.

This manner of priesthood would not cause them to feel superior to the rest of the Jewish people, a superiority that resulted from their imparting holiness to them, for in their scheme of things they would not impart holiness to other Jews — they would remain totally separate and apart.

But Korach and his band were badly mistaken: It is true that there are different categories of service — Jews who are solely occupied with spiritual matters, and other Jews whose task it is to purify and elevate the physical world through the service of "All your actions should be for the sake of heaven,"[5] and "In all your ways you shall know Him."[6]

Nevertheless, it is necessary for the *Kohanim* to bestow their sanctity upon the Jewish people so that they too may aspire to the level of "priesthood," i.e., that during certain portions of the day, even the "regular" Jew will occupy himself with Torah study and divine service, to the exclusion of all else.

Our Sages imply this when they say,[7] "Minimize your business activities and occupy yourself with Torah." A business person should not only "set aside certain portions of the day and night for Torah study,"[8] but should also "steal

---

5. *Avos* 2:12.
6. *Mishlei* 3:6.
7. *Avos* 4:10.
8. *Hilchos Talmud Torah* of the *Alter Rebbe*, 3:4.

away" time from his business affairs — *minimize* his business activities — and dedicate that time to "priesthood," to the study of Torah and divine service.

Based on *Likkutei Sichos* Vol. VIII, pp. 116-118.

Chukas-Balak   חקת-בלק

Defying Rationality

The Torah portion of *Chukas* takes its name from the word *chukas*, supra-rational Divine decree, that appears at the outset of this portion in reference to the laws of the Red Heifer.

The word *chukas* itself is etymologically related to *chakikah*, to engrave and hew out.[1] What is the connection between supra-rational Divine decrees and engraving?

Mitzvos are divided into three categories: *Eidos*, Testimonies; *Mishpatim*, Laws; and *Chukim*, Decrees. *Eidos* are commandments that serve as a testimony and remembrance of important events. *Mishpatim* are laws dictated by human intellect as well as by Divine intellect. *Chukim* are decrees that have no rational explanation.

A Jew instinctively desires to perform G-d's will.[2] This desire emanates from the essence of the Jewish soul, which transcends intellect. This instinct most often finds expression in the performance of *Chukim*.

When a person performs *Eidos* and *Mishpatim*, the soul's essential desire is not fully revealed, since the intellectual aspect of these *mitzvos* clouds the soul's purely supra-rational desire to fulfill G-d's will. *Chukim*, however, do not have the "excess baggage" of logic. Therefore, performance of the *Chukim* reveals the soul's essence.

The connection between *Chukim* and engraving lies in the fact that the superiority of *Chukim* over *Eidos* and *Mishpatim* is similar to the superiority of engraving over writing:

Writing is accomplished by joining ink to paper. Since the ink and the letters formed by it remain a separate entity

---

1. *Likkutei Torah* beginning of portions of *Chukas* and *Bechukosai*.
2. See *Rambam* conclusion of ch. 2 of *Hilchos Geirushin*.

from the paper upon which they are written, they therefore conceal that part of the paper upon which they appear. However, engraved letters are composed of the very substance upon which they are engraved, and therefore do not conceal it.

Since intellect tends to conceal the soul's essence, the performance of *Eidos* and *Mishpatim* is similar to writing, in that the intellect conceals the soul's essential desire to fulfill G-d's will just as written letters conceal the paper upon which they are written.

Chukim, however, are performed in a wholly supra-rational manner; there is nothing about them that would tend to obscure G-d's will and desire. They are therefore likened to engraved letters.

Chassidus explains[3] that there are actually two forms of engraving: letters engraved in a normal fashion and letters formed by hewing the material clear through. In the former, the letters in some small way do impede the brilliance of the stone in which they are engraved, and in this they are somewhat similar to written letters; in the latter, this impediment does not exist.

Within *Chukim*, too, we find two manners of *Chukim*: those that have some relationship to intellect — similar to an engraved letter; or *chukah* such as the commandment of the Red Heifer, that has no relationship to intellect — similar to a letter formed by hewing the stone through and through.

We thus understand that the performance of those *Chukim* that have some relationship to intellect lacks the degree of revelation found in the performance of the *chukah* of the Red Heifer. It is only in performing the latter kind of decree, where intellect does not enter the picture, that the soul's essence is revealed in all its glory.

Based on Likkutei Sichos Vol. VIII, pp. 124-129.

---

3.   *Ma'amar Ain Omdin 5667; BaSukkos 5710.*

The Mitzvos As Chukim

The opening section of the Torah portion *Chukas* describes the purification ritual of the *Parah Adumah*, the Red Heifer, one of the foremost suprarational commandments — *Chukim* — of the Torah.

At the beginning of the portion, the verse says:[1] "This [the laws of the of *Parah Adumah*] is the *chukah* of the Torah...." Our Sages ask:[2] Would it not have been more appropriate for the Torah to state "This is the *chukah* 'of the *Parah Adumah*,'" rather than "of the *Torah*"?

They answer[3] that the verse's terminology indicates that the suprarational decree of *Parah Adumah* is indeed "the Torah" — it is a foundation and *chukah* for the entire Torah, in that all *mitzvos* are to be viewed as *Chukim*.

This is so because all *mitzvos* are in essence G-d's Will, and as such transcend human logic; even *mitzvos* that are logical are manifestations of Divine Will that have been drawn down and clothed in reason.

This is why *all* commandments, including the eminently logical, are to be performed not out of any rational imperative but simply because G-d has decreed them. This is reflected in the text of the blessing made for all *mitzvos*, "...and He has *commanded* us."

Thus, by stating "This is the *chukah* of the Torah...," the verse is informing us that although *mitzvos* are generally divided into rational and suprarational commandments, the essential component of *all mitzvos* is suprarational in nature.

The above enables us to understand the advice of the *Mishnah* in *Avos*:[4] "Be as careful in [the performance of] a minor *mitzvah* as of a major one...."

A person may well ask: How is it possible to perform "a minor Rabbinic regulation," as scrupulously as the most major of commandments? Especially so, when the Torah it-

---

1. *Bamidbar* 19:2.
2. *Likkutei Torah*, beginning of *Chukas*.
3. See *Likkutei Torah* ibid.; commentary of *Or HaChayim* on this verse.
4. 2:1.

self — the "Torah of *Truth*" — classifies one commandment as major and the other as minor.

According to the above, however, the answer is clear: With regard to the logical aspect of *mitzvos*, there do indeed exist differences in commandments — rational and suprarational, major and minor, etc. However, with regard to the *essence* of the *mitzvos*, they are all expressions of the Divine Will; no differences exist. They are all suprarational, all major.

Just as this is so with regard to the *mitzvos* themselves, so too regarding the effect they have on the person who performs them.[5] Fulfilling any of these expressions of Divine Will — no matter how seemingly minor — utterly unites the individual with G-d; going against any expression of Divine will — no matter how seemingly minor the infraction — has a major detrimental effect on the person's attachment to Him.

What enables the Jew to feel that the observance of even a seemingly minor commandment has an effect on his overall connection with G-d?

It derives from the essence of the Jew's soul, an essence that itself wholly transcends logic.[6] This finds expression in the famous saying:[7] "A Jew neither desires nor is able to be separated from G-dliness."[8]

Understandably, it is almost impossible to expect that the unity felt by the essence of a person's soul be consciously perceived throughout the year. Nevertheless, when this feeling is roused during special times of the year, it leaves an impression on the person's ongoing level of rational spiritual service, so that the person is able to be aware of the positive or negative import of his every action.

There is a lesson here with regard to one's efforts in helping a fellow-Jew: It is not enough to merely help one's

---

5. See *Tanya* Ch. 24; *Kuntres U'Mayon* 3:3ff.
6. See *Likkutei Sichos IV*, p. 1056ff; Volume VIII, p. 129ff.
7. *HaYom Yom* p. 73.
8. See *Tanya* Ch. 18 and onward.

fellow perform the "major" *mitzvos;* one must realize that *all mitzvos* are major, and the performance of even a seemingly "minor" one can carry a person to the greatest heights.

Based on *Likkutei Sichos* Vol. XIII, pp. 67-70.

Pinchas   פינחס

Jewish Leadership — Torah and Royalty

The Torah portion of *Pinchas*[1] recounts how Moshe asked G-d to "appoint a man over the community" to be its next leader, so that the Jewish people will not become "like sheep that have no shepherd." G-d replied to Moshe: "Take Yehoshua... and lay your hands upon him."

In explaining how a Jewish king is appointed, the Rambam states:[2] "The first king of a dynasty cannot be appointed save by the court of 70 [-one] elders and a prophet, as was the case with *Yehoshua*, who was appointed by Moshe and his court [of 70 elders]." The Rambam is thus of the opinion that Yehoshua was invested as a king.

Accordingly, the following must be understood:[3] The Rambam rules[4] "When a king is appointed, he is to be anointed with anointing oil." Why then did Moshe merely lay his hands on Yehoshua and not anoint him?

The *Midrash*[5] notes that Moshe had anticipated that his children would inherit his mantle. G-d, however, told him: "'He who plants the date palm [merits that he] eats its fruits.'[6] Your children.... did not occupy themselves in Torah. Yehoshua.... since he served you with all his might, is worthy of serving the Jewish people."

How was it possible for Moshe to assume that his sons would inherit the mantle of leadership when he knew they were guilty of "not occupying themselves in Torah"?

---

1. *Bamidbar* 27:15-23.
2. *Hilchos Melachim* 1:3.
3. This question is asked by the *Minchas Chinuch* in his glosses to *Rambam* ibid.
4. *Hilchos Melachim* ibid. 5-7.
5. *Bamidbar Rabbah* 21:14; *Tanchuma Pinchas* 11.
6. *Mishlei* 27:18.

Our Sages explain[7] that Moshe hoped to be succeeded by *two* leaders, one to serve as king and military commander, and the other to lead in Torah. It was in the former position that he hoped to be succeeded by his children. G-d, however, replied: "Only one will lead them... Yehoshua will be their king... and [be their] preeminent Torah scholar, for 'Two kings cannot make use of the same crown.' "[8]

The reason Moshe's request for two leaders was rejected must be understood. While it is true that "Two kings cannot make use of the *same* crown," Moshe desired that his position be divided into two *distinct* "crowns" — the crown of royalty and the crown of Torah scholarship. Why could they not be separated, with the crown of royalty being inherited by Moshe's children?

The true function of a Jewish king is described by the Rambam.[9] Not only must the king provide the Jewish people with their material needs,[10] but his goal must be to "uplift the true religion," i.e., to see to it that the laws of the Torah are carried out.

Thus, in the Jewish context, regency is an extension of the Jewish high court, whose purpose is to be "the pillars of Torah law for all the Jewish people."[11] The king must ensure that the Torah laws issued by the high court are obeyed by the populace.[12]

This is why in the Jewish scheme of things, kingship and Torah leadership cannot be viewed as two distinct entities. Rather, they are one continuum; splitting royalty and Torah scholarship results in "two kings utilizing the *very same* crown."

The reason Yehoshua's appointment to leadership came about through Moshe's laying on of hands and not through anointment will be understood accordingly:

---

7. *Megaleh Amukos, Ofen Alef.* Quoted in *Yalkut Reuvaini, Bamidbar* 27:15.
8. *Chulin* 60b.
9. Conclusion of ch. 4 of *Hilchos Melachim.*
10. See *Berachos* 3b.
11. *Rambam,* beg. of *Hilchos Mamrim.*
12. See *Likkutei Sichos XIX* p. 166ff.

The regal aspect of Yehoshua's leadership was a direct result of, and wholly secondary to, his Torah leadership. It therefore followed that the mantle of Torah leadership, a mantle transmitted through *semichah*[13] — the laying on of hands — took precedence; anointment was entirely unnecessary.

Based on *Likkutei Sichos* Vol. XXIII, pp. 198-205.

13. See *Sanhedrin* 14a; *Rambam Hilchos Sanhedrin* beg. of ch. 4.

A Commensurate Reward

In commenting on the verse[1] "Pinchas the son of Elazar the son of Aharon beheld this... and he took a spear in his hand," *Rashi* notes: "He saw what was transpiring and reminded himself of the law that zealous individuals may attack one who is intimate with a heathen woman."

The Torah goes on to say that as a reward for his zealousness, G-d granted Pinchas "eternal priesthood, to him and his descendants after him."[2]

How was it possible for Pinchas to receive the priesthood as a reward for his actions? While Pinchas no doubt deserved a great reward, the priesthood is seemingly not something that can be given as a reward, rather it is a natural state of being.

Up until then, Pinchas was not a priest, for "The priesthood was only given to Aharon and his sons who were anointed with him, and their progeny who would be born *subsequent* to their anointment."[3] Pinchas, however, was born earlier and thus was not included in the priesthood. Since Pinchas was excluded from the priesthood, how did he suddenly become a priest?

1. *Bamidbar* 25:7.
2. Ibid. verse 13.
3. *Zevachim* 101b.

The sin of illicit relationships is harsher than other sins in that it occupies the individual entirely and involves the person's essence. As harsh as this sin is, the sin of intimacy with a heathen woman is even harsher. The reason for this is because other illicit relationships do not cross the boundaries that G-d established between the Jewish people and other nations, while intimacy with a heathen woman does, inasmuch as the child born as a result of such a relationship is not Jewish. Thus, a person who is involved in this type of relationship takes his ability to procreate — a power that stems from his soul's essence — and utilizes it to father a non-Jewish child!

We must, however, understand the following: Since the division between Jew and non-Jew is a boundary that was placed within creation, how is it possible for a Jew to — Heaven forfend — overstep this boundary by being intimate with a heathen women and fathering a non-Jewish child?

A Jew's ability to choose freely results from "Man's being similar to Us" — he is likened, as it were, to G-d. Just as G-d can do whatever He pleases, so too can the Jew choose to do as he wills.[4]

Since G-d is not at all limited by laws of nature (so much so that the He is not limited to the separation between Jew and non-Jew, for it was He that chose to make that separation in the first place), so too can a Jew utilize his freedom of choice to choose that which is the opposite of holiness — fathering a non-Jewish child.

This is also why Pinchas was rewarded for his actions with "eternal priesthood," even though priesthood is a natural state of being. Since the sin that elicited Pinchas' zealous response was one that consisted of breaching the boundaries between Jews and non-Jews, therefore he was rewarded — measure for measure — with a priesthood that could come about only by a Divine elimination of the natural barriers Pinchas faced in obtaining the priesthood.

Based on *Likkutei Sichos* Vol. VIII, pp. 150-156.

---

4. *Likkutei Torah, Emor* 38b.

Division By Lot

In the Torah portion *Pinchas*,[1] G-d tells Moshe that *Eretz Yisrael* is to be apportioned to the tribes by lot. Division by lot was deemed to be so important that this method was chosen though it resulted in disproportionate allotments of land.[2]

What is so special about division by lot?

There are three distinct aspects regarding the Jews' possession of Torah:[3]

a) Torah is considered the *inheritance* of the Jewish people, as the verse states:[4] "The Torah commanded to us by Moshe is the heritage of the congregation of Jacob"; b) Torah is the *acquisition* of the Jewish people, as our Sages say:[5] "G-d said, 'I have sold you the Torah'"; c) the Torah was granted to us as a *gift* — "G-d gave the Jewish people three fine gifts... Torah, *Eretz Yisrael*, and the World to Come."[6]

That the Torah can be at the same time an inheritance, a purchase and a gift can be understood if one considers the differences between these three things.

Inheritance has nothing to do with the qualities or standing of the person that inherits;[7] young and old, rich and poor, great and small inherit equally.

When a person purchases something, however, he must pay for the object.

In both instances the receiver must have some tangible connection to the object received: an inheritor must be related to the legator, while a purchaser must pay for the item that is sold to him.

---

1. *Bamidbar* 26:52-56.
2. See *Rashi* ibid., verse 54.
3. Cf. *Hemshech V'Kochah 5637* chs. 66,68; *Ma'amar, Torah Tzivah, 5654; 5702.*
4. *Devarim* 33:4.
5. *Shmos Rabbah* 33:1. See also *Berachos* 5a.
6. *Berachos* ibid. See also *Bereishis Rabbah* 6:5.
7. See *Niddah* 43b.

This is not so with regard to a gift. No relationship is necessary between a giver and a receiver; gifts can be simply an expression of the giver's kindness.

The same is true with regard to these three things as they relate to the Jews' possession of Torah:

Each and every Jew is part of the "congregation of Jacob," and as such Torah is his or her rightful heritage. Thus we find that every Jew "possesses" a letter in the Torah that is uniquely his.[8] This also explains why the obligation to study Torah applies equally to all Jews, for Torah is every Jew's heritage, and as such can and should be studied or recited by all Jews, whatever their station in life.[9]

The "acquisition" of Torah refers to that part of Torah which is acquired through the effort of cogitation. As such, it is similar to an object acquired in exchange for something else of value. Concerning this level of Torah it is written:[10] "Prepare yourself for the study of Torah, for it does not come to you through inheritance."

With regard to this level of Torah, differences between Jews indeed exist, for each person's intellectual capacity differs from that of his neighbor,[11] so that the degree of Torah understanding varies from individual to individual.

Calling the Torah a "gift" refers to those aspects of it that are beyond any man's grasp, and therefore must be granted as a gift from G-d.

Thus, this concept of the Torah as gift differs from both the description of it as a heritage received as a result of a Jew's — finite — right of inheritance, and as an object "purchased" by man's — finite — comprehension.

This third level of Torah is also referred to as "lot"; just as a gift depends wholly on the giver, so too the outcome of

---

8. See *Im Ruach HaMoshel 5695*.
9. See *Rambam, Hilchos Talmud Torah* 1:8; *Shulchan Aruch Admur HaZakein, Orach Chayim*, beginning of Ch. 155.
10. *Avos* 2:12.
11. See *Sanhedrin* 38a.

a lot depends strictly on G-d's choice.[12] "Lot" thus alludes to that which transcends man's intellect.

The quality of *Eretz Yisrael* is such that "G-d's eyes are on it at all times"[13] — G-dliness is revealed there to a degree not found in the rest of the world. That such a state exists within this physical world cannot be the result of man's limited service; it is a gift from above.

Eretz Yisrael thus had to be divided by lot, reflecting action at a level that emanates wholly from Above.

Based on Likkutei Sichos Vol. XIII, pp. 114-121.

---

12. See *Teshuvos HaGe'onim* — Jerusalem, 5720 — Sect. 60; Responsa *Chavas Ya'ir*, Sect. 61.

13. *Devarim* 11:12.

Matos-Masei   מטות-מסעי

Console the Father — Console the Child

The Torah portions of *Matos* and *Masei* are combined and read on the same Shabbos in two cases: when that Shabbos precedes the month of *Menachem Av* (and is thus the day during which the month is blessed), or when that Shabbos is itself the first Shabbos of *Menachem Av*.

Our Rabbis comment that all the Torah portions are connected to the time period during which they are read.[1] It follows that the portions of *Matos* and *Masei* are connected with the month of *Menachem Av*.

This connection is even more germane than the link between these portions and the three-week period of quasi-mourning known as *Bein HaMitzarim*, when these two portions are invariably read.[2]

It is the Jewish custom — Jewish custom itself being considered as sacred as Torah[3] — to refer to the month of *Av* (while blessing this new month) by the name *Menachem Av*.

The literal meaning of *"Menachem Av"* is "Consoling the Father." The Jewish people console their Father in Heaven, as it were. And G-d, our Father, is in need of consolation, in light of the statement of our Sages[4] that G-d says: "Woe to the Father who exiled His children."

The connection between *Menachem Av* and the Torah portions of *Matos* and *Masei* will be understood accordingly. A Jew wishes for consolation during this month. But he wants consolation not so much for himself as for his Father.

---

1. *Shaloh, Cheilek Torah SheBiksav*, 297a.
2. See *Shaloh* p. 366ff.
3. See *Yerushalmi Pesachim* 4:1; *Tosafos* titled *Nifsal, Menachos* 20b; *et al.*
4. *Berachos* 3a.

This concept is stressed in the portion of *Matos* as well as in the portion of *Masei*:

The Torah portion of *Matos* relates how G-d commanded Moshe to battle the Midianites, saying: "Exact the retribution of the *people of Israel* from the Midianites...."[5] However, when Moshe relayed this command to the Jewish people he said: "...to exact the retribution of *G-d* from Midian."[6] Comments the *Sifri*:[7] Moshe said to the Jewish people: "You are not avenging flesh and blood; you are avenging *He who spoke and the world came into being*."

This theme is mirrored in the portion of *Masei*, when the verse states:[8] "You shall not defile the land... in which I dwell; for I, G-d, dwell among the Jewish people." Says the *Sifri*:[9] "Jews are loved [by G-d]. Even when they are defiled, the *Shechinah* is in their midst... Jews are loved [by G-d]; wherever they are exiled the *Shechinah* is with them... and when they return, the *Shechinah* returns with them."

Thus, exile affects not only the Jewish people; the *Shechinah*, too, is in exile, as it were. The Jews' redemption is thus a redemption for the *Shechinah* as well. Understandably, the redemption of the *Shechinah* is of greatest import. This is why *Menachem Av* — "Consolation of the Father" emphasizes G-d's consolation.

Still, we must understand why it is that *Menachem Av* does not mention the sons' consolation — the consolation of the Jewish people.

This is because a Jew is rooted so deeply in G-d that his wants, desires, state of exile, etc., are not considered his alone; if he is exiled, his Father is automatically in a state of exile, as it were. Conversely, the Father's consolation is the consolation of His children. There can therefore be no

---

5. *Bamidbar* 31:2.
6. Ibid. verse 3.
7. Ibid.; see also *Rashi* ibid.; *Bamidbar Rabbah* 22:2; *Tanchuma, Matos* 3.
8. *Bamidbar* 35:34.
9. Ibid.

greater consolation for the children than *Menachem Av* — the "Consolation of the Father."

Based on *Likkutei Sichos* Vol. XXIII, pp. 214-220.

On The Move

The Torah portion *Masei* begins by stating:[1] "These are the journeys of the Children of Israel who left Egypt...." The Torah then goes on to recount all the places where the Jews resided during their 40-year trek from Egypt to the Promised Land.

Our Sages[2] ask: By recounting the places where the Jewish people camped rather than the journeys themselves, the Torah is indicating that the resting places are more important than the journeys. This being so, the verse should have stated: "These are the *encampments*...," rather than "These are the *journeys*..." Especially so, since the Jews spent the majority of these 40 years in their encampments, and not in travel.

The ultimate purpose of both the Jews' travels and encampments was, of course, to enter *Eretz Yisrael*. The encampments were therefore also termed "journeys," for they served no purpose in and of themselves.

In commenting on the verse, "These are the journeys of the Children of Israel who left Egypt...." the Baal Shem Tov notes[3] that the 42 journeys of the Jewish people from Egypt to *Eretz Yisrael* are mirrored in the 42 spiritual journeys undertaken by each and every Jew from the time of his birth — his personal departure from "Egypt" — to his arrival at the edge of the "Land of Life."

Understandably, the "rest stops" and "encampments" along the way refer to the various stages of spiritual growth to be experienced during life's journey.

---

1. *Bamidbar* 33:1.
2. *Alshich* ibid. See also *Klei Yakar* and *Orach Chayim* ibid.
3. Quoted in *Degel Machne Efrayim*, beginning of portion *Masei*.

But the previous question reoccurs: Surely, since the emphasis is on man's accomplishments — his "encampments" — the verse should have stated "These are the *encampments*," rather than "These are the *journeys*"?

In order for man to accomplish all that he is capable of, he must be constantly "on the move." We thus find the following difference between "stopping" and "moving" in terms of man's service:[4]

Even when a person rises from level to level, if the new level is comparable to the previous one, the individual has not truly departed from the lower level, and is considered to be "stationary."

"On the move" means there is no comparison between a person's former state and his present one — the individual has totally departed from his previous level.

The verse therefore emphasizes "the *journeys*," indicating that a Jew should never be satisfied with moving from one level to a comparable one. Rather, he must constantly "journey" in a manner whereby his next stage is infinitely higher than his current one.

This latter manner of "travel" contains two elements: *departing* from the previous level and *attaining* the infinitely higher one. As long as there has not been a complete departure from the former level, the higher level cannot be attained.

This, then, is the meaning of "These are the *journeys* of the Children of Israel *who left Egypt*...." Why was it necessary for there to be many "journeys" in order to leave Egypt; it would seem that with the first journey the Jewish people already departed Egypt?[5]

Egypt is symbolic of spiritual limitations. Thus, the "encampments" — the spiritual achievements *en route* — did not constitute complete redemption from "Egypt." In order to arrive at the Promised Land, there had to be a *total depar-*

---

4. See *Likkutei Torah, Shlach* 38d; *Tze'enah U'ri'enah 5660; Sefer HaMa'amarim 5671* p. 69ff.
5. See *Likkutei Torah, Masei* 88c.

ture from previous "encampments," for each stopping — no matter how lofty the waystation — itself represented a lingering within the state of "Egypt."

Based on *Likkutei Sichos* Vol. XXIII, pp. 224-227.

ספר דברים
Devarim

Devarim

דברים

Gad & Reuven — Going Ahead of the Jewish People

At the conclusion of the Torah portion of *Devarim*, Moshe relates how he told the tribes of Reuven and Gad that their warriors were to "go forth ahead of their Jewish brethren"[1] and lead them in battle. *Rashi* explains:[2] "Since they were mighty, they would go forth ahead of the Jewish people in battle and the enemies would succumb to them, as is written:[3] 'he tears as prey the arm and head.'"

The tribes of Reuven and Gad went "ahead" of the Jewish people in two ways: a) they forged ahead of the other Jews as a separate and distinct entity; b) they also placed themselves at the head of the Jewish army.

In terms of man's spiritual service, these two methods of doing battle represent two ways of vanquishing the enemy — the evil inclination:[4]

By "going forth ahead of their Jewish brethren" the warriors of Reuven and Gad placed themselves at much greater risk than the rest of the nation — evidence of *mesirus nefesh*, total self-sacrifice. In spiritual terms, this translates into divine service that transcends intellect — a manner of service that emanates from the soul's core.

The other tribes, however, did not place themselves at particular risk. In spiritual terms this relates to a lesser degree of divine service — service limited to one's comprehension, and which reflects the soul's more extrinsic levels.

This explains why the children of Gad would "tear as prey the arm and head," i.e., with one blow they would

---

1. *Devarim* 3:18.
2. Ibid.
3. Ibid. 33:20.
4. *Bereishis Rabbah* 54:1.

sever the enemy's arm and head. When logic is one's only weapon in the battle against evil, it is impossible to nullify all the forces of darkness with one blow, for a particular manner of service is required in order to defeat each evil power.

But when one calls upon the all-encompassing spiritual power of self-sacrifice, a power so great that it obliterates every aspect of evil, then it is possible to vanquish *all* the evil — the "arm and head" — at one blow.

Ultimately, even *mesirus nefesh* alone does not suffice; it is necessary for *mesirus nefesh* (i.e. the tribes of Gad and Reuven) to influence the intellect, emotion, speech and action (i.e. the other tribes) as well. This is accomplished in two ways:

a) *Mesirus nefesh* clothes itself in intellect, emotion, etc., so that one's performance of Torah and *mitzvos* is fueled by it.[5] The main aspect of an individual's spiritual service remains the day-to-day study of Torah and performance of *mitzvos; mesirus nefesh* is invoked merely as a means to enhance this service, and not as an end in itself.[6]

b) *Mesirus nefesh* becomes an end unto itself: be it in a situation that requires actual self-sacrifice, or one that requires *mesirus nefesh* in *potentia*, such as during the *Ne'ilah* prayer of *Yom Kippur*.

This aspect of *mesirus nefesh* too, although not clothed in intellect and emotion, has the ability to affect them. For, as explained in *Tanya*,[7] when the power of *mesirus nefesh* is aroused, it *automatically* affects one's intellect, emotions, speech and action.

These, then, are the two manners in which the tribes of Gad and Reuven went to war: At the outset of spiritual service they placed themselves at the head of the Jewish army, i.e., *mesirus nefesh* merely served as the "head" and conductor of the intellect and emotions, etc.

---

5. See *Tanya* conclusion of ch. 25.
6. Cf. *Likkutei Sichos IV* p. 1022ff.
7. Ch. 19.

Thereafter came the higher degree of *mesirus nefesh*, wherein these two tribes would forge ahead on their own. That is, *mesirus nefesh* was aroused as an entity unto itself.

Based on *Likkutei Sichos* Vol. IX, pp. 1-13.

From G-d's Mouth to Moshe's

At the beginning of the Book *Devarim* the verse states: "In the fortieth year, on the first day of the eleventh month, Moshe spoke to the Children of Israel regarding all that G-d had commanded him for them."[1]

What, exactly, did Moshe say?

The *Seforno* explains[2] that Moshe repeated all the Torah given up to that time. Indeed, this is one of the reasons why the Book of *Devarim* is also known as *"Mishneh Torah,"* the *"Repetition* of the Torah."[3]

Our Sages note[4] that the Book of *Devarim* differs from the first four Books of the Torah in that the latter are "from G-d's mouth," while *Devarim* is "from Moshe's mouth."

This does not — Heaven forfend — imply that the words in *Mishneh Torah* are not G-d's. Rather, as *Rashi* explains:[5] "Moshe did not say *Mishneh Torah* to the Jews on his own, but as he would receive it from G-d he would repeat it to them."

Since the words of *Mishneh Torah* too are not Moshe's words but G-d's, why are the first four Books of the Torah considered to be from "G-d's mouth" while the Book of *Devarim* is considered to be from "Moshe's mouth"; what difference is there between the first four Books and the fifth?

---

1. *Devarim* 1:3.
2. Ibid.
3. See *Chagigah* 6b; Commentary of *Rashi* beginning of Torah Portion *Behar*.
4. See *Zohar III*, 261a. See also *Megillah* 31b; *Shach* and *Or HaChayim* beginning of *Devarim*.
5. *Sanhedrin* 56b.

The inherent sanctity of Torah is such that it completely transcends this physical world;[6] in order for it to descend within this world an intermediary is necessary — one who is both higher than this world yet within it. This intermediary bridges the gap between the sacred Torah and this corporeal world.

Moshe served as the intermediary, inasmuch as he combined aspects of this world with higher levels. His humility was truly otherworldly; concurrently, he attained the highest degree of completeness possible for an earthly being.[7]

Information flows through an intermediary in one of two ways:[8]

a) The information passes through but does not become united with the intermediary; all he does is bring about its descent.

b) The communication becomes so wholly unified with the intermediary that it is refashioned — personalized — by its passage through him. This, in turn, enables the recipients to receive the information according to their own personal levels of intellect.

An example: When intellect is transmitted through one's fingers, e.g., when one jots down an idea or paints a picture, the fingers do not refashion the thought. However, when a thought is drawn down with emotion, the emotion will color and change the intellect accordingly.[9]

Herein lies the difference between the first four Books of the Torah and *Mishneh Torah*: In the first four, Moshe served as a go-between in the first manner, and Torah remained a communication "from G-d's mouth," while in *Mishneh Torah* His words were clothed within Moshe's intellect, and are therefore considered to be "from Moshe's mouth."[10]

---

6. See *Midrash Tehillim* 90:3; *Bereishis Rabbah* 8:2; *Zohar II*, 49a.
7. See *Devarim Rabbah* 11:4; Commentary of the *Rambam* to *Cheilik* — Seventh Fundament.
8. See *Or HaTorah, Shemini, Ma'amar* titled *Yayin v'Sheichar* ch. 6, *Panim b'Panim 5659* (pp. 194-195); *Oteh Or 5700*.
9. See *Ma'amar* titled *Yayin v'Sheichar* mentioned above; *Hemshech 5666*, p. 425.
10. See also *Tiferes Yisrael* of the *MaHaral*, ch. 43.

What is the advantage of having Torah clothed in Moshe's intellect? Seemingly, this involves a descent in sanctity.

When a flow of divine knowledge is not clothed in the intellect of a human intermediary, it eludes comprehension, for such knowledge is by definition beyond the grasp of the receiver, and the intermediary did nothing to make it more accessible.

Thus, were Torah to have been transmitted only in the manner of the first four Books (i.e. "from G-d's mouth"), it would have been impossible for the Jews to truly comprehend it. When Moshe, however, repeated the Torah to them in his own words (i.e. "from Moshe's mouth"), it became comprehensible.

Based on *Likkutei Sichos* Vol. XIX, pp. 9-12.

Vaes'chanan   ואתחנן

Shema and Torah Study —
Together, Yet Worlds Apart

The Torah portion of *Vaes'chanan* contains the commandments to recite *Shema* and study Torah.[1] Although both
commands are found in the same verse, they are very different.

The duty to recite the *Shema* involves reciting it twice
daily, "when you lie down and when you rise." Each recitation is an entity unto itself, the proof being that the blessing
for its recitation is itself recited twice daily, in the morning
and in the evening.

The obligation to study Torah, however, is not divided
into the two separate times, but is a single, ongoing obligation that continues throughout the day and night. This is
why the blessing for Torah study is recited only once a day.

Seemingly, the very opposite should be the case: Torah
study is bound up with comprehension and comprehension
varies according to time — when a person is rested he will
think more clearly, etc. Since comprehension is affected by
time, it would be logical to link the command of Torah study
— an act that requires comprehension — to time, and to its
division of day and night.

The *mitzvah* of reciting the *Shema*, however, requires *a
constant and unalterable* acceptance of the yoke of the Heavenly Kingdom and G-d's Unity. Thus, it stands to reason
that this command should not be subject to the changes that
result from the division of night and day.

---

1. *Devarim* 6:7.

Nonetheless, we find that the commandment of *Shema* is linked to time, while the command to study Torah defies the divisions of time.

Why is this so?

Man's life is subject to the division of days, for "Days separate one from the other"[2] — days divide time into distinct entities. To have a complete "day," night and day must be combined, as the verse states,[3] "...there was evening and there was morning, one day."

This also hints at the ultimate purpose of man's service — to transform this nethermost world into a dwelling place for G-d. The implication is that man should not negate physicality, but rather that this lowly world, seemingly separate from the spiritual realms, should become a dwelling place for G-d.

This is accomplished when the physical organism itself comes to realize that its whole essence derives from G-d. When this connection is felt by a corporeal being, G-d's absolute unity is revealed.

An allusion to this concept can be found in the Torah when it states: "...there was *evening* and there was *morning*, *one* day." The implication is that the Divine intent is to combine and unite the darkness and corporeality of "evening" with the luminosity and ethereality of "morning," so that together they form one day.

This idea of unity within diversity lies at the heart of the *Shema*, wherein the Jew declares: "*Shemah Yisrael*... the L-rd is *One*," thus "crowning G-d and making Him reign 'above, below and on all four sides'"[4] by revealing His light and oneness within this physical and spiritually dark world.

Thus, connecting the *mitzvah* of *Shema* with the time periods of day and night emphasizes the unification of light and darkness, physical and spiritual, so that together they

---

2. *Nazir* 7a. Cf. *Zohar III*, 94b: "Each and every day does its own [particular] work."
3. *Bereishis* 1:5.
4. *Berachos* 13b.

form "one day" — the revelation of G-d's unity within this world.

Torah, however, is likened to fire, as the verse states:[5] "My words are like fire, says the L-rd." Our Sages explain:[6] "Just as fire is impervious to [ritual] impurity, so too is Torah impervious to [spiritual] impurity." In other words, while Torah clothes itself in material reality and deals with physical matters, it remains detached from physicality.

Since Torah views the world from its own perspective rather than becoming one with creation, it follows that the obligation to study Torah is not subject to the limitations of night and day.

Based on *Likkutei Sichos* Vol. XIV, pp. 21-23.

5. *Yermiyahu* 23:29.
6. *Berachos* 22a.

Lessons of Tefillin

In the Torah portion *Vaes'chanan* the commandment of *tefillin* is conveyed in the following manner: "You shall bind them as a sign upon your hand, and they shall be for a re- minder between your eyes."[1]

Because the verse begins by saying, "You shall bind them as a sign upon your hand," and only then goes on to say, "and they shall be for a reminder between your eyes," the *Gemara*[2] gleans that the hand *tefillin* are to be donned be- fore the head *tefillin*.

The *Gemara* goes on to say that with regard to removing the *tefillin* the order is reversed: first the head *tefillin* are re- moved and only then are the hand *tefillin* removed. For "and *they* shall be for a reminder between your eyes" indicates that "whenever the head *tefillin* are worn there must be two"

1. *Devarim* 6:8.
2. *Menachos* 36a.

— both hand and head *tefillin*; inevitably, then, the head *tefillin* are removed first.

Since "The entire Torah is likened to *tefillin*,"[3] it follows that just as the term *tefillin* refers to both the hand and head *tefillin*, so, too, within the service of Torah and *mitzvos* there are aspects of both the hand and head *tefillin*.

The hand *tefillin*, placed upon the *biceps* opposite the *heart*, is indicative of service of the heart, fear of G-d and acceptance of the Divine yoke, while the head *tefillin*, which is placed adjacent to the brain, symbolizes the service of the mind.

This concept is also stressed in the *Shulchan Aruch*, which emphasizes that the commandment of *tefillin* entails "placing them upon the biceps opposite the heart and upon the head adjacent to the brain, so that we remember the miracles and wonders that He has done for us, these miracles indicating G-d's unity, and that it is He who possesses the might and power...."[4]

Moreover, an integral part[5] of the *mitzvah* of *tefillin* is that we "submit to G-d's service our soul, which is in the *brain*, as well as the desires and thoughts of the *heart*. By donning *tefillin* a person will be mindful of the blessed Creator and restrict his pleasures."[6]

In a more general sense there are two overall aspects: The hand *tefillin* relate to feelings and emotions — fear and awe of G-d, and practical *mitzvos*; the head *tefillin* relate to intellect and Torah.

Herein lie two important lessons: The fact that the hand *tefillin* are to be donned first indicates that fear and awe of G-d must precede Torah knowledge. This is in keeping with the dictum of the *Mishna:*[7] "Anyone whose fear of sin comes before his wisdom, his wisdom will endure; but anyone

3. *Kiddushin* 35a.
4. *Shulchan Aruch Admur HaZakein, Orach Chayim* 25:11.
5. See *Bach* on *Tur, Orach Chayim* 268, titled *VeYechavein*.
6. *Shulchan Aruch Admur HaZakein*, ibid.
7. *Avos* 3:9.

whose wisdom precedes his fear of sin, his wisdom will not endure." Or as the *Zohar* states:[8] "Fear of G-d is the doorway to wisdom."

This thought is elaborated on in *Tanya*,[9] where it states: "One must constantly bear in mind that the beginning of divine service, as well as its core and root... requires first arousing the innate fear which lies hidden in the heart of every Jew not to rebel against the Supreme King of Kings, the Holy One, blessed be He."

Then comes the second lesson: "Whenever the head *te-fillin* — the service of intellect and Torah study — are 'worn' there must be two; the hand *tefillin*, fear of G-d, must be present as well."

For fear and awe of G-d is not only a *prerequisite* to the study of Torah, but must also be found alongside and together with the intellectual pursuit of Torah and G-dliness. Only then can a person be assured that "his wisdom will endure."

Acting in such a manner enables an individual to reach that level of Supernal fear and awe that is the hallmark of the sanctity achieved through Torah study.[10]

It is with regard to this loftier level of fear that our Sages state:[11] "If there is no wisdom, there is no fear of G-d," and concerning which the verse states:[12] "He has commanded us to observe all the statutes so that we may fear Him."

Based on *Likkutei Sichos* Vol. XIX, pp. 47-54.

---

8. *Zohar I* 7b.
9. Ch. 41.
10. *Tanya*, conclusion of ch. 23; ch. 43; *Likkutei Torah*, *Vaes'chanan* 9c and onward.
11. *Avos* 3:17.
12. *Devarim* 6:24.

Eikev   עקב

The Healing Effect of "Heeling"

The Torah portion of *Eikev* is named for the word *"eikev"* in the portion's first verse: "Because *(eikev)* you listen to these laws and safeguard and keep them...."[1] *Eikev* also means "heel." This gives rise to a number of commentaries by our Sages. Among them:

a) *Eikev* refers to those *mitzvos* that people treat lightly and "tread upon with their heels,"[2] or "toss under their heels."[3] The verse thus implies that those commandments, too, shall be obeyed.

b) *Eikev* alludes to the time just before the coming of Moshiach — "On the heels of Moshiach." The verse is thus telling us that close to Mashiach's coming Jews will surely obey G-d's commands. This is in keeping with the Torah's assurance[4] that prior to Mashiach's coming the Jews will return to G-d.[5]

When there are several commentaries on the same verse in the Torah, and especially on the same word, the explanations are interrelated.[6] What then is the relationship between the two above-mentioned comments on *Eikev*?

Immediately following the words "Because *(eikev)* you listen to these laws and safeguard and keep them," the Torah goes on to state: "G-d your L-rd will [therefore] keep his covenant and kindness that He swore to your fathers."

Divine beneficence may come about in one of two manners:

---

1. *Devarim* 7:12.
2. *Rashi* ibid.
3. *Tanchuma* ibid.
4. *Devarim* 30:2. See also *Rambam Hilchos Teshuvah* 7:5.
5. *Or HaTorah* beginning of *Eikev*; ibid. p. 491; ibid. p. 504.
6. See *Likkutei Sichos III*, p. 782.

a) It may be engendered as a result of a person's good actions (i.e. he *earns* it), or it may be purely an act of G-d's kindness, whereby He showers goodness even upon the unworthy.

b) G-d acts in a beneficent manner towards the Jewish people because of his covenant with our forefathers, for which reason Jews must receive all manner of good, even if they are — Heaven forfend — unworthy, and even if G-d is not "feeling" particularly well-disposed towards them.

It would seem that in this instance G-d has no choice, as it were, in the matter; He must provide the Jewish people with all manner of good because of the "covenant and kindness that He *swore* to your fathers."

This being so, how is it that the verse makes G-d's "covenant and kindness" dependent on the Jews' good behavior — "*Because* you listen...."? After all, the whole point of the covenant is that He will act kindly toward the Jews even when their behavior is wanting?

Conversely, when Jews do indeed "listen to these laws," performing even those *mitzvos* that may be taken lightly, then it follows that they will *earn* G-d's beneficence. At such times it becomes unnecessary for G-d to provide His benevolence because of His "covenant, kindness and oath."[7]

Man enjoys that which he works for. Present a person with a gift that is wholly unearned and the recipient will accept it with a sense of shame, aware that he has done nothing to make himself worthy of the gift. Since G-d desires to provide the Jewish people with *complete* goodness, He therefore established that *all* Divine beneficence should come as a "reward" for service.

For this reason, even that goodness which every Jew receives as a result of the "covenant and kindness that He swore" must also be engendered by spiritual toil. Furthermore, when a person does indeed "listen to these laws" he receives Divine beneficence that is truly limitless — in

---

7. See *Klei Yakar, Devarim* 7:12.

keeping with G-d's infinite "kindness that He swore," rather than a reward commensurate with the person's limited service.

The merit of service is particularly felt at the conclusion of the Exile, when Jews are "on the heels of the Moshiach." For then the darkness of exile is particularly intense and the Jews' spiritual might is waning; at that time Jews perform *mitzvos* not out of any sense of personal delight, but out of self-sacrifice to G-d.

This quality found at a time when Jews are "on the heels of the Moshiach" also finds expression in the performance of those commands that a person tends to take lightly.

When a person performs *mitzvos* out of a sense of self, he will naturally differentiate between those that he deems more important — the level of "head" — and those that he deems of lesser importance — at the level of "heel." When, however, *mitzvos* are performed solely because G-d has so commanded, then "head" *mitzvos* and "heel" *mitzvos* will be performed with equal intensity.

Based on Likkutei Sichos Vol. IX, pp. 71-74.

"Heels Over Head"

The Torah portion *Eikev* begins with the verse, "Because (*eikev*) you listen to these laws and safeguard and keep them, G-d your L-rd will keep His covenant and kindness that He swore to your fathers."[1]

The Hebrew word *eikev* not only means "because," but also "heel." Thus *Midrash Tanchuma*[2] explains that "these laws" refers to *mitzvos* that seemingly lack significance, so that people tend to "ignore them and cast them under their heels."

---

1. *Devarim* 7:12.
2. Ibid.

Superficially, it would seem that the Midrash is inferring that these seemingly unimportant commandments are treated so lightly by some individuals that they do not observe them at all.

However, if this were indeed so, what is the connection between their non-performance and their being "cast under the heel" — if they are not performed at all then they are "cast out entirely," not merely "cast under the heel"?

Truly, the *Midrash* is not referring to people who maintain that these "insignificant" *mitzvos* need not be performed, and surely it does not allude to those individuals who defile them by casting them under their heels.

Rather, the *Midrash* is making reference to those persons who recognize that all *mitzvos* are to be performed, no matter how inconsequential they may seem, only that these individuals prioritize the order of their performance, delaying the performance of *mitzvos* that they treat lightly — they cast their performance "under their heels."

These persons maintain that they will first see to it that the "head," i.e., the most important and stringent matters, will be performed properly. Afterward they will see to those *mitzvos* that are in close proximity to the head — *mitzvos* that are slightly less major. Only at the very last will they think about observing "heel *mitzvos*," and surely going above and beyond the letter of the law through the beautification and enhancement of these *mitzvos* will be put off to the very end.

Such individuals contend that one cannot possibly begin with the "heel"; order dictates that one must first do those things that are of greatest import and only then can one begin to think about deeper piety, enhanced performance, beautification of *mitzvos*, etc.

Although such thinking has a certain validity,[3] it is absolutely vital that divine service begin with faith and acceptance of G-d's yoke, not with the dictates of logic. And the

---

3. See *Mo'ed Kattan* 9a.

Jewish faith exhorts the individual to be as scrupulously observant of the seemingly minor *mitzvos* as the major ones.

For the quintessential aspect of all *mitzvos* is that they unite the individual with G-d.[4] This applies to all the *mitzvos*, without the slightest difference between "major" and "minor" *mitzvos*, "head *mitzvos*" or "heel *mitzvos*." It is therefore out of place to think about a sequential order to the performance of *mitzvos*.[5]

Thus we also observe that the condition which enabled the Jewish people to receive the Torah and become a nation was their prefacing "We shall do" to "We shall hear" — a totally illogical sequence.[6]

For a Jew's spiritual beginning, similar to the beginning of the Jewish nation as a whole, must be with faith and acceptance of the divine yoke and not with intellect; even those matters that are readily understandable must be performed out of a sense of faith and G-dly submission.

So too, children — people at the beginning of their lives — should know not only about the natural, i.e., logical, events that transpired with the Jewish people, but the miraculous, i.e., faith and belief, as well. This instills a firm foundation of faith in G-d.

This manner of conduct is especially important in times of exile, when the Jewish people are "like a sheep surrounded by 70 wolves"[7]: When we transcend our self-imposed order and are equally fervent in our performance of all commandments, then G-d too foregoes the "order" of natural events, and the "Great Shepherd protects His sheep,"[8] and abundantly provides them with children, health and sustenance.

Based on *Likkutei Sichos* Vol. XIX, pp. 89-93.

---

4. *Likkutei Torah, Bechukosai* 45c; *Rebbe Omer 5700*, conclusion of ch. 1 and onward.
5. See *Kuntres U'Mayon* p. 22.
6. See *Shabbos* 88a.
7. *Tanchuma, Toldos; Esther Rabbah* 10:11; *Pesikta Rabosi* ch. 9.
8. *Tanchuma, Toldos; Esther Rabbah*, ibid.

Re'eh   ראה

Three Torah Portions and their Haftoros

The Ninth of *Av* marks the destruction of both Holy
Temples. Three *Haftoros*, known as "The Three [*Haftoros*] of
Punishment," are read on the three *Shabasos* that precede the
Ninth of Av. Then, on the Shabbos following the Ninth of
Av, there begins the series of "The Seven [*Haftoros*] of Con-
solation."

The first *Haftorah* of consolation is *Nachamu*, which accompanies the Torah portion of *Vaes'chanan*. The *Haftorah* of
VaTomar Tzion follows the week after, and is read in conjunction with the portion *Eikev*. This, in turn, is followed by
the *Haftorah* of *Aniyah So'arah* that is read in connection with
Re'eh.

All matters relating to Torah are precise. Surely, the jux-
taposition of these particular Torah portions with these particular *Haftoras* is not mere happenstance. What is the relationship between these portions and their *Haftoros*?

The destruction of both Holy Temples caused much
more than mere physical annihilation; it also caused
G-dliness to depart, as it were, from this world.[1] This occurrence is annually relived on the Ninth of *Av* — and following this occurrence it is necessary to begin spiritual service
anew.

Every new beginning, particularly a new spiritual beginning, must first be empowered by G-d and receive His
blessing — an "arousal from Above that precedes the
arousal from below."[2] This is why we read *Vaes'chanan* on
the first Shabbos after the Ninth of *Av*. It is then that spiritual service begins anew, and it is then that we ask for G-d's

---

1. See *Zohar I*, 210a; ibid. *III*, 20b, 75a.
2. See *Likkutei Torah, Vayikra* 2b.

blessing in this quest — a plea implicit in the word *Vaes'chanan*. Our Sages explain that *Vaes'chanan* means a plea for "an undeserved gift,"[3] i.e., a gift not necessarily commensurate with our spiritual efforts.

Appropriately, then, we also read the Haftorah of *Nachamu*: "Be consoled, be consoled My people, says your G-d"[4] — a form of blessing and consolation that comes entirely from Above.

However, merely receiving G-d's gift does not suffice; it is necessary for man to rouse himself — "an arousal from below" — and serve G-d as well. This second stage is alluded to in the portion of *Eikev*, which informs us that even man's lowest level of *eikev* — a level that does not perceive G-dliness at all[5] — is sublimated to G-dliness, so that it too "listens" and hearkens to G-d's word.

This concept is further buttressed by the *Haftorah* of *Eikev, VaTomar Tzion*, wherein the Jewish people — "forsaken and forgotten" — bitterly lament their estrangement from G-d. And this heartfelt lament is wholly a result of the Jews' own spiritual service, a manner of service that heightens their spiritual sensitivity and causes them to mourn their lack of closeness with the Creator.

While the degree of service that "listens" to G-d is laudable, it is not the ultimate. In the highest form of service, a person attains so rarefied a level that he is able not merely to hear, but also to *see*, G-dliness. It is this third stage that is hinted at both in the Torah portion as well as in the *Haftorah* of *Re'eh*.

The opening words of this portion are: *"Re'eh Onochi* — See [that] I [G-d]....,"[6] this means that a Jew is to see and behold G-d Himself. Anything less than that, the Jew should find wholly unsatisfactory.

---

3. *Sifri, Devarim Rabba, Tanchuma* and commentary of *Rashi* on *Devarim* 3:23.
4. *Yeshayahu* 40:1.
5. See previous essay.
6. *Devarim* 11:26.

This gives rise to the lament in the *Haftorah* of *Re'eh, Ani-yah So'arah*, wherein the Jewish people express their anguish at their "tempestuous [spiritual] impoverishment that can find no consolation"[7] merely through the words of the prophets, for they desire to be united with and consoled by G-d Himself.

Indeed, G-d accedes to their request and assures them, "It is I, and I alone, who shall console you."[8] Granting their request is G-d's response to the Jews' service — "an arousal from Above that follows the arousal from below."

This also explains why *Eikev* is always read during the month of *Av* and *Re'eh* is read either on the Shabbos that blesses the month of *Elul* or on *Rosh Chodesh Elul* itself. *Av* is the month during which G-d gave vent to His Divine wrath;[9] *Elul* is the month during which He expresses His Divine mercy.[10] During the former month we feel mostly the distance, gloom and concealment epitomized by *eikev*. When the month of *Elul* comes, during which the Thirteen Attributes of Divine Mercy are dominant, then G-d is seen in all His glory, for: "It is I, and I alone, who consoles you."

Based on *Likkutei Sichos* Vol. IX, pp. 76-78.

---

7. *Yeshayahu* 54:11.
8. Ibid. 51:12.
9. *Zohar, Shmos* 12a.
10. See *Shulchan Aruch Orach Chayim* 581; *Likkutei Torah, Re'eh* 32a and onward.

"Cleave to Him"

We are told in the Torah Portion *Re'eh*,[1] "Follow G-d your L-rd, fear Him, observe His commandments, hearken to His voice, serve Him and cleave to Him." On the words "cleave to Him," *Rashi* explains: "Cleave to His ways, per-

---

1. *Devarim* 13:5.

form acts of loving kindness, bury the dead, visit the sick, just as G-d has done."

Rashi's comment must be understood: Since, according to *Rashi*, the verse means to tell us that we should cleave to G-d's ways and act as He does, why doesn't the verse explicitly state "cleave to His ways" rather than "cleave to Him?"

Moreover, since the command to cleave to G-d's ways is stated as *"cleave to Him,"* it is understandable that the ultimate unity with G-d is accomplished specifically through following G-d's example and performing acts of *loving kindness.*

In other words, the highest form of cleaving to G-d can only be accomplished through these latter actions, and not by performing the actions and commandments referred to earlier when the verse declared "obey His commandments."

This, too, must be understood: **All** *mitzvos* bring about an attachment between man and G-d; what greater attachment is achieved by doing those things that fall under the heading of "cleaving to G-d"?

G-d commanded us to perform *Mitzvos,* and we perform them because we are so obligated. It therefore follows that the attachment achieved by performing *mitzvos* is one in which the performer is continuously aware of his own self; it is *he* who is becoming attached to G-d through *his* performance.

This is not so with regard to "cleaving to G-d." Although "cleaving to G-d" begins as the result of a command, the performance, completion, and totality of the command involves the total loss of any sense of self, for the person is wholly engulfed within Him — he cleaves to Him.

The difference between *mitzvos* in general and performing those actions that result in "cleaving to Him" is thus the difference between "attachment to G-d" and "cleaving to G-d":[2]

---

2. See *L'ma'an Tizkeru 5568; V'Haya Eikev 5673.*

"Attachment to G-d" — the state achieved through the regular performance of Torah and *mitzvos* — is similar to attaching two separate objects one to another and tying them together. Even after the objects have become bound together, they are still viewed as two things. "Cleaving to G-d," however, is so strong a form of unification that there are no two separate entities — they are truly one.

We thus understand that the same act — extending a loan for example — when performed with the intent of "cleaving to G-d" is infinitely greater than the same act performed as a separate *mitzvah*; the latter lacks total loss of self and only attains attachment — not cleaving — to G-d.

This also explains why the verse states "cleave to Him." Although this requires "cleaving to His ways," no action is specified, for the intent here is not to speak of the act itself — "His ways" — but the *result* of the act; when one is so at one with G-d, following in His ways will come as a matter of course.

Thus it is told of the *Alter Rebbe* that on Fridays towards evening he would *automatically* fall asleep, since it was then a time of sleep Above.[3] I.e., his cleaving to G-d was so intense that the proper actions — "ways" — followed spontaneously.

Acting in such an unprompted and unpremeditated manner in consonance with G-d's desires reveals the tremendous degree of innate cleaving that a Jewish soul has to G-d. When the Torah commands us to "cleave to G-d," it empowers all of us to reveal our latent qualities.

Based on *Likkutei Sichos* Vol. XIV, pp. 53-63.

---

3. *Toras Sholom* p. 13.

Shoftim שפטים

Two Forms of Witnesses

In the Torah portion of *Shoftim* we learn: "The testimony of one witness does not stand against a person with regard to any sin or iniquity that he may have committed; a case can be established [only] through the testimony of [at least] two or three witnesses."[1]

Specifically, there are two categories of witnesses: a) witnesses who verify specific facts or events;[2] b) witnesses who were themselves an integral part of the events.[3]

An example of the first category are witnesses to a loan, whose sole purpose is to verify the deed. They have no part in the legal transaction; even if the loan were transacted without witnesses the borrower is no less obligated to repay the lender.

An example of the second category are witnesses to a marriage; their presence constitutes an integral part of the ceremony itself; according to Jewish law[4] a couple cannot become husband and wife without the presence of bonafide witnesses.

These two categories of witnesses, witnesses who verify and witnesses who are an integral part of the event itself, exist within a spiritual context as well.

Scripture states:[5] "'You are My witnesses,' says the L-rd." In commenting upon this verse, the *Zohar* provides two explanations:[6] a) "You" refers to the Jewish people; b) "You"

---

1. *Devarim* 19:15.
2. See *Kiddushin* 65b.
3. See *Tumim* 90:14.
4. *Kiddushin* ibid.; *Rambam Hilchos Ishus* 4:6; *Tur* and *Shulchan Aruch Even HaEzer* 42:2 and commentaries ibid.
5. *Yeshayahu* 43:10; ibid. verse 12.
6. *III* 86a.

refers to heaven and earth, concerning which it is written,[7] "Today I call heaven and earth as witnesses before you." These two sets of witnesses, the Jewish people and heaven and earth, correspond to the two previously described categories of witnesses in the following manner:

The testimony of witnesses is only germane to a matter that is otherwise concealed; something that is revealed to all does not require witnesses.[8]

In a spiritual sense this means witnesses are not needed to testify to the fact that G-d provides life, for this is known to all.[9] One need but observe the manner in which the universe is conducted and one will readily perceive G-d's handiwork and the Divine life force that vivifies all creation.

Even with regard to G-dliness that can only be believed in but not perceived, witnesses and testimony are superfluous. For although this degree of G-dliness cannot be grasped intellectually, intellect itself decrees that there are levels of Divinity that go beyond the bonds of intellect. Once a thinking person concludes that G-dliness must permeate this world in order for it to exist, he will eventually realize that the degree of G-dliness that provides this world with life is not the most critical; there are levels that entirely transcend the world and man's intellect.

Therefore, with regard to this level as well, the testimony of witnesses is not germane, for though this level of G-dliness is not in a state of revelation — it is suprarational — nevertheless, intellect itself demands that it exist. Therefore, this level too falls within the purview of "something that will eventually be revealed to all," concerning which testimony does not apply.

Testimony and witnesses do, however, apply to G-d's *essence*, which is totally concealed from intellect, and indeed is

---

7. *Devarim* 30:19.
8. *Likkutei Torah, Pikudei* 4a and onward. See also discourse titled *VaYakam Eidus* ch. 1, in *Sefer HaMa'amarim 5700.*
9. See *Likkutei Torah, Vaes'chanan* 6a and onward; ibid. *Emor* 31b and onward; *Sefer HaMitzvos* of the *Tzemach Tzedek, Mitzvos HaAmonas Elokus* ch. 1, et al.

concealed from any revelatory level. Here, witnesses are necessary to *reveal* His essence. This is accomplished in ways reflecting the two types of witnesses:

The infinite power vested within heaven and earth serves as "ascertaining witnesses" to G-d's true infinitude; the Jews' ability to draw down G-d's essence within this world through their spiritual service is the form of witnessing wherein the witnesses are "witnesses who are an integral part of the event itself."

Jews are able to accomplish this because they are rooted in G-d's essence; they are therefore able, through their service of Torah and *mitzvos*, to draw His Essence into this world.

Based on *Likkutei Sichos* Vol. XIX, pp. 188-196.

Emotions — A Tree of the Field

In the Torah portion *Shoftim* we are commanded to treat trees with respect, for "Man is a tree of the field."[1] What is the resemblance between the loftiest creature and lowly vegetation?

The special quality of plants and trees lies in their attachment to the earth, the source from whence they derive their existence and nourishment. This is particularly true with regard to trees. Other plant life, such as grain, vegetables, etc., do not exist in such a continually attached state, for they soon wither and die. The fact that trees are able to withstand winter's frosts and summer's heat indicates that they have a particularly strong attachment to the earth, an attachment that enables them to endure difficult times and continue to bear fruit.

Man is a microcosm;[2] just as the world as a whole is composed of inanimate matter, vegetable matter, animals

---

1. *Devarim* 20:19.
2. *Tanchuma, Pikudei* 3. See also *Avos d'Reb Nasan* ch. 31:3.

and men, so too are these qualities to be found within each and every individual.

A person's emotive traits are likened to vegetation,[3] for they embody growth and development. And although intelligence grows as well, intellect also has an "animal" aspect in that it constantly undergoes movement and change, similar to an animal's ability to roam. Further, man's emotive traits tend to be self-limiting — a kind person is inevitably gentle, a severe person will almost always deal with others in a stern manner. For this reason too, the emotive traits are likened to vegetation.

Comprehension, however, understands things as they truly are, not as the person wishes them to be. The conclusions drawn from a concept will vary according to the concept itself, leading sometimes to kindness and sometimes to severity.

Just as in the macrocosm, vegetation is unique in its constant unification with its source, so too within man, the emotive powers are always attached to a person's essence. This also explains why emotional traits and tendencies are so powerful, and why it is so very difficult for a kind person to become severe, etc.

By likening man to "a tree in the field," the Torah is in effect telling us that the true test of an individual is not so much his intellectual qualities but his emotional ones; it is they that take the measure of the man.[4]

It follows that man's labor and toil with regard to self-improvement is to be directed more towards refining his emotional traits than towards refining his mind;[5] perfecting and polishing one's emotive character has the greatest impact on a person's essence.

In fact, refining one's emotive traits is deemed to be so important that intellectual comprehension is not considered

3. *Torah Or* 4a.
4. See *Hemshech Te'erav III*, p. 1221.
5. See *Ma'amarim* titled *Al Ta'atzar* p. 6ff, *Ain HaKadosh Baruch Hu Ba 5685; VaYisa Aharon 5694*.

complete if it does not affect one's emotions — "Know this day and take [this knowledge] unto your heart."[6]

Just as this is so with regard to each individual, so too regarding the Jewish people as a whole:

All Jews are descendants of Avraham, Yitzchak and Yaakov, and as such are constantly attached to them and their qualities. The main qualities of the Patriarchs lay not so much in matters of intellect as in emotion,[7] for Avraham epitomized kindness and love, Yitzchak severity and fear, Yaakov mercy and beauty — the three traits that encompass the emotional spectrum.[8]

These sterling qualities — the "trees of the field" — are the birthright of each and every Jew. They must merely be revealed, refined and developed to the greatest possible extent.

Based on *Likkutei Sichos* Vol. XXIV, pp. 115-119.

---

6. *Devarim* 4:39.
7. See *Torah Or*, beginning of Torah portion *Va'eira*. See also *Tanya* ch. 18.
8. See *Tanya* ch. 3; *Torah Or* 1b.

Seitzei   תצא

A New Home and its Guard-Rail

In the Torah portion of *Seitzei* we learn[1]: "When you build a new home, you must place a guard-rail around your roof." The purpose of the guard-rail — as the Torah itself goes on to say — is to keep people from falling off an unenclosed roof.

In a spiritual context, the meaning of this commandment is as follows:

Our Sages tell us[2] that "One's wife is [considered as] one's [entire] home," so much so that Rabbi Yossi said:[3] "I never called my spouse 'my wife'...but 'my home.' "

In this context, "when you build a new home," refers to the beginning of one's marriage. When a person marries and sets up a home, he must take upon himself the yoke of earning a livelihood. At such a time a person's spiritual status may easily plummet.

The Torah therefore reminds the individual that since he is beginning a new home and a new lifestyle, with a greater degree of immersion in physicality, he must build a guard-rail. Clearly his previous manner of spiritual service will not suffice, and he must take upon himself additional guard-rails so as not to take a spiritual tumble in thought, speech, or deed.

At times man's body is also referred to as his home.[4] In terms of man's spiritual service, this alludes to the general service of *birurim*, wherein man seeks to purify and elevate his body and his portion in the physical world.

---

1. *Devarim* 22:8.
2. *Mishnah* beginning of *Yoma;* See *Gemara* ibid. 13a; *Likkutei Sichos XVII* p. 172ff.
3. *Shabbos* 118b, explained in *Likkutei Sichos* ibid.
4. *VaYovo Amalek 5688*, conclusion of ch. 1.

This manner of service is known as a *"new* home," for prior to the soul's descent into this world it had not the foggiest notion as to what the physical world and the spiritual service within it entails.

Furthermore, since the corporeal is infinitely distant from the spiritual, the service of purifying and uplifting this physical world is truly something new. When a Jew serves G-d in this manner, the world itself becomes an abode for G-d.

This concept of an abode for G-d is also something "new." Prior to this manner of service, the degree of G-dliness that manifested itself in this lowly world was restricted. However, as a result of this manner of service, this physical world becomes an abode for G-d — G-d Himself is manifest within this world.[5]

Understandably, building such important new edifices has a tremendous impact upon the builder. He, too, is refined and uplifted in a "new" and infinitely greater manner — to a point that his soul reaches an even higher state of existence than it enjoyed prior to its descent within a body.[6]

The "vessel" that must serve as a receptacle to this new and lofty level of elevation is the act of self-nullification. For the only way one can attain a degree of infinite elevation is to totally nullify oneself before G-d, thereby freeing oneself from the limiting encumbrances of one's previous level.[7]

This, then, is the inner meaning of a guard-rail. The protective and preventive measures — the "guard-rail" — that the person undertakes in the course of his spiritual service are an expression of his self-abnegation and acceptance of the Heavenly Yoke. This enables him to be a fit vessel to the *"new* home."

There is a practical lesson in this: A person should not shut himself off from the rest of the world; he must build a

---

5. See *Tanchuma, Naso* 16; *Tanya* beginning of ch. 36.
6. See *Sefer HoArochim-Chabad I*, entry titled *Ahavas HaShem — HaHosafah Sh'bah Al Yedei Hanefesh HaB'hamis* Ch. 4, and places cited there, *et al.*
7. See *Torah Or* 6c; *Hemshech 5666* p. 12ff, p.18ff, *et al.*

"home," a dwelling place, for G-d in this nethermost world. For it is only through the descent within this world that the ultimate and truly new ascent is accomplished, Above as well as below.

On the other hand, one must know that in order to transform the physical into a vessel for G-dliness, a person must make a guard-rail — he must remain apart from the physical world's grossness and corporeality. While it is true that he must busy himself with physical things, they should remain insignificant to him; he knows and feels that the only reason he occupies himself with corporeality is in order to fulfill the Divine intent of transforming this world into a home for G-d.[8]

Based on Likkutei Sichos Vol. XIX, pp. 208-214.

---

8. See also *Likkutei Sichos* X, p. 103ff.

Marriage & Divorce — Divine Style

The vast majority of laws relating to Jewish marriage and divorce are derived from verses in the Torah portion *Seitzei*.[1]

The relationship between husbands and wives is similar to the relationship between G-d and the Jewish people. It thus follows that marriage and divorce as experienced between mortal spouses derives from the "marriage" and the so-called "divorce" between G-d and the Jewish people.

The marriage of G-d and the Jewish people took place when He gave them the Torah, as the *Mishnah* states:[2] "'The day of His marriage' — this refers to *Mattan Torah*."

Although according to Jewish law betrothal requires an act by the groom, i.e., the groom gives the bride an object of value and states: "You are consecrated to me...," this act

---

1. *Devarim* 24:1 and onward.
2. *Ta'anis* 26b. See also *Bamidbar Rabbah* 12:8.

must have the full consent of the bride; a woman cannot be married against her will.[3]

The same was true with regard to G-d's betrothal and marriage of the Jewish people when He gave them the Torah: G-d revealed His great love to the Jewish people in order to rouse their love for Him,[4] so that the Jewish people would *desire* to be "married" to Him. Although this love for G-d resulted from G-d's arousal of the emotion within them, and did not come about of the Jews' own volition, it had so profound an effect on them that their love for Him became part and parcel of their very being.

Thus the *Rambam* states as a point of law[5] that *every* Jew, even one who is on an extremely low spiritual level, "desires to perform all the *mitzvos* and distance himself from transgressions." It is simply that this desire is sometimes concealed and must be brought to the fore.

Just as the Jewish people's love for G-d permeates their being, and is always whole and absolute, so too with regard to His love for them: it permeates *His* entire essence, as it were, and something that is part of one's essence is not subject to change.

This blissful state of marriage between G-d and the Jewish people existed until the period of exile, at which time there came about a state of "divorce," as the *Gemara* records:[6] "The Jewish people responded to the prophet with a telling rejoinder...'A woman who was divorced by her husband — can one party possibly then complain about [the conduct of] the other?' "

This means to say that since during times of exile, G-d is not found in a revealed manner among the Jewish people; it is as if He had divorced them.

---

3. *Kiddushin* 2b; *Tur* and *Shulchan Aruch* ibid., beginning of section 42.
4. *Torah Or* 98d.
5. *Hilchos Geirushin* conclusion of ch. 2.
6. *Sanhedrin* 105a. See also *Yirmeyahu* 3:8: "I sent her away and gave her her bill of divorce"; *Psichta* of *Eicha Rabbah* 4: "They were punished by divorce."

In truth, however, G-d's love for the Jews is so essential to His being that even when this love is suppressed to the extent that He metaphorically "divorces" them, He is still very much with them; the "divorce" is not really a divorce at all. Truly, it is nothing but a temporary separation, which He will rectify when He once again reveals His essential love for them; remarriage will not be necessary.

Accordingly it is to be understood that the "temporary separation" engendered by exile reveals a depth of the relationship between G-d and the Jewish people that is even more profound than that revealed prior to the "divorce."

Before the estrangement, one could have thought that the connection between G-d and the Jewish people was predicated upon their performance of Torah and *mitzvos*. When we observe, however, that during periods of exile, when the Jewish people are wanting in their performance of Torah and *mitzvos*, G-d loves them all the same, this proves that His love is not based on any external factor, but is truly an intrinsic and essential love.

Based on *Likkutei Sichos* Vol. IX, pp. 143-150.

Savo   תבוא

The Connection Between Savo and Chai Elul

The eighteenth day of *Elul*, or *Chai Elul*, marks the birthdate of both the Baal Shem Tov,[1] founder of the Chassidic
movement, and the Alter Rebbe,[2] founder of Chabad Chas-
sidism. This day invariably falls either on or near the Shabbos during which the Torah portion of *Savo* is read.

All Jewish festivals and auspicious occasions on the
Jewish calendar are alluded to in the Torah portion read
during the week when they occur.[3] Understandably, *Chai
Elul* is thus alluded to in the portion of *Savo*.

Where in this portion can one find this connection?

Savo begins by relating the laws of *Bikurim*, the first
fruits that the Jews were obliged to bring immediately upon
"coming to the land that G-d your L-rd is giving you as a
heritage, occupying and settling it."[4]

Our Rabbis note[5] that the qualification "occupying and
settling it" comes to teach us that the obligation of *Bikurim*
did not begin until after the 14 years during which *Eretz Yisrael* was conquered and divided among the tribes.

The verse is modified in this way for the following reason: The true meaning of "coming to the land" is that of
coming into it *entirely*. This is in keeping with the saying of
our Sages:[6] "A partial entry is not considered an entry at all."
The word "coming,"[7] therefore means "occupying and set-

---

1. In the year 5458 (1698).
2. In the year 5505 (1745).
3. *Shaloh, Cheilek Torah SheBiksav* beginning of Torah portion *Vayeishev*.
4. *Devarim* 26:1.
5. *Zevachim* 118b.
6. *Chulin* 33b.
7. See *Kiddushin* 37b.

tling it," for only then were the Jews considered to have truly entered the Land.

This, then, is the connection between *Savo* and *Chai Elul*, the birthdate of the two great Chassidic founders:

Chassidus is unique in its ability to rouse the spirit, mind and heart so that a Jew's service of Torah and *mitzvos* is in the manner of *savo* — a complete immersion, with every fibre of one's being suffused by spiritual service.

The importance of this manner of service will be understood by explaining the difference between man's intrinsic and extrinsic states of being; intrinsic referring to man as he exists in relation to himself and extrinsic to man as he exists relative to others.

In terms of spiritual service, this means the following: When a person does something in an external and extrinsic manner, he and the thing he is doing remain two distinct entities.

When, however, a person does something from his innermost self, then his being immerses itself in that which he is doing, for in relation to man's innermost core there exists nothing outside of himself. Thus, when a person acts in this manner, even a specific, seemingly external, action is tied up and united with his innermost self; he and the act are united.

Herein lies that which is unique about Chassidus: Chassidus, as part of "the soul of Torah,"[8] reveals a Jew's quintessential life force in all aspects of Torah and *mitzvos*,[9] and the unique quality of this life force is that it totally unites with that which it enlivens.[10]

For the life force does not add anything to that which it vitalizes — a live body possesses no more parts than a dead corpse. The life force is thus not separate from that which it energizes, rather it is the *soul* of the enlivened body, and

---

8. *Zohar III* 152a.
9. See *On the Essence of Chassidus*, ch. 6 and onward. See also *Sefer HaMa'amarim 5708* p. 295ff.
10. See *Ki Imcha 5700* ch. 2; *Yichayeinu 5701* ch. 2, *et al.*

because of it each and every aspect of the body is a living entity.

The reason is that a person's "life" is his soul and innermost essence, and as explained earlier, that which is part of a person's innermost core becomes wholly one with the object with which it unites. Thus, the body in which a life force dwells is entirely permeated by it.[11]

Exactly so is the effect of Chassidus on Torah and *mitzvos*: It is possible for a Jew to study Torah and perform *mitzvos* while remaining separate from them. Chassidus, however, enables every Jew to reveal the innermost aspect of his life force — his holy Jewish soul. And in relation to that level — the quality of *savo* — each and every Jew is truly one with all of Torah and *mitzvos*.[12]

Based on Likkutei Sichos Vol. XIX, pp. 244-247.

---

11. See *Hemshech Te'erav* ch. 210.
12. See also *Likkutei Torah, Behar* 40b-d.

The Bikurim Offering and Declaration

The portion *Savo* opens with the commandment of *Bikurim*, the first fruit offering. During the offering ceremony, the person bringing the fruit would say:[1] "An Aramean [Lavan] tried to destroy my father [Yaakov]... he descended to Egypt... G-d brought us out from Egypt with a mighty hand ... He brought us to this area... I am now bringing the first fruit of the land that G-d has given me."

Ostensibly, the reason for mentioning G-d's rescue of Yaakov from Lavan's clutches and the miracle of the Exodus was to thank G-d for His many kindnesses,[2] these kind-

---

1. *Devarim* 26:5-9.
2. *Rashi* 26:5.

nesses culminating in His giving the Jews "this land flowing with milk and honey."[3]

However, if the purpose were merely to enumerate G-d's many acts of goodness toward the former slaves, why not also mention His splitting of the sea, His providing them with manna, and the many other things that enabled the Jews to survive in the desert for 40 years?

We must conclude that the saving of Yaakov from Lavan and the extrication of the Jewish people from Egypt are singularly connected to the commandment of *Bikurim*. What is the connection?

The obligation to bring *Bikurim* only began after the Jewish people entered *Eretz Yisrael* and settled the Land, as our Sages note[4] that the *mitzvah* of *Bikurim* only began after the 14 years during which *Eretz Yisrael* was conquered and divided among the tribes.

We thus discern that the bringing of *Bikurim* served not only to offer thanks for the actual gift of *Eretz Yisrael*, but more importantly for the fact that the Jewish people were now settled there in a permanent manner, for only then did they experience the true joy of being residents in their own land, fully enjoying the fruits thereof.

In order to emphasize this, the person bringing *Bikurim* was to remember those permanent places of residence in which our ancestors found things going so badly that they were faced with extinction. Thus, Aram and Egypt are particularly noted, for it was there that our ancestors lived on a permanent basis — 20 years in Aram and 210 years in Egypt — and were faced with extinction.

This also explains why the declaration recited while bringing *Bikurim* focuses more on the Jewish experience in Egypt and the subsequent Exodus than on Yaakov's experience with Lavan, for it was specifically in Egypt — not in Aram — that the Jewish people found themselves for so many generations.

---

3. *Devarim* ibid.
4. *Zevachim* 118b.

On a deeper level, the answer as to why only these two events are mentioned in the *Bikurim* recitation is as follows:

Chassidus explains[5] that a tree's fruit is analogous to the soul clothed within a body. The command of *Bikurim* involves uniting the soul as it is found below with its source Above, this being known as Supernal *Bikurim*.

More specifically, the offering of *Bikurim* entails the elevation of the lower level to the higher one, while the recitation of the verses that accompany the *Bikurim* offering alludes to the drawing down of G-dliness from Above, i.e., the soul's source Above illuminates and unites with the soul below.

Both Lavan and Egypt are thus mentioned during the *Bikurim* recitation, for both entailed a spiritual descent, inasmuch as Yaakov's descent to Lavan as well as the Jews' descent to Egypt (and thereafter G-d's descent into Egypt to liberate them) are perfect examples of a higher level descending to a lower one.

There is a lesson here for all of us: A person should not be content with merely serving G-d through his own elevation by Torah and prayer. Rather, he must also draw down G-dliness into the world, even unto the choicest matters therein — just as *Bikurim* was brought from the choicest of fruit[6] — thereby transforming physical reality into a vessel for G-dliness.

Based on *Likkutei Sichos* Vol. XIV, pp. 93-98.

---

5. *Or HaTorah, Savo* p. 1040ff.
6. *Rambam* conclusion of *Hilchos Isurei Mizbeiach*.

Nitzavim   נצבים

Freedom of Choice, and Choosing Freely

One of the central themes of Judaism is Free Choice. This issue is addressed at some length in the concluding verses of the Torah portion *Nitzavim*,[1] where we are told: "...I have set before you [a free choice] between life and good, and death and evil... I have placed before you life and death, the blessing and the curse.... Choose life."

What, exactly, impels a Jew to freely choose good over evil?

The Jew's choice of good over evil, sacred over mundane, is rooted in the fact that the essence of a Jew's soul is one with G-d.[2] Indeed, the power possessed by every Jew to choose freely — "man being like one of Us"[3] and able to freely act as he chooses, just as G-d can freely do exactly as He pleases[4] — lies in the fact that his soul is rooted in G-d.

Although the soul's essence has no desire other than G-dliness, the soul has descended to be clothed within a physical body, and as a result it is possible for it to choose something other than goodness and holiness.[5]

Moreover, even as the soul exists in its pristine state, the concept of Free Choice still applies, in the sense that there is not any particular benefit or merit that compels the soul to choose G-d; it does so freely because its essence is one, as it were, with Him.

When choice results from reason it is inherently limited — the choice only goes so far as the reason. Since man's rea-

---

1. *Devarim* 30:15-20.
2. *Kvod Malchuscha 5660;* Conclusion of *Hemshech Tik'u 5670.*
3. See *Bereishis* 3:22.
4. See *Rambam, Hilchos Teshuvah* beginning of ch. 5; *Likkutei Torah, Emor* 38b.
5. See *Likkutei Torah* ibid.

son is intrinsically limited, his reasoned free choice is necessarily limited as well. Thus, when the soul's essence chooses G-d because of something that transcends reason, the intensity of this choice is limitless.

Moreover, it may be argued that when choice comes as a result of logic, then it is not truly *free* after all; the person was compelled to act by force of logic. For the compulsion of logic is just as strong, if not stronger, than brute force.[6]

When, however, the soul's essence desires and chooses G-d because of its own intrinsic being, then the choice is such that anything other than G-dliness and goodness is utterly negated.[7]

While rooted in the soul's essence, freedom of choice is *revealed* on a conscious level ˙in man's intellect,[8] for only when a Jew actually has before him the two paths of good and evil and chooses good is it apparent that he freely chose good and G-dliness over evil and unholiness. Intellect, and intellect alone, has the capacity to find merit in each of the two paths.

Accordingly, the connection between Free Choice and the Torah reading is readily understood: *Nitzavim* always precedes *Rosh HaShanah,* at which time we endeavor to arouse within G-d a desire to choose the Jewish people. This is expressed in the verse recited before the blowing of the *shofar* on *Rosh HaShanah:* "He *chooses* our heritage for us, the glory of Jacob, whom He loves eternally."[9]

Here, too, there are two aspects to G-d's decision. There is no basis in reason for G-d's choice of the Jewish people. So penetrating and meaningful is this choice that G-d says: "I cannot possibly exchange them for any other people,"[10] for there exists "Israel and the King alone."[11]

---

6. See *Likkutei Sichos IV* p. 1309.
7. See *Likkutei Sichos* ibid., p. 1341, *XI* p. 7 fn. 58.
8. See places cited in fn. 2. See also *Likkutei Torah, Nitzavim* 46c; *Likkutei Sichos VI* p. 113 fn. 47.
9. *Tehillim* 47:5.
10. Introduction to *Rus Rabbah* 3. Cf. *Pesachim* 87a and onward.
11. See *Zohar III* 32a.

Yet this choice is *revealed* in this world when we see that the Jews have become "G-d's treasure from the *midst of all the nations*"[12] — other nations exist alongside the Jewish nation, and yet He chooses us, thereby making His love for us revealed to all.[13]

Rosh HaShanah is the day when everything returns to its primordial state,[14] and thus G-d must choose us anew. When we choose G-d, not only logically but also because of our soul's essence, then He in turn is moved to choose and reveal His choice of us as "His treasured nation," manifesting this decision by showering us with all manner of good.

Based on *Likkutei Sichos* Vol. XIX, pp. 274-282.

---

12. *Shmos* 19:5.
13. See commentary of *Rashi* on *Shmos* ibid. See also *Tanya* ch. 49.
14. *Pri Etz Chayim, Sha'ar Rosh HaShanah* ch. 1; *Likkutei Torah, Nitzavim* 51b; *Siddur Im Dach* 244d and onward, *et al.*

Motivations for Repentance

In the Torah portion *Nitzavim* we read:[1] "There shall come a time when you shall experience all the words of blessing and curse that I have presented to you, and you will reflect on the situation... You will then return to G-d your L-rd... with all your heart and all your soul."

It is clear from the above, as well as from the further verses, that every Jew will ultimately return to G-d in complete repentance; even one who has strayed far from the path of righteousness will "return to G-d" upon experiencing "all the words of... curse."

Accordingly, we must understand the verse's intent when it states "all the words of *blessing*." It is understandable that curse and misfortune can lead a person to broken-

---

1. *Devarim* 30:1-2.

MOTIVATIONS FOR REPENTANCE

heartedness and repentance. But how does experiencing "blessing" rouse an individual to repentance?[2]

The Torah speaks here of repentance that is so intense that it leads a person to return to G-d "with all his heart and soul." Understandably, the factor that induces a person to repent so mightily — his feeling of pain emanating from the curse — must itself be extremely powerful. What makes the pain so intense?

The Torah explains by stating "you shall experience *all* the words of blessing and curse," i.e., the detailed fulfillment of the curse will come *after* having first experienced the blessing.

Experiencing misfortune after having first experienced a period of blessing is far more painful than never having experienced goodness at all. For example, a person who was once rich and then became a pauper feels the pain of poverty far more than does an individual who has always been poor.

Thus, it is specifically through blessing followed by curse that a person can reach so lofty a degree of repentance that he will return with "all his heart and all his soul."

But this raises another question: The verse is explaining how G-d will bring *each and every* Jew to full repentance. But if this degree of repentance can only be reached when blessing precedes curse, how then can a person who has known only the curse attain full repentance?

Earlier on the Torah states[3] — according to *Rashi's* commentary — "Behold I [immediately] place before you a blessing.... Blessing so that you fulfill [the condition of obeying] the commandments.... " G-d starts off every Jew with blessing.

Thus, every Jew began his life with blessing. The complete repentance that comes only when blessing precedes curse is therefore available to all those who are in need of repentance.

---

2. See commentaries of *Shach* and *Orach Chayim* ibid.
3. Ibid. 11:26-27.

The above also relates to the days that precede *Rosh Ha-Shanah*, "the day of great judgment," during which the portion of *Nitzavim* is read.

G-d promises to provide *all* Jews with blessing, regardless of their spiritual station, adding only that *everlasting* blessing is dependent on a person's fulfilling the commandments.

The reason for G-d's generosity is plain: Each and every Jew is likened not only to a prince[4] but also to a king[5]; they are therefore eminently entitled to receive all manner of good.

As the *Gemara* states[6] with regard to feeding Jewish laborers: "Even if you were to provide them with a repast that equals [King] Shlomoh's during his heyday, you have still not fulfilled your obligation, for they are children of Avraham, Yitzchak and Yaakov." Since "That which G-d commands the Jewish people to do He does as well,"[7] He surely provides the Jewish people with all manner of good.

Surely, each and every Jew then fulfills the condition of obeying the commandments, and G-d's blessings will last forever.

This ensures that, come *Rosh HaShanah*, a person will engage in *Teshuvah Ila'ah*, the superior level of repentance wherein the individual's spirit reunites with G-d in a joyful manner.[8] Especially so when the first day of *Rosh HaShanah* falls on *Shabbos*, so that the service of *Shabbos* is that of *Teshuvah Ila'ah* — a degree of *Teshuvah* that is performed with great joy.[9]

Based on *Likkutei Sichos* Vol. XIV, pp. 118-121.

4. *Shabbos* 67a; *Zohar I* 27b.
5. *Berachos* 9b; Introduction to *Tikkunei Zohar* 1b.
6. *Bava Metzia* 83a.
7. *Shmos Rabbah* 30:9.
8. *Likkutei Torah*, beginning of portion *Ha'azinu*.
9. *Iggeres HaTeshuvah* ch. 11.

Rosh HaShanah   ראש השנה

Coronation, Teshuvah and Shofar

In commenting on the verse, "Seek the L-rd while He may be found, call upon Him while He is near,"[1] our Rabbis note:[2] "These are the ten days between Rosh HaShanah and Yom Kippur." These days are commonly referred to as the *Aseres Yimei Teshuvah*, the "Ten Days of Penitence."

This comment needs to be clarified: "*Between* Rosh Ha-Shanah and Yom Kippur" implies that Rosh HaShanah and Yom Kippur are not part of the ten-day count,[3] while "These are the *ten days...*" makes it clear that Rosh HaShanah and Yom Kippur are indeed included, inasmuch as there are only seven days between Rosh HaShanah and Yom Kippur.

Evidently, Rosh HaShanah and Yom Kippur possess aspects of penitence which cause them to be included within the "Ten Days of Penitence."

In addition to the above, we find yet another aspect to Rosh HaShanah: "The *mitzvah* of the day is the sounding of the shofar."[4]

What is the relationship between the three above-mentioned aspects of Rosh HaShanah, and what is the order of their spirituality?

Clearly, the essential aspect of Rosh HaShanah precedes all else. Moreover, since the *mitzvah* of *Teshuvah* transcends all other *mitzvos* (for *Teshuvah* is able to rectify one's failure to perform the other *mitzvos*), it follows that *Teshuvah* precedes the *mitzvah* of the day — the sounding of the shofar.

---

1. *Yeshayahu* 55:6.
2. *Rosh HaShanah* 18a.
3. See *Ta'anis* 5a; *S'dei Chemed, Klalim* 2:72.
4. *Rosh HaShanah* 27a.

But what exactly is the fundamental aspect of Rosh Ha-
Shanah? The *Gemara* explains[5] that it consists of crowning
G-d as our King. Until that is accomplished, no service of
mitzvos can take place, for "First accept My Kingship and
then [you can] accept My decrees."[6] It also follows that
Teshuvah — the purpose of which is to rectify any shortcom-
ings in the performance of the King's decrees — can also
come about only after accepting G-d's Kingship.

In terms of spiritual accomplishment: Performing G-d's
decrees results in an attachment to G-d's revealed will.
Teshuvah also relates to Divine will, since repentance for
failing to perform G-d's will is not applicable to that level of
service which transcends will. Accepting G-d's reign and
dominion, however, brings an attachment to Him that
eclipses every level of revelation.

The above factors also serve to indicate the importance
of the Jewish people, since it is they who are able to attain an
absolute degree of unification with G-d, which in turn enables them to elicit from Him a desire to reign over the
world as a whole and the Jewish people in particular.

All this is alluded to by the holiday being named *Rosh
HaShanah*, "*head* of the year," rather than simply "*beginning
of the year*":[7]

It is termed "head" because the head possesses the following qualities: a) It is far superior to and removed from all
other bodily parts; b) The head contains and encompasses
the life force that animates the rest of the body; c) The head
constantly monitors and directs all other parts of the living
organism.

These three qualities are also found within *Rosh HaShanah*, the "*head* of the year":

Just as the head is superior in quality to the rest of the
body, so too is the essential aspect of Rosh HaShanah — ac-

---

5. *Rosh HaShanah* 16a, 34a.
6. See *Mechiltah, Shmos* 20:3; *Toras Kohanim, Acharei* ch. 13; *Yalkut Shimoni, Shmos*
    ibid.
7. See *Likkutei Torah, Savo* 41c; beginning of *Ateres Rosh.*

ceptance of G-d's reign and kingdom, a level of service that achieves total unification with G-d Himself — superior to the spiritual service of the rest of the year.

Precisely as the head encompasses and provides life to the rest of the body while retaining it loftiness, so does the *Teshuvah* of Rosh HaShanah have a connection to *mitzvos*, while retaining its superiority to them and encompassing them all.

And the good resolutions and the *mitzvah* of Shofar on Rosh HaShanah affects the performance of *mitzvos* the whole year through — exactly as the head directs all other aspects of the body.

Based on *Likkutei Sichos* Vol. IV, pp. 1144-1146.

Vayeilech   וילך

Vayeilech and Yom Kippur —
Revealing Divine Kingship and Jewish Unity

The Torah portion *Nitzavim* is always read prior to Rosh HaShanah[1]. When the portion *Vayeilech* is separated from *Nitzavim* and is read separately, it will be read on the Shabbos before Yom Kippur. This indicates that the portion *Vayeilech* is related to Yom Kippur.

What is the relationship?

Rosh HaShanah and Yom Kippur share a common theme: the arousal within G-d of a desire to choose the Jewish people as His subjects. Jews are thus inscribed and sealed for a new year filled with all manner of revealed and palpable good. The two days differ however, in that only the *inscription* for the new year occurs on Rosh HaShanah, while the actual *sealing* — the culmination of the process begun on Rosh HaShanah — takes places on Yom Kippur.[2]

The Alter Rebbe explains the connection of *Nitzavim* to *Rosh HaShanah* in this way:[3] As previously mentioned, Rosh HaShanah is when G-d extends His kingship and dominion over the Jewish people.[4] This is accomplished when Jews unite so that they are all as one.[5]

This concept of Jewish unity is also at the heart of the opening statement of *Nitzavim*: "Today you are all standing before G-d your L-rd — your leaders, your tribal chiefs... your woodcutters and water drawers."[6] The verse tells us

---

1. *Rambam, Hilchos Tefilah* 13:2; *Tur* and *Shulchan Aruch, Orach Chayim 428.*
2. See *Rosh HaShanah* 16a-b.
3. *Likkutei Torah*, beginning of the Torah portion *Nitzavim*.
4. *Rosh HaShanah* 16a; ibid. 34b.
5. *Likkutei Torah* ibid.
6. *Devarim* 29:1.

that, notwithstanding the different levels of individual Jews, all stand united before G-d.

This aspect of Jewish unity is also the focal point of *Vayeilech*. The portion begins by saying that "Moshe went and spoke the following words to *all* Israel,"[7] i.e., he spoke to all Jews in an identical fashion. The portion concludes with Moshe addressing "the entire assembly of Israel"[8] — all of them together in a united manner.

Moreover, the commandments taught in *Vayeilech* — *Hakhel* and the writing of a *Sefer Torah* — are *mitzvos* that stress the unity of the Jewish people.

"*Hakhel* — Gather together the people"[9] encompasses all Jews "men, women, children and proselytes"[10] — equally. Indeed, that is why this commandment is termed *Hakhel*, which means "congregation." In this case, those who congregate lose their individual identity and form an entirely new totality.

Writing a *Sefer Torah*, too, stresses the concept of unity, for while Jews differ greatly in their comprehension of Torah, all are equal with regard to writing a *Sefer Torah*.

Although the theme of both *Nitzavim* and *Vayeilech* is Jewish unity, there is a difference between these two Torah readings. As mentioned earlier, Rosh HaShanah and Yom Kippur share a common feature, namely, the arousal within G-d of a desire to choose the Jewish people as His subjects. This theme begins on Rosh HaShanah, continues throughout the Ten Days of Penitence, and culminates on Yom Kippur.

The difference between Rosh HaShanah and Yom Kippur in this regard will help us understand the differences in the unity of the Jewish people as expressed in *Nitzavim* and as expressed in *Vayeilech*.

Rosh HaShanah accomplishes Divine Kingship at its supernal source, while Yom Kippur completes the drawing

---

7. Ibid. 31:1.
8. Ibid. verse 30.
9. Ibid. verse 12.
10. Ibid.

down of this aspect so that it will be revealed in this world. Since all this is accomplished through Jewish unity, it follows that the same differences will exist with regard to Jewish unity.

Jewish unity on Rosh HaShanah is mainly that of Jews united Above — in their source and root; Yom Kippur expresses this unity down here below. Because of this, Jewish unity is expressed on Yom Kippur physically as well as spiritually.

Consider: There is no difference among Jews with regard to their observance of the Five Afflictions on Yom Kippur — the prohibition against eating, drinking, etc. Differences may exist between the performance of a good deed by a righteous person and the performance of the same deed by a simple person. However, with regard to a prohibitive command — not to eat, drink, etc. — all Jews are equal in their observance.

Herein lies the difference between *Nitzavim* and *Vayeilech*. While both address the theme of Jewish unity, *Nitzavim* speaks of uniting disparate levels of Jews, while the unity spoken of in *Vayeilech* is such that all Jews are addressed equally.

Based on *Likkutei Sichos* Vol. XIX, pp. 298-304.

Ha'azinu   הַאֲזִינוּ

Teshuvah, Torah, and Mitzvos —
Essence, Heaven, and Earth

The Torah reading of *Ha'azinu* opens with Moshe's words: "Listen heaven and I will speak; hear earth the words of my mouth."[1] With these words Moshe called upon heaven and earth to bear witness concerning his admonitions and exhortations in the "Song of *Ha'azinu*" regarding the Jews' performance of Torah and *mitzvos*.[2]

Sifri[3] offers the following reasons for Moshe's selection of heaven and earth as witnesses:

a) " 'Listen heaven' — because Torah was given from heaven; 'hear earth' — because upon it the Jewish people stood when they [accepted the Torah and] said 'All that G-d spoke we shall obey and hear.' "

b) " 'Listen heaven' — they did not perform those commandments that are bound up with [the astronomical calculations of] "heaven," namely, adding a leap month and establishing the beginning of new months; 'hear earth' — they did not perform those commandments that are bound up with earth, namely, Gleanings, Forgotten Sheaves...."

c) " 'Listen heaven' — they did not perform any of the commandments that are bound up with "heaven"; 'hear earth' — they did not perform any of the commandments that are bound up with the earth."

Torah and *mitzvos* were, of course, given by G-d, who is infinitely higher than either heaven or earth. In seeking to encourage a more perfect obedience to G-d's will, it seems logical to stress that Torah and *mitzvos* were given by Him,

---

1. *Devarim* 32:1.
2. *Rashi* ibid.
3. Ibid.

rather than focusing on the fact that they are connected to heaven and earth. Why the emphasis on heaven and earth?

A Jew is expected to serve G-d in two opposite ways: on one hand he is expected to serve with pure and simple faith and with acceptance of the Heavenly Yoke — elements that derive from the soul's essence. On the other hand, his service must permeate his intellect and emotions so that they too understand and experience G-dliness.

In practical terms, this means that a Jew is to draw down and connect his soul's essence with his inner powers, so that not only does he serve G-d in thought, word and deed out of simple faith, but he also comprehends G-dliness in his mind and loves and fears Him in his heart.

Moreover, a Jew is expected not only to serve G-d in the general and ongoing manner of regular Torah and *mitzvos*, but also through repentance, *teshuvah*. This level of service — a level that emanates from the soul's essence and seeks the innermost aspect of G-dliness — must permeate a person's intellect and emotion as well.

This is why when Moshe desired to rouse the Jews to the service of Torah and *mitzvos*, the performance of which was to reflect not only pure faith but the inner powers of intellect and emotion, he mentioned that Torah and *mitzvos* were given *through* heaven and earth.

He did this in order to arouse within Jews *their* level of heaven and earth, i.e., their loftier inner powers of intellect and thought which are likened to heaven,[4] and the lesser powers of emotions, speech and action which are likened to earth.

These three levels — the soul's essence, the soul's "heaven," and the soul's "earth" — find general expression in the three manners of *teshuvah*: (1) an expression of the soul's essence, (2) the service of Torah study — an expression of the soul's intellect, and (3) the performance of *mitzvos* — an expression of the soul's "earthy" aspect.

---

4. *Likkutei Torah, D'rushei Shabbos Shuvah* 64c.

It is to these forms of service that the *Sifri* alludes in its three commentaries. The first comment of the *Sifri* speaks of service the mainstay of which is intellect and "heaven." The second comment speaks of the performance of *mitzvos* concerning which we say that "action is what is most important" — the level of "earth." The third comment speaks of *teshuvah*, for which reason *Sifri* states: "they did not perform *any* of the commandments" — a sorry state of affairs that necessitates *teshuvah*, which emanates from the soul's very essence.

Based on *Likkutei Sichos* Vol. IV, pp. 1154-1158.

Ha'azinu   האזינו

Shabbos Teshuvah   שבת תשובה

The Teshuvah of Shabbos Teshuvah

The Torah portion *Ha'azinu* begins with Moshe saying:[1] "Listen heaven and I will speak; hear earth the words of my mouth." The *Sifri* notes[2] that concerning heaven Moshe used an expression denoting closeness, *ha'azinu*, while regarding earth he used an expression indicating distance, *v'sishma*, for Moshe was "close to heaven and distant from earth."

All of Torah serves to instruct each and every Jew. Since it tells *us* "listen heaven and hear earth," it is evident that like Moshe, we are expected to become "close to heaven and distant from earth." How are we to reach so rarefied a level?

Ha'azinu is often read on the Shabbos between Rosh Ha-Shanah and Yom Kippur, a Shabbos known as "*Shabbos Teshuvah*," a "Shabbos of Repentance."

The simple reason for the name is that this Shabbos falls within the *Aseres Yimei Teshuvah*, the "Ten Days of Peni-tence." However, since every aspect of Torah is extremely precise, it is to be understood that the name "*Shabbos Teshu-vah*" serves to indicate that *Shabbos* enhances repentance, so that the *Teshuvah* of this Shabbos is superior to the *Teshuvah* of the other "Ten Days of Penitence."

What is the connection between *Shabbos* and a superior form of *Teshuvah*?

The Alter Rebbe explains[3] that the *Teshuvah* of *Aseres Yimei Teshuvah* involves the soul's essence, while *Teshuvah* during the rest of the year involves only the soul's internal

---

1. *Devarim* 32:1.
2. Beginning of *Ha'azinu*.
3. *Likkutei Torah, Savo* 43d

powers. Thus, the former period of *Teshuvah* is far superior to the latter.

These two times for *Teshuvah* also correspond to the two general levels of repentance, the lower level — whose purpose is to rectify man's sins, and the higher level — which sees the soul returning and cleaving to its Source.[4]

In a general sense, these two forms of *Teshuvah* are mirrored in the difference between spiritual service during the week and spiritual service on Shabbos: During the week man is involved in mundane affairs, seeking to elevate the physical world to holiness. This corresponds to the lower level of repentance, in which the service is that of reuniting the soul's internal powers with G-dliness.

On Shabbos, however, mundane labor is prohibited, for the sanctity of the day is such that man transcends the physical; his labor on that day involves achieving ever-higher levels within the framework of holiness.[5]

Thus the *Teshuvah* of Shabbos is the loftier level of *Teshuvah*, whereby the soul is elevated and cleaves to its Source.[6] The superiority inherent in the *Teshuvah* of "*Shabbos Teshuvah*" as compared to repentance during the other days of the "Ten Days of Penitence" will be understood accordingly:

The seven days between Rosh HaShanah and Yom Kippur correspond to the seven weekdays of the entire past year; each day of the seven rectifies the misdeeds committed on that weekday in the year just past, with Sunday rectifying for all past Sundays, Monday for all Mondays, etc.

Therefore, although the *entire* period of the *Aseres Yimei Teshuvah* involves the superior form of *Teshuvah*, nevertheless, since the weekdays of the *Aseres Yimei Teshuvah* involve atonement for the *weekdays* of the past year, it follows that the weekday *Teshuvah* is not the loftiest form.

Shabbos, however, is the *Teshuvah* for past Shabbasos, which themselves are inherently superior in service and

---

4. *Iggeres HaTeshuvah*, ch. 8ff; *Likkutei Torah*, beginning of *Ha'azinu*.
5. *Torah Or* 13a, 65b-c, 113a; *Likkutei Torah*, *Balak* 72a and onward.
6. *Iggeres HaTeshuvah*, ch. 10; *Likkutei Torah*, *Shabbos Shuvah* 66c.

Teshuvah. It therefore follows that the *Teshuvah* of *Shabbos Teshuvah* is the loftiest of all the *Aseres Yimei Teshuvah.*

It is the attainment of this level on Shabbos Teshuvah that enables each and every Jew to be like Moshe — "close to heaven and distant from earth."

Based on Likkutei Sichos Vol. XIV, pp. 143-147.

Sukkos   סוכות

Yom Tov, Chol HaMoed & Shabbos Chol HaMoed

Our Sages call all Jewish holidays "Festivals for Rejoicing."[1] Nevertheless, Sukkos is the only festival designated as
"The Season of our Rejoicing."[2]

We thus understand that there are different degrees of
joy, and that the joy of Sukkos — "The Season of our Rejoicing" — possesses the greatest degree of all. Moreover, the
joy that accompanies Sukkos is a revealed and palpable
dimension of joy. This may be seen from the fact that the
term "Season of our Rejoicing" was established by the Rabbis to be part of our holiday prayers — something performed by all Jews. Thus, the additional measure of joy present during Sukkos is felt by even the humblest Jew.

Furthermore, during the time of the *Beis HaMikdash*,
when the physical world enjoyed a greater degree of spiritual refinement, the greater degree of Sukkos joy permeated
the physical world.

The festival of Sukkos is also known as *Chag HaAsif*, the
"Festival of Ingathering," for it also celebrates the gathering
of the harvest. And during the time of the *Beis HaMikdash*,
with "Every person under his grape arbor and fig tree," the
bountiful harvest caused a palpable joy.

That the world's physical refinement enabled spirituality
to take a more concrete form was indicated by the fact that
physical offerings were brought when the *Beis HaMikdash*
was standing, while nowadays prayer acts in their stead.
Here too, the reason is that during times of exile the physical
world is less refined, so we cannot serve G-d by bringing
physical offerings, for the physical is now too coarse.

---

1. Text of *Amidah* & *Kiddush*.
2. Ibid.

SUKKOS

Although the joy of reaping the harvest experienced on Sukkos existed in its physical sense only during the times of the *Beis HaMikdash*, the *spiritual* aspect of reaping exists today. For the holiday of Sukkos follows close on the heels of the month of *Elul* and the awesome time of Rosh HaShanah, Yom Kippur, and the Ten Days of Penitence. The Jew's service during this most important period in the Jewish calendar results in a bountiful spiritual harvest during the festival of Sukkos.

Although all of Sukkos is the "Season of our Rejoicing," the emotion felt on the actual *Yom Tov* days of Sukkos is greater than that felt on *Chol HaMoed*, the intermediate days. This is readily understandable when one considers that the only labor permitted on *Yom Tov* is that which relates to the preparation of food for the day. Since the gratification is immediate, this hardly constitutes true *labor*, for the individual is instantly recompensed by pleasure.

This is not so with regard to the labor permitted during *Chol HaMoed*: during that period, all types of essential labor — *Davar Ha'Avud* — are permitted, even if gratification will only come in the distant future.

Thus, during *Chol HaMoed* the individual cannot possibly be as joyous as on *Yom Tov*, for his preoccupation with toil keeps him from fully enjoying the festival.

But this is only true of the weekdays of *Chol HaMoed*. When *Shabbos Chol HaMoed* comes, all labor is prohibited - even that which is permitted on *Yom Tov* — and joy is once again heightened. Moreover, the joy attainable then is even greater than that attainable on *Yom Tov* itself. This is because the pleasure and delight obtained through labor permissible on *Yom Tov* is found on Shabbos as a matter of course — on Shabbos "All of one's labor has been completed." Additionally, Shabbos delight is engendered without any need for labor, while *Yom Tov* needs the labor that precedes it, and which acts as a stepping stone to *Yom Tov's* joy and delight.

Based on *Likkutei Sichos* Vol. XIV, pp. 418-420.

Sukkos — Revealing the Concealed

Our Sages inform us[1] that those spiritual matters that are in a state of concealment during Rosh HaShanah and Yom Kippur are revealed during the festival of Sukkos.

Rosh HaShanah and Yom Kippur each possess three distinct aspects, one greater than the other:[2]

a) The unique *mitzvos* of those days — on Rosh HaShanah the sounding of the shofar and on Yom Kippur the *mitzvos* of fasting, repentance and confession.

b) The fact that both Rosh HaShanah and Yom Kippur are part of the "Ten Days of *Penitence*," with penitence transcending *mitzvos.*

c) The *essential quality* of those days — on Rosh HaShanah the aspect of accepting G-d as King, and Yom Kippur the fact that "The very day [of Yom Kippur] brings atonement"[3] — a degree of atonement that far surpasses that achieved through *Teshuvah,* repentance.

Although these three aspects are part of both Rosh HaShanah and Yom Kippur, in a more general sense each aspect is tied to one of the three festivals of the month of *Tishrei:* Rosh HaShanah, Yom Kippur and Sukkos.

Rosh HaShanah clearly manifests its role as "head" of the year; it is the time when G-d is *crowned* King. This ability to crown G-d as King also indicates the Jews' absolute unity with Him, a union which makes it possible to bring about a desire to reign within G-d.

Yom Kippur, the "Day of *Forgiveness*," when "The very day brings atonement," plainly displays that it is the day on which forgiveness is granted for transgressing the King's decrees. This too is indicative of an essential union between G-d and the Jewish people.

The festival of Sukkos is the time when Jews are immersed in and unite with G-d through the performance of

1. *Siddur Im Dach 235b.* See also *Likkutei Torah, Nitzavim* 48b, *Rosh HaShanah* 54c ff.
2. See previous essay on Rosh HaShanah. See also *Likkutei Sichos IV,* p. 1149ff.
3. *Shavuos* 13a.

mitzvos — Sukkah, Esrog and Lulav, etc. Indeed, the performance of *mitzvos* is indicated by the name of the holiday itself — *Sukkos*.

As mentioned above, all aspects that are concealed on Rosh HaShanah and Yom Kippur are revealed during Sukkos. Therefore, although the main feature of Sukkos is the performance of *mitzvos*, the festival also reveals the themes of Rosh HaShanah and Yom Kippur.

In describing the Sukkos festival, the Torah states: "On the fifteenth day of this seventh month is the Festival of Sukkos....."[4] So, too, with regard to dwelling in the sukkah the verse states: "You shall dwell in sukkos for seven days."[5] As nothing else is cited as a reason for the festival, clearly the essential feature is the sukkah itself.

With regard to the *mitzvah* of Esrog and Lulav, the verse states:[6] "You shall take for yourselves *on the first day*," thereby indicating that the *mitzvah* of Esrog and Lulav is not the essential aspect of the first day of *Sukkos*, i.e., it is not intrinsic to the holiday itself.

Only after the Torah commands Esrog and Lulav does it go on to say:[7] "and you shall rejoice before the L-rd your G-d for seven days" — the commandment of rejoicing during Sukkos being the third aspect of the festival.

The essential connection between Jews and G-d — a relationship wherein all Jews are equal, and which is expressed in accepting G-d's Kingship on Rosh HaShanah — is revealed within the essential aspect of Sukkos: a unity that finds expression in the fact "All Jews are fit to dwell in the selfsame sukkah."[8]

Every Jew's bond with G-d is expressed through *Teshuvah* — the main aspect of Yom Kippur — and manifests itself through the command of Esrog and Lulav, the Lulav serving

---

4. *Vayikra* 23:34.
5. Ibid., verse 42.
6. Ibid., verse 40.
7. Ibid.
8. *Sukkah* 27b.

as a symbol that Jews were victorious in *atonement* on *Yom Kippur*.[9]

Finally, the connection of the Jew to G-d through the performance of *mitzvos* is revealed in the *mitzvah* of *rejoicing* on Sukkos — the privilege of performing G-d's commands being the cause of their rejoicing.

Based on *Likkutei Sichos* Vol. XIX, pp. 350-354.

---

9.   *Tanchuma, Emor* 18. See also *Vayikra Rabbah* ibid., 2.

Berachah   ברכה
Simchas Torah   שמחת תורה

Shehecheyanu for Torah

The second day of *Shemini Atzeres* is known as *Simchas Torah*, "The Joy of Torah." The *Ramo* explains[1] that this day is so named "because we then rejoice and feast in honor of the conclusion of the Torah" — on *Simchas Torah* we complete the Torah by reading the final portion of *Berachah*.

Thus the previous Lubavitcher Rebbe explains that the blessing of *"Shehecheyanu"* recited on *Simchas Torah* applies not only to the holiday itself, but also to the joy of concluding the Torah.[2] But this must be understood. The joy of *Simchas Torah* is related to the *"conclusion* of the Torah," but the blessing of *"Shehecheyanu"* is invariably recited over something *new*.

The text of the *"Shehecheyanu"* blessing reads: "Shehecheyanu — You have granted us life, *v'kiyemanu* — and granted us existence, *v'higiyanu* — and enabled us to reach *lizman hazeh* — this occasion."

In general, when one thanks another he first thanks him for those things that are of lesser significance and then for matters of greater import. Accordingly, the order of the *"Shehecheyanu"* blessing should have been reversed, first thanking G-d for our existence, and then for embuing that existence with life.

When a person thanks G-d for granting him existence and life, thereby enabling him to "reach this occasion," he may well ask: Was his life up till now truly lived in a manner such that it is fitting to thank G-d with *"Shehecheyanu"*?

---

1. *Orach Chayim*, conclusion of ch. 669. See also *Tur* ibid.
2. *Sefer HaSichos 5705* p. 55.

Quite possibly the majority of his life had not been filled with pleasure but with pain.

The blessing therefore begins by thanking G-d for granting life: Just as when a person is alive all parts of him are equally living, so too the quality of the life referred to by *"Shehecheyanu"* is that which encompasses all aspects of man equally, for which reason he is obligated to thank G-d.

Without Torah it is impossible for an individual to say that his life is full of things that cause him to offer G-d thanks; even if he enjoys mostly good times, he still cannot consider himself to be vitally alive, as most of a person's time is occupied with food, drink and sleep, earning a living, etc.

A Jew, however, is inextricably bound to the "Torah of life," and is therefore able to imbue *all* that he does with life; even while engaged in mundane affairs he cleaves to G-d by remembering that *"All your actions* should be for the sake of Heaven,"[3] and "In all your ways shall you know Him."[4]

The result? "And you who cleave to the L-rd your G-d are *entirely alive,"*[5] every moment of every day. Thus a person can and must thank G-d for granting him life and enabling him to reach this occasion.

However, according to this explanation of "life," the original question remains: what is there to cause a person to thank G-d for "existence;" it seems to require a far fainter degree of thanks.

Life need not necessarily be that of a soul within a *body;* quite the contrary, the soul as it exists Above, unencumbered by a body and constantly cleaving to G-d, is considered to be much more "alive."

We therefore give G-d additional thanks for the descent of the soul within the body; thanks that the body, which *in and of itself* can only be said to *exist* (for it lacks all spiritual sensitivity) is thus imbued with true life. We can then be

---

3. *Avos* 2:12.
4. *Mishlei* 3:6; *Tur* and *Shulchan Aruch, Orach Chayim* 231.
5. *Devarim* 4:4.

grateful not only for the soul — life, but for the body as well — existence.

When a Jew lives a Torah life throughout the year, both he and Torah are imbued with a much greater degree of Divine illumination during *Simchas Torah*; it is a new and loftier Jew and Torah, as it were. Jews therefore rejoice with Torah and recite the blessing of *"Shehecheyanu."*

Based on *Likkutei Sichos* Vol. XIX, pp. 371-378.